THE PIANO TRIO

The Piano Trio

Its History, Technique, and Repertoire

BASIL SMALLMAN

CLARENDON PRESS · OXFORD

1990

Oxford University Press, Walton Street, Oxford OX2 6DP
Oxford New York Toronto
Delhi Bombay Calcutta Madras Karachi
Petaling Jaya Singapore Hong Kong Tokyo
Nairobi Dar es Salaam Cape Town
Melbourne Auckland
and associated companies in
Berlin Ibadan

Oxford is a trade mark of Oxford University Press

Published in the United States
by Oxford University Press, New York

British Library Cataloguing in Publication Data
Smallman, Basil, 1921–
The piano trio: its history, technique, and
repertoire.
1. Piano trios, to 1988
I. Title
785.7′03621′09
ISBN 0–19–318307–2

Library of Congress Cataloguing in Publication Data
Smallman, Basil.
The piano trio: its history, technique, and repertoire/Basil
Smallman.
p. cm.
Bibliography: p.
Includes indexes.
ISBN 0–19–318307–2: $57.00 (U.S.)
1. Piano trio.   I. Title.
ML 1165.S6   1989
785′.28193———dc20

Typeset by Latimer Trend & Company Ltd, Plymouth
Printed in Great Britain by
Courier International Ltd., Tiptree, Essex

To my grandchildren
Daniel and Anna

Preface

References to the nature of the piano trio, and to its history and repertoire, are common enough in general musical literature; but specific information is often traceable only in widely diverse and not readily accessible sources, such as specialist articles, individual composer studies, and the prefaces to modern editions of the music. A primary aim, therefore, of the present study is to assemble this material in all its variety, and to attempt through it to create a unified picture of the genre's development, particularly in relation to the major stylistic changes which have occurred in music generally during the last two hundred years. The output of trios over the whole period has been very large and, as with the much cited iceberg, it is the 'tip' only which remains clearly evident in present-day concert life; the other, and much larger, part, comprising many half or wholly forgotten works, lies 'submerged'—and not always with justice—on the shelves or in the store-rooms of numerous libraries. In the present survey, in order to preserve manageable proportions, the focus is placed chiefly on the accepted masterpieces of the genre; but sufficient reference is made to the 'submerged' elements to indicate not only their profusion but also their seriousness of artistic purpose, and to suggest to performers and students in general that avenues may remain open for rewarding exploration.

Some slight difficulties with trio terminology are minimized by a judicious use of upper and lower case, respectively, for ensembles and individual works, and inverted commas to identify the second sections of minuets and scherzos. Thus, such a phrase as 'the "trio" section of the third movement of the third trio in the set, dedicated to the Triumviri Piano Trio', though inelegant to a degree, is at least comprehensible. However, as a minor exception, a special use of capitals and quotes is reserved for the 'Archduke' Trio and the relatively few other works in the repertoire with nicknames.

Music examples are provided to illuminate a number of

detailed points, but the reader is advised to consult the scores wherever possible in order to reach a fuller understanding of the topics under discussion.

I am most grateful to the staff of the West Sussex County Library in Chichester, and particularly to Mrs Elizabeth Smart, Music Librarian, for their untiring efforts in securing books, scores, and other study material for me; also to the Librarians of the Royal Academy of Music and the Royal College of Music for permission to consult their collections. I gratefully acknowledge the assistance of the following publishing houses in supplying me with study scores of a number of modern piano trios: Boosey and Hawkes; J. and W. Chester/Wilhelm Hansen, London; Faber Music; Novello and Co.; Oxford University Press; Schott and Co.; Stainer and Bell; and Universal Edition (London). Extracts from the following works are reproduced by kind permission of the publishers: Frank Bridge, Piano Trio No. 2, © 1930 (Augener), Stainer and Bell; Earle Brown, Piano Trio © 1972, and Dominic Muldowney, Piano Trio, © 1985, Universal Edition (London); Alexander Goehr, Piano Trio, © 1970, and Bohuslav Martinů, Piano Trio No. 1, © 1931, Schott and Co.; Jonathan Harvey, Piano Trio, © 1977, Novello and Co.; Charles Ives, Piano Trio, © 1955, Peer International Corporation, New York, and William Elkin Music Services; Alun Hoddinott, Piano Trio No. 2, © 1987, and Alan Rawsthorne, Piano Trio, © 1963, Oxford University Press; Gabriel Fauré, Piano Trio, © 1923, Editions Durand S.A., Paris/United Music Publishers, and Requiem, © 1901, Editions Hamelle, France/United Music Publishers, Maurice Ravel, Piano Trio, © 1915, Editions Durand S.A., Paris/United Music Publishers; Albert Roussel, Piano Trio in E♭, © 1905, Editions Salabert, Paris/United Music Publishers.

B.S.

June 1988

Contents

1 Introduction

I T seldom happens that the origins of an artistic form can be assigned with confidence to a particular date or identified with a specific creative artist; usually such beginnings are obscured by the number and variety of the factors that contribute to them, or by the inconsistencies which appear inseparable from the evolutionary process. In the case of the piano trio, however, the criteria applicable to its fully fledged form are sufficiently precise to make the pin-pointing of a date, or at least a narrow period of origin, more than usually feasible. The genre represents, as we shall see, the culmination of an extended process of development, during which a great deal of music was written for the trio ensemble (usually in the earlier stages, harpsichord, violin or flute, and bass) under the guise of the so-called accompanied sonata. It was not, however, until the end of the eighteenth century that the conditions were gradually created for it to adapt fully to the ideals associated with classical chamber music. In order for this to happen three specific criteria had necessarily to be accepted as paramount: that the strings (and most crucially, for historical reasons, the cello) should be granted near-equal partnership with the keyboard; that the scoring should be unequivocally for the piano rather than the harpsichord,[1] and most importantly, that all three instruments should be accorded, as nearly as possible, an equal share in the sonata argument through the exchange and alternation of thematic material. During the last quarter of the century a number of composers came near to reaching these ideals, among them K. F. Abel, C. P. E. Bach, J. C. Bach, Carl Stamitz, and Ignaz Pleyel, and the works they produced, though still basically sonatas of the accompanied variety, began to include increasingly independent roles for the strings and to specify the

[1] Essentially that it should have been *conceived by the composer* in terms of the fortepiano. The publishers, in order to maximize sales, continued to stipulate 'for harpsichord or piano'. Mozart's mature piano trios, for example, were published as *Sonate per il clavicembalo ò forte-piano con violino e violoncello.*

fortepiano as at least a possible alternative to the harpsichord. But the equitable distribution of the sonata elements among the instruments, essential to the classical style, remained largely absent. It was absent also in the trios of Haydn, despite his position as a principal founder of Viennese classicism. In the long series of keyboard trios he composed between 1784 and 1796, he came close to adopting the essential criteria of the fully developed forms; but by not fully emancipating the strings, he failed to sever entirely his links with the traditional accompanied sonata, with its keyboard-dominated style. It remained, therefore, for Mozart to provide the definitive breakthrough to the fully formed piano trio, at first tentatively, in 1776, with his Divertimento in B flat, K254, the cello line of which lacks independence, and then with growing assurance, from 1786 (our 'pin-pointed' date), with the first three of the great series of trios written in Vienna—K496 in G, K498 in E flat (the clarinet trio) and K502 in B flat. In these works we find for the first time clear signs of a successful marriage between large-scale sonata structures and fine trio scoring, involving to a marked degree shared interest and ingenious thematic distribution.

The piano trio, which was destined to become one of the most widely cultivated of chamber forms, second in importance only to the string quartet, was, by comparison with the other major instrumental forms of the period, a late arrival on the scene in the Vienna of classical times. One clear reason for the delay was the tardy progress made in contemporary piano construction. Necessarily the full development of the trio (and all other forms of concerted chamber music with piano) had to wait upon the evolution of a truly efficient instrument, one with enough power to match the strings in the ensemble and sufficient mechanical capability to ensure clarity in the attack and release of notes and precise damping. It is hardly surprising therefore that Mozart did not attempt major works for strings and keyboard—neither the piano trio, the piano quartet, nor the mature violin sonata—until his discovery in the late 1770s of the superbly responsive 'Viennese' pianos of J. A. Stein and Anton Walter, whose instruments represent major milestones in the history of piano construction. The composer's admiration for Stein's instruments is made clear in a notable letter which he wrote to his father from Augsburg in October 1777. 'In whatever way I touch the keys', he declared, 'the tone is always even. It never jars, it is never stronger or weaker or entirely absent; . . . his instruments have this special advantage over others that they are made with an escape action. Only one maker in a hundred bothers about this.'[2] It was only with pianos of this smoother, and indeed brighter toned, variety that it became possible to achieve the complex ensemble writing, involving a high degree of integration between the keyboard and its instrumental partners, which the fully developed chamber style demanded. Somewhat similar is the situation observable in the evolution of the keyboard concerto. Whereas in the early concerto the orchestral accompaniment had frequently to be severely restrained or even eliminated during the 'solo' sections in order to preserve the soloist's audibility, at later stages of development the growing power and efficiency of keyboard instruments made possible altogether richer, more complex supporting textures, often involving wind instruments as well as strings.

A second, and equally important, reason for the trio's protracted development lay quite simply in the sheer difficulty of writing really effective chamber music for piano and strings. On the one hand there was the problem of reconciling the structural imperatives of the sonata style with the need to distribute thematic material equitably among the instruments; and on the other the difficulty of attaining, through judicious scoring, an appropriate blend and balance in an ensemble comprising instruments of non-equivalent tonal character and dynamic strength. That these requirements did not prove easy to fulfil, even for Mozart, is evident from the large number of trio sketches and half-finished attempts which he left. Furthermore, since the provision of an independent, but fully integrated, role for the cello presented him with some of his most severe difficulties, it was only natural that he should have postponed his development of the trio until he had first mastered the problems of the violin sonata, a task in which he was intensively engaged from the end of 1777.

In one important respect the retarded development of the trio brought with it positive benefit, since it enabled the new form at the point of its first maturity to profit directly from technical and aesthetic advances which had already taken place in other princi-

<hr>

[2] E. Anderson (ed.), *The Letters of Mozart and his Family*, 2nd edn., rev. M. Carolan and A. H. King (London, 1966), i. 328.

pal forms of the period—concerto and opera, as well as chamber music of all kinds. When, in 1786, the first true piano trios appeared, Haydn had already brought the string quartet to an advanced state of development and was currently engaged on the six works contained in his Op. 50 set. And Mozart, himself, had not only completed his six quartets dedicated to Haydn, but had also recently finished *Le nozze di Figaro* and three of his greatest piano concertos, K482 in E flat, K488 in A, and K491 in C minor, all of them works rich in compositional features of significance for the growth of the piano trio. Quartet writing, for example, provided essential insights into the use of motivic integration and contrapuntal resource in composing for small ensembles; the concerto demonstrated effective methods of distributing thematic and accompanimental material between keyboard and strings; and opera, by providing lively examples of the handling of soloists, both individually and in ensemble, suggested ways in which a vivid dialogue style might be made appropriate to a purely instrumental medium. Samples of the influence of each of these major forms are discoverable in the variation finale of K496 in G, the first of the mature trios of 1786—string quartet and concerto textures in variations 2 and 6, respectively, the latter recalling in particular the finale of the great G major concerto, K453; and a remarkable anticipation, in the second half of variation 5, of parts of the terzettino, 'Soave sia il vento' from the first act of *Così fan tutte*.

From his experience with Vienna's rich concert and operatic life Mozart gained the resource to develop not only the piano trio and the piano quartet, but also virtually every other major chamber form of the late classical period, those involving wind, stringed, and keyboard instruments in a remarkable variety of groupings. After his death in 1791 there remained to be established only two further large-scale chamber genres involving strings and piano—the cello sonata and the piano quintet. Haydn, on the other hand, working for much of his life within the relatively more restricted orbit of the court at Esterhàza, preferred to focus particularly on the single genre of the string quartet and to explore it in depth and with extraordinary fecundity. He too, of course, wrote piano trios, particularly after relinquishing his full-time position at Esterhàza in 1790; but these works, as we have seen earlier, represent more a stirring end to the traditional accompanied sonata form than any new departure of vital significance for the future of the genre. They are none the less compositions of outstanding vigour and imagination whose special virtues will be examined in greater detail in the next chapter.

Although antecedents of the classical piano trio are not greatly in evidence before the middle of the eighteenth century, there are a few early indications of the important solo part the keyboard was eventually to play in chamber music. Notable examples are provided by various of the flute, violin, and gamba sonatas (often described as 'en trio') by J. S. Bach, dating from around 1720, in which the harpsichord abandons its usual continuo function and begins to undertake a new obbligato role. As if substituting for an absent player (probably a not uncommon requirement) the keyboardist's right hand contributes over the bass line a separate contrapuntal strand to the texture, sometimes also with chordal enrichment, in full equality with the solo wind or stringed instrument, and thus points the way towards a new type of artistic partnership in chamber music.[3] This method is well exemplified in Bach's bass viol sonata in G (BWV 1027) which the composer transcribed from a trio sonata (for two flutes and continuo) of his own composition in the same key (BWV 1039). In this case the original flute lines are allotted, with necessary adjustments, to the solo gamba and the harpsichordist's right hand, providing in the process an altogether different sonority from that of the original work.[4]

Also of much significance from the late Baroque period are experiments made by some of the French clavecinistes, who sought a reversal of the traditional instrumental functions by placing the keyboardist in the forefront as soloist and relegating the strings (either violin alone, or violin and cello/bass viol) to a simple accompanying role. This new genre, the Parisian origins of which were investigated in detail some fifty years ago by the

[3] In her study of the trios of C. P. E. Bach—'C. P. E. Bach and the Trio Old and New', *C. P. E. Bach Studies*, ed. S. L. Clark (Oxford, 1988), 83—M. Fillion adopts the term 'obbligato duo donata' for solo string or wind sonatas with realized harpsichord, derived from, or written in the style of, trio sonatas; and reserves the term 'keyboard trio' or *terzetto* for keyboard sonatas with a subordinate accompaniment for violin and cello.

[4] See H. Eppstein, 'J. S. Bachs Triosonate G-dur (BWV 1039) und ihre Beziehungen zur Sonate für Gamba und Cembalo G-dur (BWV 1027)', *Die Musikforschung* 18 (1965), 126–37.

Dutch scholar Edouard Reeser, subsequently became categorized consistently as the 'accompanied sonata'.[5] Amongst its earliest exponents was Jean-Joseph Cassanéa de Mondonville (1711–72) whose reputation in Paris rested at least as much on his operas as on his instrumental works, since in 1752 he became involved in the *Querelle des bouffons* as a leading champion of the national school. His accompanied sonatas, published in 1734 as his Opus 3, under the title *Pièces de clavecin en sonates avec accompagnement de violon*, were very probably the first of their type.[6] Collections of a similar nature by other French composers followed shortly afterwards, including Rameau's *Pièces de clavecin en concert* (1741) and Louis-Gabriel Guillemain's *Pièces de clavecin en sonates* (1745).[7] Rameau's set shows several particularly elaborate and forward-looking characteristics. Scored for harpsichord and a choice of accompanying instruments ('*un violon ou une flûte, et une viole ou un 2ᵐᵉ violon*') it comprises nineteen short movements grouped into five suites each of which contains four movements, except No. 5 which has only three. Although the dominant role falls to the harpsichord in these pieces, the other parts are by no means always simply accompaniments. Moving beyond the self-imposed limitations of his fellow composers Rameau grants both the violin and the cello (or their substitutes) a full share in the proceedings in several of the movements, contributing solo passages, imitative counterpoints, echo effects, and scalic decorations in a colourful baroque manner. Not only is the music full of lively contrapuntal interest, but it contains many features of scoring suggestive, when allowance is made for differences of style, of the piano trio of later times. Rameau's publication, however, was exceptional for its period; more usual was the method, evident in the Mondonville and Guillemain collections, of reducing the accompanying part (or parts) to a position of such extreme subordination *vis-à-vis* the keyboard that it mattered relatively little whether or not it was actually present. In adopting this approach these composers appear to have been responding to

---

[5] See E. Reeser, *De Klaviersonate met Vioolbegleiding in het parijische Musiekleven ten Tijde van Mozart* (Rotterdam, 1939), 43 ff.

[6] See W. S. Newman, *The Sonata in the Classic Era*, 2nd edn. (New York, 1972), 617; and D. Fuller, 'Accompanied Keyboard Music', *Musical Quarterly* 60 (1974), 239–40.

[7] Examples of accompanied sonatas by Mondonville, Guillemain, and others are to be found in an appendix to Reeser, *De Klaviersonate met Vioolbegleiding*.

a growing trend of the period, as is indicated in the following extract from the preface (*Avertissement*) to Guillemain's set:

When I composed these 'Pièces en Sonates' my first thought was to make them only for the clavecin without including an accompaniment, having noticed that the violin covered the clavecin a little too much, which keeps one from distinguishing the true melody [*sujet*]. But to conform to the present taste, I did not feel that I could dispense with the added part, which requires an extreme softness of execution in order to let the clavecin itself be heard readily. If one wishes one can play these sonatas with or without accompaniment. They will lose none of their melody, since it is all complete in the clavecin part, which will be the more convenient for those who do not have a violinist available.[8]

Guillemain neglects to say why the 'present taste', to which he deems it wise to conform, should have demanded the addition of a violin part which interfered so greatly with the audibility of the melodies. He might, not unreasonably, have pointed out that a frequent and attractive function of the accompanying instrument, often referred to in the prefaces of the period, was to give unison support to the weak-toned keyboard melodies, thereby sustaining and highlighting them, and to enrich the middle of the texture with chords, arpeggios, and a variety of simple, imitative counterpoints. It is interesting to notice from the composer's comments how major a concern problems of balance were to musicians at this time (and how markedly different, incidentally, from those of present-day string players in harness with a concert grand piano). Frequently directions are to be found in scores and parts of the period for the accompanying violin to use a mute, or adopt a lower level of dynamics, in order to avoid overpowering the delicate sound of the keyboard instrument.

With the general shift in musical style which took place around the middle of the century, in which multi-strand polyphony gave way increasingly to new homophonic approaches, keyboard instruments came into particular prominence as the ideal media for the latest types of sonata, providing as they did for a single performer to combine melody and accompaniment, to effect ready variations in style, to range freely over a wide compass, and to create swift, dramatic changes of texture. One might well

---

[8] Quoted in Newman, *Sonata*, 621–2. This preface is very similar to the one given in Rameau's *Pièces de clavecin* and may well have been modelled on it.

expect this development to have hastened the demise of the accompanied sonata, but in fact quite the reverse was the case. Although the solo sonata gained greatly in importance and was widely cultivated, the accompanied type none the less maintained its hold and continued to offer much scope for inventive treatment. Particular advantages of the form were the warmth and colour which, as we have seen earlier, a violin could impart to the relatively restrained melodic surface of a harpsichord or fortepiano sonata, and the enrichment of the middle of the texture it could achieve by means of held notes or simple chord and arpeggio patterns. Furthermore, a welcome element of variety could frequently be introduced by allowing the violin to take over entirely as soloist in short melodic passages, or to insert attractive echo phrases and snatches of imitation. In cases where the cello was also used—and this was the practice principally of German composers—its limited but useful function was to double and strengthen the comparatively weak bass notes of the keyboard part.

However, in addition to such technical and aesthetic reasons, the accompanied sonatas gained popularity through the scope they provided, with their simple string parts, for amateur musicians to enjoy the pleasures of ensemble playing without overtaxing their abilities. This social aspect is well brought out by various of the titles and published prefaces encountered at this period. Boccherini, for example, describes his Op. 7 collection of 1770 as *Sei conversatione a tre*, and makes it clear that they are designed to meet the requirements of the *amatori* of music. And Charles Avison, in the preface to his harpsichord sonatas, Op. 7, which have accompaniments for two violins and cello, provides a definition that is apt enough for domestic music-making at all periods and in all styles:

This kind of music is not, indeed, calculated so much for public entertainment, as for private Amusement. It is rather like a conversation among Friends, where Few are of one Mind, and propose their mutual Sentiments, only to give Variety, and enliven their select Company.

Also, at the height of the vogue for this much favoured genre, it was not unusual to find amateur musicians advertising their skills through the local press in order to seek out kindred spirits for mutual musical pleasure. A familiar example, which moves pleasantly enough across the class barriers of the time, is a notice which appeared in the *Wiener-Zeitung* in 1789: 'Wanted by a nobleman, a servant who plays the violin well and is able to accompany difficult keyboard sonatas'.[9]

A continuing supply of readily accessible works for amateurs was provided by minor composers of the period, such as Kozeluch, Vanhal, Sterkel, and Hoffmeister, whose numerous accompanied sonatas were praised more for their tunefulness and technical simplicity than for any deeper musical characteristics. In a review published in Vienna's *Musikalische Real-Zeitung* in 1789, for example, Sterkel's trios were commended to the readers precisely because they showed 'no excess of modulations to remote keys, no awkward difficulties or neck-breaking passages; but pleasant melody, well-ordered progress and—what is so rarely achieved by today's fashionable composers—tonal unity'.[10] Still further examples of suitable accompanied works resulted from the addition of optional string parts to solo keyboard sonatas, or the arrangement for trio of works originally written for other combinations. Noteworthy instances of the former kind, from late in the century, are J. C. Bach's *Sei sonate per il cembalo ò il forte piano*, published by Johann André with an added violin part marked '*Composto dal editore*', and Mozart's B flat piano sonata, K570, which was issued with a violin part (possibly also by André) not originally intended by the composer; and typical of the latter variety are the keyboard trio versions of string quartets by Pleyel, published by Artaria between 1788 and 1790.[11]

Within the complex web of developments leading to the fully formed piano trio, special significance attaches to the work of a group of German composers who settled in Paris during the third quarter of the century, and built for themselves a considerable reputation in chamber composition: J. G. Eckard, L. Honauer, H. F. Raupach, and Johann Schobert, of whom the first named was probably the finest keyboard player and the last the best

[9] Cited in K. Geiringer, *Haydn* (London, 1932), 38.

[10] *Musikalische Real-Zeitung* for the year 1789, No. 45. p. 336: quoted in K. Komlós, 'The Viennese Keyboard Trio in the 1780s: Sociological Background and Contemporary Reception', *Music and Letters* 68 (1987), 229.

[11] See Komlós, 'The Viennese Keyboard Trio (Sociological Background)', 226. The vogue for transcriptions seems particularly to have affected Mozart's G major trio, K496, which appeared in nine versions, one of them involving a clarinet quartet and another, of the slow movement only, an orchestra.

composer. Schobert's output, in addition to some solo keyboard sonatas, includes numerous duos, trios, and quartets in which the harpsichord is accompanied by either a single violin, a violin and cello, or two violins and cello.[12] All four musicians were particularly important, however, for the influence they exercised on the seven-year-old Mozart when he stayed in Paris between November 1763 and April 1764, during an extended journey across Europe with his father Leopold and sister Nannerl, which led eventually to London. In a letter written early in 1764 Leopold declared that in Paris

it is the Germans who are masters, as far as published music is concerned. Among them Schobert, Eckhard and Honauer are particularly appreciated . . . M. le Grand, a French clavier-player, has abandoned his own style completely and now writes sonatas in our manner. Schobert, Eckhard, Le Grand and Hochbrucher have all brought us their engraved sonatas and presented them to my children.[13]

Leopold appears to have held no very high opinion of Schobert, apparently because he took little trouble to disguise his envy of Nannerl's extraordinary keyboard ability—'this mean Schobert', he called him. But his son was strongly drawn to the ethos of the older man's music, its 'true passion, seriousness and fatalism', as Einstein describes it.[14] Already in 1762, the child composer had written two keyboard sonatas (K6 and K7) and these, with added violin parts, were published in Paris in 1763 as his Op. 1, together with a pair of similar accompanied works (K8 and K9), in the Schobert manner, as his Op. 2. Subsequently, in London, a further six sonatas were engraved (K10 to K15) in which the keyboard part is supported not only by an accompanying violin (or flute) but also by a cello to reinforce the bass ('*avec l'accompagnement de Violon ou Flaute Traversière et d'un Violoncelle*'). No doubt the young Mozart, keen though his musical sensibilities clearly were, was indulging at this point mainly in a childish form of imitation; and no doubt he received considerable help from his father, particularly in devising the additional string parts. But it is not hard to see in these earliest essays of his the beginnings of an evolutionary path that was to lead first to the classical violin

---

[12] Modern edn., ed. H. Riemann, in *Denkmäler deutscher Tonkunst*, 39.
[13] Anderson, *Mozart Letters*, i. 37.
[14] Einstein, A., *Mozart: His Character, His Work* (London, 1946), 125.

sonata in 1778, and then after a further eight years to the fully fledged piano trio.[15]

Influence at least equal in importance to that of the 'Paris Germans' was exercised on the young Mozart by Johann Christian Bach, whom the eight-year-old composer first encountered on his arrival in London in April 1764. Some two months earlier Christian Bach had published a set of six harpsichord sonatas with accompaniments for violin, or German flute, and cello, and it is entirely likely that Mozart was provided with an opportunity to study these and probably also to perform them.[16] The sonatas, all cast in Bach's favourite two-movement structure, involve a sonata-form first movement of modest proportions and limited key-range, followed by either a minuet finale in binary form or a simple rondo movement. The principal role is allotted consistently to the harpsichord and, apart from one special instance, the accompanying parts are wholly restricted, the cello in particular being tied unremittingly to the keyboard bass line. The exceptional case is the first movement of the last sonata in the set (Op. 2 No. 6 in E flat), where the treble instrument has an unusually florid part, frequently pitched well above the keyboard's top line, which creates the impression of a genuine duet sonata. However, even in this movement, the cello line has virtually no independence but glumly continues its routine supporting role.

Fourteen years later, in September 1778, J. C. Bach published in London a further set of accompanied sonatas (Op. 15 Nos. 1–4) which shows some interesting progress towards the classical piano trio concept. Particularly noteworthy in these works are the occasional bursts of cello independence which indicate a growing urge towards a more viable string partnership in the ensemble. A passage such as that in Example 1, which occurs quite unpredictably in the final movement of Op. 15 No. 1, must surely have taken many an unwary eighteenth-century cellist by surprise. In

[15] Among works by the young Mozart, in which he borrowed openly from the composers he had met on his travels are three harpsichord concertos, K107, based on sonatas by J. C. Bach (*Tre sonate del Sgr. Giovanni Bach ridotte in concerti dal Sgr. Wolfgango Mozart*) dated 1765, and a further collection of four concertos, K37 to K41, based on sonata movements by Raupach, Honauer, and others, written in 1767. A keyboard sonata by Raupach with violin accompaniment was at one time misattributed to Mozart and included as No. 6 in the Köchel catalogue.

[16] Modern edn., ed. E. Warburton, in *Johann Christian Bach, 1735–1782, The Collected Works*, 39 (New York, 1988).

Ex. 1

other respects these later works show relatively little stylistic advance on their predecessors of 1764. The piano is indicated as an acceptable, and perhaps even preferred, alternative to the harpsichord; and the German flute is no longer suggested as a substitute for the violin. But the structural patterns are hardly any different, and the harmony and key schemes only slightly richer; and nowhere does the violin part match the lively character of Op. 2 No. 6, mentioned above. Clearly these works provide a significant link in the chain from the accompanied sonata to the classical piano trio; but, lacking as they do an organic, integrated treatment of the instrumental parts in relation to the whole sonata concept, they remain at, rather than over, the threshold of the burgeoning piano trio genre. The crucial differences of approach may be seen by comparing the brief excerpt from Christian Bach, given above, with the passage in Example 2 from Mozart's E major trio, K542, written ten years later. Whereas Bach's sudden cello solo is an isolated phenomenon, a simple continuation of a four-bar phrase initiated by the violin, Mozart's cello part (as also

his violin line) is fully independent and fully integrated into a
closely wrought contrapuntal texture in which each strand has a
role of equal significance.

With the growth of the mature piano trio, the accompanied
sonata began inevitably to wither. The stark inequality of musical
interest and technical demand between the keyboard and string
parts was sufficient to ensure the older form's demise. But it was
not a rapid decease, and examples of the genre by such minor
composers as Adalbert Gyrowetz (1763–1850), Anton Reicha
(1770–1836), and Joseph Wölfl (1773–1812) continued to appear
until well into the second decade of the nineteenth century. Also,
rather curiously, the terminology associated with the form tended
to linger on in various more or less inappropriate contexts, such as
Beethoven's Op. 30 violin sonatas, which were described in their
first edition as 'for pianoforte with violin accompaniment'. In
more recent times the accompanied sonata has failed to hold a
place on the concert platform, partly because of its inherently
dilettante nature, which is alien to modern ideas, and partly

because of its generally insubstantial repertoire. Only where the actual music is of unimpeachable quality, as in the late Haydn trios, has the imbalance of interest within the ensemble not proved an insuperable obstacle.

Like the traditional accompanied sonatas, the earliest piano trios were designed mainly for the enjoyment of amateur performers in the home—in contrast to the string quartets of the period which were more frequently conceived in terms of professional performers.[17] Often the composer himself would act as pianist and invite suitable string-playing friends to join him for an evening of pleasurable music-making. Something of the general approach is conveyed by a postscript which Mozart attached to a letter of 17 June 1788 to his friend and benefactor, Michael Puchberg: 'When can we make a little music again at your place? I have written a new trio!'—the work in question being very probably the E major trio K542, composed around that time.[18] It is not clear whether Puchberg himself was intended to participate, but, as an amateur bass player of some repute, he may perhaps have been expected to take the cello line. At later stages, as the technical demands of the string parts increased, it became customary to 'borrow' players from professional string quartets for the performance of trios, very often with the composer functioning still as pianist. Thus, Beethoven and Schubert both called upon the services of Ignaz Schuppanzigh (founder of the Rasumovsky Quartet) as violinist and either Nikolaus Kraft or Joseph Lincke as cellist, while Schumann relied on Ferdinand David (Joachim's teacher) as violinist, Julius Rietz as cellist, and his wife Clara as pianist; and later in the century Brahms and Dvořák played their own works with members of the Cologne and Bohemian Quartets, respectively. It was only during the twentieth century that specialist professional trios began to be formed in any number, one of the earliest and most distinguished being the Thibaud–Casals–Cortot Trio, founded in

---

[17] See Komlós, 'The Viennese Keyboard Trio (Sociological Background)', 222, for further details about the popularity of the genre with amateur, and particularly, lady pianists in the late eighteenth century.

[18] Anderson, *Mozart Letters*, ii. 916. Also often referred to as the 'Puchberg' trio is the Divertimento in E flat, K563 for string trio of Sept. 1788; however, the date of Mozart's letter discounts the possibility that this was the work referred to. Very possibly both compositions were intended to be offered in gratitude to the friend who had provided Mozart with so much help, financial and otherwise.

1905. Happily, the growth of professional ensembles did little to dampen the enthusiasm of amateurs; indeed, as expert performances became increasingly available, new ideals of musicianship were established, towards which domestic groups of sufficient technical skill were only too eager to aspire.

2 The Late Eighteenth Century: Mozart and Haydn

FOLLOWING his early experiments with the accompanied sonata Mozart delayed for over ten years before again embarking on concerted chamber works for one or more strings and piano. During the intervening period the string quartet was the chamber form which principally engaged his attention, together with the solo piano sonata. When, in 1778, he began again to explore the combination of piano and strings, it was particularly to the violin sonata that he turned, his interest having been sparked by a new constructive principle, the elements of which he had encountered in some sonatas (*Divertimenti da camera*) by the Saxon Kapellmeister Joseph Schuster. A reference to this discovery occurs in a letter which he sent to his father from Munich on 6 October 1777. 'Schuster's sonatas', he wrote, 'are not bad ... if I stay on I shall write six myself in the same style, as they are very popular here.'[1] The new structural device which Mozart identified in these works, and sought to develop in his own violin sonatas (his 'Clavierduetti mit Violin' as he called them), was a crucially important one. It involved the elevation of the violin from its customary accompanying role to one of near-equal partnership with the keyboard, by entrusting it with a large share of the melodic material in alternation with the piano, and with the opportunity to contribute significantly to the whole texture by means of imitations, counterthemes, and transitional passage-work.[2] In relation to chamber music with piano this new technique brought about a revitalization akin to that produced in the string quartet by Haydn's energetic exploration of textural

[1] E. Anderson (ed.), *The Letters of Mozart and His Family*, 2nd edn., rev. M. Carolan and A. H. King (London, 1966), i. 300.
[2] For a discussion of the developing role of the violin in Mozart's duo sonatas, see W. Fischer, 'Mozarts Weg von der begleiteten Klaviersonate zur Kammermusik mit Klavier', *Mozart Jahrbuch* (1956), 16.

integration and motivic development from his Op. 20 set of 1772 onwards.

The only Mozart composition to involve the piano trio combination at this period was the Divertimento in B flat, K254, dated August 1776. Though customarily regarded as the first of the developed Mozart trios, this work is hardly more than an elaborate accompanied sonata. Composed over a year before the Schuster-inspired violin sonatas, it is notable for its unusually active violin part, particularly in the second and third movements;[3] but not surprisingly it shows little sign of alternation and exchange of ideas between the instruments in the mature sonata manner. Furthermore the cello's role is a very humble one, amounting to little more than a doubling of the keyboard bass-line at the unison or the octave below. No special significance attaches, incidentally, to Mozart's use of the term 'divertimento' for this work, which has a full-scale sonata structure; the expression was commonly used for major chamber compositions of all types at this period and carries with it no implication of lightness of style or musical intention.[4] The titles adopted by Mozart for his mature trios of the 1780s are 'Terzett' and, exceptionally (in the autograph of K496 only), 'Sonata'. The designation 'Piano Trio' appears not to have been in general use at the time, though a version of it is to be found in a letter by Leopold Mozart, of January 1778, in which he refers to his son's Divertimento K254, as ' Trio für Clavier ex B und recht, recht vortreflich' (Trio in B flat for piano and very, very splendid).

During the 1770s Haydn was also engaged in writing simple trios of the accompanied sonata type, for harpsichord, violin, and cello, which he too described by the term 'divertimento' or sometimes 'partita'.[5] Though by no means insignificant these works give few indications of the powerful piano trio style he was to cultivate during the last decade of the century. Rather surprisingly, Haydn appears to have neglected the violin sonata; no fully authenticated example of the genre by him has

---

[3] Fischer, in 'Mozarts Weg', p. 30, points to the increased equality between the violin and keyboard roles in this work, citing in particular the opening of the rondo finale.

[4] See J. Webster, 'Towards a History of Viennese Chamber Music in the Early Classical Period', *The Journal of the American Musicological Society*, 27 (1974), 212.

[5] See M. Fillion, 'The Accompanied Keyboard Divertimenti of Haydn and his Contemporaries, c. 1750–1780', Cornell Univ. diss. 1982.

survived;[6] and consequently, he never wholly absorbed the Mozartian system for parcelling out thematic material between the keyboard and one or more stringed instruments. This appears to have been one important instance where the interaction of ideas between the two composers, so clearly evident in the symphony and string quartet, failed to operate. As a result, when they came at the end of their careers and at the height of their powers to make their most significant contributions to the piano trio form, they approached their task from quite different viewpoints. For Mozart, essential scope had to be provided for all three instruments to combine, alternate, imitate, and vie with each other on equal terms and in numerous ingenious and expressive ways. The piano he treated, logically enough, as a concertante instrument on the basis of his experience with the piano concerto, but always with the restraint necessary to allow the strings their full share of the musical argument. In effect he applied to the trio the classical criteria regarding integrity and equality of interest in the parts with much the same rigour as both he and Haydn had already done in relation to the string quartet. Haydn, on the other hand, took the keyboard part as the core of the piano trio, providing for it music of great brilliance and formal subtlety. The strings he was content to confine to a largely colouristic role, as a means of adding warmth to the melodic lines and imparting strength to the bass, but never of dictating the formal structure in any significant way. The violin is granted some independence in the later trios, sometimes taking short solo passages and often supplying beautifully .crafted inner parts or imitative counterpoints; but the cello rarely has more than a very restricted role, functioning mainly in support of the bass-line in the manner of the older accompanied sonatas. In the process he deliberately cultivated an old-fashioned, even somewhat 'crippled' form; but through his imaginative treatment of it he managed to imbue it with entirely new life. Mozart's system, when expanded by Beethoven, became the accepted ideal for virtually all later trio

---

[6] A violin sonata in G major by Haydn, available in several modern editions, is almost certainly an unauthentic version of a piano trio (Hob. XV. 32): see A. Tyson, 'New Light on a Haydn Trio (XV: 32)', *Haydn Yearbook*, 1 (1962), 203. Tyson conjectures that the trio, which was issued in London by Preston (possibly in conjunction with another publisher, Bland) in 1794, at the time of Haydn's second visit to England, may actually have been composed in 1792, during his first visit. The apparently spurious version, for violin and clavier alone, can be traced to an edition produced by Artaria in Vienna, also during 1794.

composition. But Haydn also, by the example of his masterful piano writing and structural inventiveness, exerted a profound influence on the future of the genre, aspects of his style reappearing transformed in the work of numerous trio composers of the succeeding generation.

The five great piano trios of Mozart were produced, according to his personal catalogue (the autograph *Verzeichnüs aller meine Werke*), during a two-year period from 1786 to 1788 in the following succession: K496 in G, K498 in E flat (the clarinet trio), and K502 in B flat in July, August, and November respectively of 1786; and K542 in E and K548 in C in June and July of 1788. In addition to these works there exist also the little G major trio, K564, apparently also dating from 1788, but of uncertain origin, and a surprisingly large amount of 'workshop debris' in the form of sketches and trio fragments, which bear clear witness to the difficulties the composer experienced with the medium.[7]

We are not perhaps sufficiently accustomed to the idea of Mozart as a composer who had to work hard at composition, to struggle with intractable material, to reject first thoughts and constantly refashion his ideas in the manner of Beethoven. But the evidence suggests that chamber music, in particular, may have caused him much difficulty. An obvious example, somewhat parallel to that of the piano trios, is provided by the six string quartets which he dedicated to Haydn in 1785. In his dedicatory letter he described his offering as the 'fruit of long and strenuous endeavour', an assertion borne out not only by the two-year period needed to complete the works but also by the numerous false starts, modifications, and corrections to be seen in the manuscript sources. It is possibly significant that the two smaller of the surviving trio fragments, each consisting of some twenty bars of sketch before breaking off, are in the same keys—G major and B flat major—as the two standard trios completed in 1786. Whether or not they were first attempts at these works—and there is no positive evidence one way or the other—it is not difficult to see why the composer should have abandoned them. The B flat fragment (K Anhang 51) starts exactly like an old-style accompanied sonata, with unison and octave doublings and interpolated harmony notes for the violin, and clearly provides

---

[7] All the trios, the fragments included, are available in the *Neue Mozart Ausgabe*, Serie VIII, Werkgruppe 22/2, (Kassel 1955–).

little if any scope for the new concept of trio writing which was lurking in Mozart's imagination. And the G major section (K Anhang 52) consists of a fourteen-bar theme, apparently for piano alone, which seems to afford the strings minimal opportunity for integrated contributions, suggesting only a simple repetition from bar 15, with the violin leading.

However, even in the completed G major trio of 1786, the problems of integrating the strings are by no means always satisfactorily resolved. Like the G major fragment, mentioned above, the first movement begins with an extended piano solo, a rambling seventeen-bar theme which is more akin to transitional material than a principal subject. Subsequently, during the exposition, there is considerable exchange of thematic ideas between the violin and the piano, but little of substance for the cello to do beyond doubling the bass.[8] After the double bar, during a diffuse and surprisingly awkward development (which lingers too long for its own good in the flat supertonic), the cello suddenly comes to the fore with independent contributions, mainly scalic passages in an imitative duet with the piano left hand (see Ex. 3). This has been hailed as the moment when the piano trio first came to full maturity: but it was something of a false dawn.[9] Although the rather mechanical imitative passages bring the cello to some degree of prominence, they do little to solve the deeper problems of combining all three instruments in a genuine trio structure. Too inflexible to allow much scope for truly idiomatic writing the section resembles nothing so much as a passage for string quartet, with the strands of its texture distributed in a basic fashion between the two string players and the two hands of the pianist. More effective is the division of material between the instruments in the slow movement, particularly in a modulatory section during the development (from bar 52), where the strings link together in octaves and thirds to form a colourful partnership in opposition to the piano, and move the music progressively from E flat to the dominant of A minor. The finale, a set of six variations and coda on an extended binary-form theme, contains, as we have seen earlier, a striking range of instrumental and

---

[8] The autograph of K496, now in Paris in private hands, shows Mozart's use of red and black inks for the string parts. This, in Einstein's view, was to remind him not to neglect either of them. See A. Einstein, *Mozart: His Character, His Work* (London, 1946), 271.

[9] Einstein, *Mozart*, 271–2.

Ex. 3

mock-vocal styles. But it affords the cello only one contribution of real independence. This occurs during a strange passage in the fourth (*minore*) variation, where separate ostinato patterns are allotted to the violin and cello, while the piano weaves against them contrapuntal strands of a repetitive character. In a decidedly unusual manœuvre Mozart recalls this idea, in a major/minor version, at the end of the final variation, providing, before the final coda, a further brief chance for the cello to take the limelight.

The experimental, even technically rather insecure, character of this G major trio is not easily explainable. Only four months after its completion date (as given in the composer's catalogue) Mozart produced his B flat trio K502, in which all stylistic and technical difficulties appear to have melted away. And during the two years preceding K496 the composer had written a whole series of chamber works with piano, such as the piano and wind quintet K452, and the two piano quartets K478 in G minor and K493 in E flat, which reveal a total mastery of their respective media. Are we to suppose, then, that Mozart found trio composition particularly problematic—perhaps because, with only two string players (unlike the piano quartet) it did not provide a harmonically balanced string ensemble to set against the piano? Or is it possible that the bulk of the G major work was actually written considerably earlier than is indicated in Mozart's catalogue, and that the date given there refers only to its final completion, perhaps after a new movement had been substituted for an earlier one which had failed to satisfy the composer? Some support for this latter theory is provided by the existence among the surviving fragments of a substantial, but incomplete, movement in G major, a *minuet en rondeau* of a type quite frequently employed by Mozart for his finales. It is not unlikely, as Alfred Einstein conjectured, that this fragment was intended originally as the last movement of K496, but was rejected because of its unsuitably 'amorous' character.[10]

In fact the trio fragment in question eventually found a 'home' (and not altogether comfortably) as the middle movement of the so-called piano trio in D minor, K442. This is actually a compilation of three substantial, and almost certainly quite unrelated, trio fragments which were completed by the Abbé Maximilian Stadler and later, in 1797, issued as an apparently unified work by the publisher Johann André of Offenbach. Stadler, who was an accomplished musician and a close friend of both Mozart and Haydn, made a very reasonable attempt at completing the trio movements, though his success was understandably proportionate to the amount already supplied in each case by Mozart. The first movement fragment in D minor consists of fifty-five bars from Mozart's hand, ending with the opening phrase of the second subject, a scalic theme somewhat similar to that in the equivalent place in the first movement of K452, the piano and wind quintet. Stadler supplies an effective completion of the exposition, but is less happy with his attempt to provide a development section; excessively long and repetitious, it is too much concerned with treating each of the main themes in turn to be convincingly Mozartian. Also uncharacteristic is the way the second theme appears in a minor-key (C minor) version in the development and subsequently in the tonic major during the recapitulation—a reversal, very largely, of Mozart's normal practice. The G major fragment, which ended up as the middle movement, is a more substantial torso, comprising nearly a hundred and fifty bars of piano part and only slightly less of the string parts, and must

[10] Einstein, *Mozart* 272.

therefore have been relatively easy to reconstruct. The cello part shows some signs of independence, characteristically enough in the development section (from bar 112), but only for a brief spell before the string parts become fragmentary and the whole sketch is terminated. The main theme bears a considerable likeness to that at the start of the middle movement of Mozart's D major piano sonata, K284, of 1775, the so-called 'Durnitz' sonata; but the resemblance cannot be taken as in any way indicative of the date of origin of the sketch: 1783 is more likely or even slightly later.[11]

The third movement of the reconstructed trio presents us, perhaps, with the biggest problem of all. It is a full-scale sonata movement, and may therefore have been intended as a first movement rather than a finale, though its 6/8 time, 'hunting-horn' style is usual enough in Mozart's last movements. The composer's sketch was completed in the piano part up to the point of recapitulation, and in the string parts only slightly more fragmentarily. The task of reconstruction must therefore have been a simple, almost automatic, undertaking for Stadler, since he needed to invent nothing of significance. The resulting piece, which is probably very close to Mozart's exact intention, is one of the very finest of the composer's trio movements, and can hardly be dated earlier than 1788. Superb technically, and full of vigour and inevitability, it uses the medium in a wholly confident, fully balanced way. The cello is almost entirely emancipated, the keyboard writing is brilliantly effective, and the formal structure is finely proportioned, with a powerfully focused development section which is notable for its colourful modulatory processes and recurrent passages of imitative writing to enrich the argument. The mystery about the movement is why Mozart failed to finish it and incorporate it into a complete, published trio.

The composition which appears to have done most to unleash the new ideas about trio writing, which were germinating in Mozart's mind in 1786, was the E flat trio K498, for clarinet, viola, and piano—the so-called 'Kegelstatt' (skittle-alley) Trio. The work was almost certainly prompted, like the clarinet quintet K581, and the clarinet concerto K622, by the outstanding skill of

[11] The date of composition conventionally applied to the so-called D minor trio is 1783. Stylistic evidence supports this date, or one slightly later, for the first two movements, but suggests one considerably later, at least 1788, for the third movement.

the composer's clarinettist friend, Anton Stadler; and it is highly likely that its original performers were, in addition to Stadler, the composer himself as viola-player, and his greatly admired pupil, Franziska Jacquin, as pianist.[12] In order to deal effectively with an ensemble of so novel a character, Mozart was forced to reconsider several aspects of blend, sonority, and the disposition of material in a way which was to prove significant for all his later trio writing. With a clarinet as the principal melody instrument, one which positively demanded an idiomatic role, the problems of sharing with the keyboard were given a new focus; and with the viola in partnership fresh emphasis was necessarily placed on the tenor area of the texture, rather than the bass to which the cello, particularly at this period, was more naturally inclined. In order to simplify the structure, and thus throw increased emphasis upon the textural and scoring aspects of the work, Mozart eliminated the customary sonata-form movement at the start and replaced it with a flowing Andante of song-like character. In addition he worked, in this opening movement, with two contrasted yet complementary themes, one built in short segments and particularly suitable for providing clearly defined scoring contrasts, and the other more sustained and cantabile in style and thus appropriate for extended presentation in each of the basic instrumental colours in turn. The trio reveals to a remarkable extent Mozart's capacity for grasping intuitively the essence of a demanding new chamber medium. Once established, and with its potentialities so impressively demonstrated, this new genre (sometimes with a cello replacing the viola) provided a challenge which many later composers, as we shall see, were eager to accept.

The liberating effect which we have ascribed to Mozart's work on the clarinet trio is evident enough in the three great piano trios of standard scoring which followed, those in B flat, E major, and C major. With these works the piano trio came finally of age as a fully developed genre, significant not solely for its own time but also for its promise of later development. Although an eighteen-month gap (from November 1786 to June 1788) separated the composition of the first of these works from the other two, it is hard not to regard the three trios as a unified group, particularly as they culminate, like several other Mozartian series—the Da

---

[12] See the preface to the *Neue Mozart Ausgabe*, VIII. 22/2. xi.

Ponte operas, the quartets dedicated to Haydn, and the last three symphonies, for instance—in a work in the key of C major.[13] Whether or not 'culminate' is too strong a word to use in connection with the last trio is perhaps open to question—one to which we shall return for later consideration.

Certain general characteristics, common to all three works, may be usefully summarized here. The trios are all large-scale and in three movements (fast–slow–fast), with a structural pattern consisting normally of sonata–simple rondo–sonata rondo, the only exception being the middle movement of the C major trio which is also in sonata form. And all of them reveal to some extent the influence of the piano concerto, partly in their overall structure (three movements only, in contrast to the four-movement pattern of the contemporary symphony and string quartet) and partly also in the somewhat dominant role allotted to the keyboard, including a considerable amount of rapid passage-work against slower-moving strings. The string parts none the less display greater independence and a more subtle interrelationship with the piano than those in any earlier trios, and virtually all the thematic material is designed to be readily interchangeable between the instruments.[14] In none of the works does the cello abandon entirely its traditional role of strengthening the bass, but increasingly throughout the series the instrument emerges as an individual 'voice', presenting melodies, enriching textures, and contributing important counterthemes on a near-equal basis with its partners in the ensemble. A noteworthy example occurs in bars 61 to 64 of the second movement of K502, where the cello provides a finely crafted interior strand in the tenor register, reminiscent of some of the viola passages in the clarinet trio (see Ex. 4).

Mozart's new approach to thematic integration can be seen by comparing the beginning of the B flat trio with that of K496 in G, previously discussed. In contrast to the long, somewhat discursive theme with which the earlier work starts, the opening of K502 (shown in Ex. 5) provides a clearly etched, one-and-a-half bar phrase for the piano, supported by a sustained tonic note on the cello and answered immediately by a brief countermotif from the

---

[13] The three trios were in fact published together, as Op. 15, by Artaria in 1788.

[14] See K. Komlós, 'The Viennese Keyboard Trio in the 1780s: Studies in Texture and Instrumentation', Cornell Univ. diss. 1986, 239–62.

Ex. 4 [Larghetto]

violin (marked x), forming a tautly constructed phrase. Subsequently, the violin motif, which sounds at first like a tiny link, almost a 'fill-in', between the two limbs of the piano's initial theme, grows in importance to a point where it dominates the transition to the second subject group and plays a leading role in the development. In general, the principal theme and its counter-motif are treated separately; but at one place, in bar 117, immediately before the recapitulation, the two are joined contrapuntally in a pointed and witty manner (see Ex. 6).

Concerto influence is much in evidence in the second and third movements of the B flat trio. Both are in rondo form and both begin, typically, with a thematic presentation by the piano alone, followed by a 'tutti' restatement involving the whole ensemble. In the slow movement the successive returns of the rondo theme invite increasing elaboration, both in melodic detail and accompanimental texture. Particularly impressive is the second reprise (at bar 84) where the piano's decorated version of the main theme

Ex. 5

Ex. 6

is enriched by strong interior countermelodies on the strings, with an unusually high-lying cello part. The effect is not unlike that of a concerto reprise where, for example, wind instruments may be introduced to add warmth and colour to the scoring. In the finale the concerto effect is still further enhanced by the exceptional athleticism of the piano part; but skilful contrapuntal treatment ensures that the strings are not neglected and a texture of notable strength and purposefulness results.

The E major trio is remarkable for its clarity of structure and directness of expression. A particular characteristic of the work is its thematic repetition, often involving the statement of a melody in one instrumental colour and its immediate reprise with different scoring and a beautifully varied or extended continuation. The beginning of the first movement provides a good example of the procedure.[15] After its initial presentation by the piano alone, the twelve-bar principal theme is repeated by the full ensemble with many new points of detail, and then radiantly expanded to twenty-two bars before arriving at a full close in the tonic. As a means of clarifying and refining the texture, rests are used extensively in the string parts, and in the process superfluous doublings (particularly by the cello) are avoided and important entries emphasized. An impressive example in the first movement is the cello's dramatic entry in bar 74, by way of a V/VI♭ interrupted cadence, after five bars of rest—a moment made even

---

[15] It should be noted that some modern editions provide slightly bowdlerized versions of the first and last movements of K542. Significant discrepancies occur, as comparison with the text given in the *Neue Mozart Ausgabe* (based on the autograph MS) shows, in I, bars 3 and 138, and III, bars 64–5.

more memorable by the tangled complex of contrapuntal imitations and chromatic harmonies which succeeds it (see Ex. 7). The
simple rondo structure of the slow movement provides a framework for the exploitation of a single captivating melody, supported by delicately varied harmony. Again emphasizing repetition, the opening idea, with its charmingly phrased rising motif
(C sharp to E), occurs twelve times during the course of the
movement; and at each main entry it is given a new perspective
by subtle variations in the surrounding imitative patterns on the
strings. Effective contrast is provided by a central episode in the

Ex. 7 [Allegro]

tonic minor, still based on the original theme, where Mozart moves suddenly and delightfully into fresh territory, with elegant new turns of melody and harmony of a decidedly Schubertian character.

A sketch, some sixty bars in length, has survived of a discarded first attempt at a finale for K542. Although only a rudimentary outline, which would clearly have been much altered in any final form, the fragment shows the beginning of a rondo movement in 6/8 time, with the promise of string parts of considerable independence, the usual touchstone of Mozart's mature trio style. It seems not unlikely that the composer's rejection of this initial attempt was prompted by the over-square, unduly repetitious nature of its opening eight-bar theme. But curiously enough, in the movement which eventually replaced the sketch, a similar rigidity of outline is apparent in the main theme, though its repetitions are more widely spaced and its second four-bar phrase (reminiscent of parts of the 'Jupiter' Symphony minuet) provides an effective foil to the opening idea. Certain aspects of the movement, generally, are problematic. The gentle, ambling nature of the rondo theme (marked 'dolce' in the score) seems to be at odds with the allegro tempo indication; the cello has a rather surprisingly sparse role to play; and the second subject group introduces an untypical, and rather unwelcome, element of showiness, with extended solo passages for the violin and piano in turn, the first in triplets and the second (a variation of the first) in very rapid semiquavers. Neither passage is easy to play at the stated allegro tempo, though the fast keyboard figuration would certainly have been more manageable on the shallow-touch Stein piano of Mozart's day than it is on a modern concert grand; and neither of them fits very happily into the gentle, 'conversational' style of the music as a whole. But, undeniably, the movement also contains many delightful features, such as the splendidly contrapuntal development section, the beautiful episode in C sharp minor from bar 120, with its charming exploitation of flat supertonic harmony, and the finely judged climax at the end, during which in a moment of extreme exaltation the cello is taken up to c'' sharp (with the violin a tenth above), its highest point in any of the Mozart trios.

In contrast to the E major trio, which has always won warm critical acclaim, the final work in the series, K548 in C major, has been consistently undervalued—ever since Einstein declared that it 'lacked the vitality of invention . . . and thematic richness' of the other trios. It is difficult to agree with this verdict. The trio is typical of Mozart in the key of C major—abstract, lofty in ideas, and beautifully crafted—and it contains some of the composer's most successful scoring for the trio medium. While it is true that its first-movement themes show a degree of classical detachment, they can no more be said to lack 'thematic richness' than can the corresponding ideas in the 'Jupiter' Symphony or the C major piano concerto K503, with their reliance on plain tonic and dominant statements. Moreover, 'vitality of invention' is abundantly evident in the first movement development, an intricate contrapuntal mosaic built from tiny melodic fragments, which achieves special expressive force from the contrast between its plaintive, minor-key chromaticisms and the forthright major-key style of the surrounding sections (see Ex. 8).

An impressive instance of motivic distribution, and its use for constructive purposes, is provided by the sonata-form slow movement, one of the most profound of all Mozart's trio movements. The crucial thematic fragment in this case (marked ⓐ in Ex. 9) is drawn from the third bar of the opening theme of the movement, and consists of an arched scale passage on the piano, largely in demisemiquavers. During the development this figure is taken over in a dialogue between the strings, providing a filigreed background against which the piano, in concerto style, meditates lyrically on parts of the second theme of the movement (markedⓑ in Ex. 9), passing in rapid succession through E flat, C minor, and G minor to the dominant of D minor. Subsequently, the return to F major for the recapitulation from an A major chord is as striking as it is unexpected. A fine contrast is created by the work's rondo finale, a light and witty example of the French style. Like its predecessor in K542, it employs an abridged sonata rondo scheme in which the normal return of the principal theme at the recapitulation is side-stepped in favour of a recurrence of the second subject in the tonic key. The resulting compression adds, in the case of both works, to the intensity of the musical argument and increases the scope for a vividly climactic coda. Whether or not literally a 'culmination' to the great trio series, the C major work uncovers a new and distinctive vein in Mozart's approach to trio composition, complementing its fellow works

Ex. 8

by the variety of its expression and at least matching them in its technical assurance.

Mozart's only other piano trio, K564 in G, is an altogether different matter. A work of slender pretensions, it was possibly intended as a practice setting for beginners in ensemble playing, analogous to the *sonates faciles* which many composers of the period wrote for their piano pupils. The view, once held, that the work may originally have been a solo piano sonata, of earlier date, which Mozart, in 1788, reworked as a trio, has in recent times been challenged. Wilhelm Weismann,[16] for example, has attempted to trace the trio's origins to a chamber work—possibly a violin sonata—from the composer's Mannheim period, while Karl Marguerre,[17] on somewhat surer grounds, has inclined to the view that the work originated, in virtually the exact form in which it has survived, in 1788, believing that the peculiarities evident in its partial autograph (the addition in Mozart's hand of violin and cello parts to a pre-existent, non-autograph copy of the keyboard part) may have resulted from an attempt by the composer to restore from memory string parts which had been mislaid. The evidence remains, however, decidedly inconclusive.[18] Even more puzzling are the stylistic discrepancies apparent in some parts of the work. The second movement, a theme and variations, and the rondo finale, though surprisingly slight for the period in structure and substance, are characteristic enough and effectively arranged for the medium. But the first movement contains at least two features which raise doubts about its authenticity: one is a second subject which is merely a free variant (as opposed to a 'monothematic' recurrence) of the opening theme, and the other a restatement of the whole of the second subject group, unvaried apart from a move to the subdominant,

---

[16] W. Weismann, 'Zur Urfassung von Mozarts Klaviertrio, KV 564', in W. Vetter (ed.), *Deutsches Jahrbuch der Musikwissenschaft für 1958* (Leipzig, 1959), 35.

[17] K. Marguerre 'Mozarts Klaviertrios', *Mozart Jahrbuch*, 1960–1, 192.

[18] The supposition, now generally discarded, that the work was originally a solo piano sonata derived support at one time from the siting of the violin and cello parts in the original 'amended' score, respectively, above and below the keyboard part. However, Mozart's other trio autographs show clearly that this was his standard practice. A further indication that K564 was very possibly intended from the start as a trio is its inclusion in Mozart's personal catalogue of his works, not normally used to list arrangements. Extra details about the conflicting arguments and conjectures surrounding the work's origins can be found in the preface to the *Neue Mozart Ausgabe* VIII. 22/2. xiii.

in the middle of the development section—both decidedly unusual procedures for Mozart.

The mature trios of Mozart represent one classical pinnacle of the trio genre. They reveal a fine balance between structure and scoring, and a blend of sonorities, which were inevitably to become attenuated during the following century. 'Inevitably' because, through the technical development of the piano, and to a lesser extent the strings, and through the continued expansion of sonata structures, the nineteenth-century trio became virtually a different genre, larger and richer in conception but often lacking in the refinement and precision characteristic of the Mozartian era. The other classical pinnacle is to be found, despite their different nature, in the piano trios of Haydn. Haydn's contribution to the repertoire, produced over a period of more than thirty years, is much larger than Mozart's, and embraces the whole range of trio development from the Baroque trio sonata to the brink of the fully fledged classical type. But even at his latest stage of development, with Mozart's example before him, Haydn never advanced beyond the traditional accompanied sonata concept, with its prominent keyboard role and limited string parts. His last fifteen trios, all written after Mozart's death, resemble enhanced piano sonatas in which the background support of the strings does much to compensate for the tonal limitations and lack of sustaining power of the instruments of the period. Large in scale, the works teem with original ideas and reveal a brilliance of keyboard writing rarely matched in contemporary works for the piano alone.[19] Haydn's reasons for not liberating the strings in his last works can only be conjectured. Possibly he preferred to continue working in a style and form which he had already cultivated extensively; and he must also have recognized that any emancipation of the strings must inevitably involve some limitation of the keyboard texture, and that this could hardly fail to detract from his basic aim of writing brilliant and demanding piano music. In any case, it is unlikely that either he or Mozart were greatly concerned with the probable influence of their works on the subsequent course of trio development. Their objective was simply to supply what musicians of the time (many

[19] See A. P. Brown, 'The Solo and Ensemble Keyboard Sonatas of Joseph Haydn: A Study of Style and Structure', Northwestern Univ. diss. 1970.

of whom were their friends) wanted to play—and, of course, publishers to publish.

Certain problems of dating and authentication have made it difficult to establish a clear picture of Haydn's works in trio form. Some of the older editions, still in current use (those particularly of Peters, Litolf, and Breitkopf and Härtel), give a total of thirty-one works, of which twenty-nine are now known to be authentic Haydn and the other two probably the work of his pupil Ignaz Pleyel. More recently, Anthony van Hoboken, in his definitive catalogue of Haydn's works, includes a further ten trios, but acknowledges that some of the additional ones are of uncertain origin.[20] And H. C. Robbins Landon, in the Doblinger edition, probably the one most commonly used nowadays, gives an extended list of forty-five trios, not all of which have survived or are indisputably authentic.[21] The record is perhaps best clarified by working backwards from the fully recognized works of Haydn's maturity towards the more controversial ones assigned to his earlier years. In all there are fifteen late trios written between 1794 and 1797, chiefly during the period of Haydn's second visit to London, all of which were intended for the piano rather than the harpsichord. A further fourteen works, composed between 1784 and 1790, were designed mainly for harpsichord, and include three flute trios and an arrangement made in 1785 of an earlier baryton trio. The other sixteen works listed by Robbins Landon are of less certain date and authenticity. Eleven of them are 'attributed' works, with considerable claims to be regarded as genuine; and of the remaining five, one is of doubtful origin, two are almost certainly spurious, and two are known only from their mention in catalogues of the period.[22] For the purpose of our present survey we shall disregard all the trios written before 1784, and focus our attention mainly on the works from the composer's second London period *post* 1794.

[20] A. van Hoboken, *Joseph Haydn, Thematisch-bibliographisches Verzeichnis* (Mainz, 1957–71).

[21] See H. C. Robbins Landon, Preface to *Die Klaviertrios von Joseph Haydn*, the first complete critical edition (Vienna, 1970). Ten of the attributed works, which Haydn entitled either 'Partita' or 'Divertimento', are included in vol. i, ser. xvii of the *New Haydn Edition*. See also the worklist under 'Haydn, Joseph', in S. Sadie (ed.), *New Grove Dictionary of Music and Musicians* (London, 1983).

[22] See G. Feder, 'Haydns frühe Klaviertrios: eine Untersuchung zur Echtheit und Chronologie', *Haydn-Studien* 2 (1970), 289.

Haydn's trios are more varied in structure than Mozart's. Though he normally wrote three-movement works, with a central slow movement, there are no less than nine among the trios written after 1784 which have only two movements—either slow followed by fast, or both fast. Where a slow movement is placed first, it sometimes serves as an introduction as in Hob. XV. 21 in C major; but more usually it is a full-length variation movement, similar to those found at the opening of some of the composer's string quartets, based either on one theme or on a pair of themes. A familiar example of the single-theme type is the opening Andante of Hob. XV. 25 (the G major trio with a final rondo 'in the Gypsies stile') which has four variations on an extended binary-form melody, the first and third in minor keys (G minor and E minor) and the others in the tonic major. The third variation, in E minor, provides an example of unusually elaborate, concerto-style, violin writing, to which the piano, for once, supplies only the most reticent of chordal accompaniments (see Ex. 10). The double-theme type of variations, typical of Haydn's most mature manner, is to be found in the impressive

Ex. 10

opening movements of Hob. XV. 23 in D minor and Hob. XV. 31 in E flat minor; the second theme of the 'pair', in both instances, is in the tonic major, and in the case of the E flat minor movement forms an ingenious melodic inversion of the original *minore* melody.

Many of the finales in the late works employ rondo form, either of the simple, sectional type with contrasted episodes, or the more elaborate sonata kind. The simple rondo is used very effectively in several minuet-style finales found among the post-1784 trios, containing dance rhythms and clear-cut construction. A fine example occurs in Hob. XV. 26 in F sharp minor which, despite its serious, even rather sombre, main theme, consistently retains a lively, dance-like character. The setting of the main theme, shown in Example 11, provides some interesting insights into Haydn's methods of utilizing the strings in the ensemble. The violin's double-stopped chords at the opening add warmth by reflecting upwards the harmonic progression in the piano left hand, while the cello's position an octave below the keyboard bass serves to provide extra sonority; then, in bars 2, 3, and 4, the violin strengthens the low-pitched keyboard melody while the cello lightens the texture by moving up to coincide with the piano's bass-line. And finally, in the repeat, the cello remains at low pitch in bar 7 so as to emphasize the dark colouring at that point and to throw into relief the important bass entry in bar 8. Unlike the majority of the trios with minuet finales which, being early works tend to have only two movements, the F sharp minor trio has a complete three-movement structure. Its middle movement, interestingly enough, is a transcription of the slow movement of Haydn's symphony No. 102 in B flat, transposed up a semitone (to F sharp major), which is notable for the way it reproduces in terms of the chamber medium much detail from the original orchestral score. The preservation of the same tonic (minor and major) throughout, found also in several of Haydn's solo piano sonatas, is comparatively rare in the trios. More usually, in three-movement works, the composer changes key for the middle movement, and in a surprisingly large number of cases moves to one which is only distantly related. Among the various patterns found are: C major–A major–C major (in Hob. XV. 27), G major–E major–G major (in Hob. XV. 25), and D minor–B flat major–D major (in Hob. XV. 23), each of which favours the

Ex. 11

third-related keys which were later to prove so attractive to Beethoven. Also pointing forward to Beethoven (of the 'Arch-duke' Trio) is the device of linking movements, which Haydn employs effectively on a number of occasions, for example between the slow movement and finale of Hob. XV. 30 in E flat major.

In his final group of trios there is abundant evidence of the pleasure which Haydn took in the exercise of his mature powers. As in the 'London' symphonies of the same period, he aims continually to delight and surprise with novel turns of harmony, form, and instrumentation, all executed with complete technical assurance, and designed to intrigue the connoisseurs by thwarting their musical expectations in subtle and captivating ways. One striking example is the swerve into E (= F flat) major for a 'false recapitulation' in the finale of Hob. XV. 22 in E flat, a device which, as we shall see later, may very possibly have influenced Beethoven at a similar point in the first of his Op. 1 trios. And another is the colourful change from B major to G major, through a V/VI♭ cadential progression during the second-subject group in the first movement of Hob. XV. 28. in E major (see Ex. 12), a move which corresponds quite closely to the fine cello entry at the equivalent place in Mozart's E major trio discussed earlier. Even more remarkable, however, is the extravagantly fanciful, capricious style of composition evident in some of the last trios, with piano writing of an untrammelled character not matched elsewhere in Haydn's keyboard music, not even in his last solo piano sonatas. The extract in Example 13 from the finale of Hob. XV. 31 in E flat minor, with its wayward chromatic scales and gruff interjections in the bass from the pianist's right hand provides a splendid impression of the general style involved.

The virtuoso element of many of the 'London' trios may well have been encouraged by the keyboard skills of two ladies resident in the city, who were particularly close friends of Haydn—Rebecca Schroeter and Theresa Bartolozzi (née Jansen). Whether or not it is fair to assess the ladies' relative abilities by the character of the music dedicated to them is debatable: but the exceptional demands of the three trios ascribed to Mrs Bartolozzi

Ex. 12

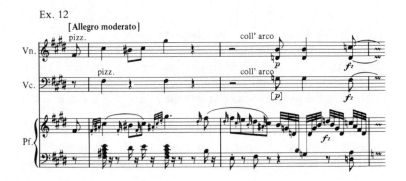

Ex. 13

(Hob. XV. 27, 28, and 29) suggest that she, in particular, was a pianist of outstanding ability. Notable features are the rapid octaves and thirds for the right hand in the first two movements, respectively, of the C major trio (Hob. XV. 27), and the swift passage-work (reminiscent of an *opera buffa* finale) and testing hand-crossings in the last movement of the same work. Elsewhere there are challenging cross-rhythms and enharmonic changes, together with numerous short cadenzas demanding neatness of execution, and an unusually full style of keyboard writing for the period. Prominent among the works dedicated to Rebecca Schroeter is the famous 'Gypsy' rondo (the finale of Hob. XV. 25) which calls for considerable resolution to preserve its moto perpetuo style, and to control its fast passages in thirds in the first *minore* episode.

Because of his self-imposed restrictions Haydn's string parts are necessarily more limited in scope; yet they contain many points of interest. Violin doublings of the surface of the keyboard part, though common, are rarely undertaken in a routine fashion;

much variety is obtained through the choice of unison or octave doublings, or by passages in thirds, sixths, or tenths in relation to the accompanied lines. Also, in some cases expressively shaped string phrases result from the free movement of unison doublings from one strand of the keyboard part to another—top, middle, and even, if it is high enough, the bass. Doublings represent, however, only a relatively small part of the violin's contributions; instances also constantly occur of finely etched counterthemes, often linked imitatively to the keyboard part, of harmonic enrichment through held notes and double-stopped chords, soft or loud according to context, and of extended solo passages. A delightful example of the type of textural richness achievable within the constraints of the style can be seen in the extract from the slow movement of Hob. XV. 27, given in Example 14. Against the second phrase of the charming principal melody, presented on the piano, both strings contribute parts of considerable independence, the cello providing colour by its movement in thirds with the keyboard bass in the second half of the first bar, and the violin inserting a delicate touch of contrapuntal interest by its initial imitative demisemiquavers. There is clearly no question of slavish doubling here.

Solo melodic passages for the violin usually involve self-sufficient paragraphs of considerable length, with the piano temporarily relegated to a subordinate accompanying role. The range of moods and styles which Haydn encompasses in these sections may be seen by comparing the sweetly lyrical melody, in bars 20 to 28 of the second movement of Hob. XV. 27, with the vigorous E flat minor theme, of Beethovenian character, in the

Ex. 14

finale of Hob. XV. 30, from bar 41, and the concerto-style, free variation in E minor from the first movement of Hob. XV. 25 (shown in Ex. 10), this last passage providing, with both repeats, no less than thirty bars of decorative solo writing. In these final trios the violin clearly fulfils an increasingly independent role; yet its contribution to the music's structure remains limited, an adjunct, even though a highly decorative one, to a largely self-sufficient piano part.

Much less independent, though far from indispensable, are the cello parts in the trios. These, contrary to commonly held opinion, do not function simply as relics of the continuo era, automatically doubling the bass-line at the unison, but serve a quite different purpose. Whereas in baroque practice it is the stringed instrument which provides the true bass-line, while the keyboard completes the harmony above it, in Haydn's trios it is the piano which is entrusted with the essential bass, while the cello contributes special strength and articulation to it according to context. Consequently there is in the cello writing a surprising amount of scope for intelligent scoring. A choice, for example, between unison and octave doublings can be significant for the sonority of the whole ensemble; the occasional doubling of an inner line in the texture can produce an unusual warmth of expression; the use of rests and register changes in the string part can shape the bass-line in a variety of telling ways; and cello support can provide effective emphasis to important, and particularly high-pitched, melodic entries in the bass. All these usages are brought together with strikingly beautiful results in the slow movement of Hob. XV. 27 in C major, a *locus classicus* of Haydn's cello writing in the trios (see Ex. 14, above).

By 1797, when the last of Haydn's piano trios appeared, Beethoven had already published his Op. 1 piano trios and set the genre on course for major new developments. However, at this period, Beethoven was by no means alone in continuing to cultivate the trio; during the next few years examples were produced by numerous lesser figures, including J. L. Dussek, Anton Eberl, Prince Louis Ferdinand, J. N. Hummel, and Beethoven's pupil and protégé, Ferdinand Ries. Dussek was the most prolific trio composer of the group, publishing at least fifteen examples of the form; but these are for the most part early works and indebted largely to the conventional accompanied sonata style. More characteristic of the period generally are the six trios by Hummel, composed between 1803 and 1822, which well exemplify the colourful, virtuosic, but rather uneven, style typical of the minor figures of the time.[23]

Hummel, who was a remarkable child prodigy, and a pupil of Mozart (sporadically between 1785 and 1788), won international fame as a virtuoso pianist, particularly on the tours he made as a boy to various parts of Europe, including visits to Edinburgh and London. Subsequently he gained widespread recognition as a composer, and eventually, in 1804, succeeded to Haydn's former post as Kapellmeister to the Esterházy court, an appointment he held for some seven years. Also, later in his career, he made an important contribution to piano technique with his three-volume 'Piano School' (*Ausführlich Anweisung zum Piano-forte Spiel*), published in 1828. His trios appear to have been modelled most closely on those of Mozart, with three-movement structures consisting typically of a sonata allegro, an aria-style slow movement in a simple sectional form, and a rondo finale, often with dance characteristics. Mozartian influence is apparent also in the concertante style of his piano writing, though, with his virtuoso background, he often ranges beyond the natural artistic restraints of his model and includes display passages of much brilliance but little matching musical substance. His trios are nevertheless genuine chamber music in which the strings are accorded a full and lively share in the proceedings. In general his first movements show good technical resource, but tend to be immoderately long for the musical ideas they are expected to support. For example, the opening movement of his Op. 83 in E major, based on some not very impressive thematic material, has an exposition section of no less than 170 bars (allegro, 3/4 time), fifteen more than the equivalent section in Beethoven's 'Eroica' Symphony. In his slow movements, on the other hand, the simpler, more sectional structures seem to work more to his advantage; his themes are more striking—indeed, often genuinely shapely and expressive— and his treatment of them brings into play rich harmonic schemes, elaborate modulatory processes, and many effective touches of scoring. Some idea of the gracefulness of the overall style can be gained from Example 15, showing part of the ending

---

[23] See D. G. Brock, 'The Instrumental Music of Hummel', Univ. of Sheffield diss. 1976.

Ex. 15

of the slow movement of Op. 93 in E flat major. For his finales Hummel usually adopts a somewhat lighter style, often incorporating popular dance elements, with or without 'nationalist' traits. In his E flat trio, Op. 96, for instance, the last movement is marked 'Rondo alla Russa', and teems with lively and attractive melodic ideas. Written in 1823 it may possibly have been intended to reflect the composer's impressions of the visit he paid to St Petersburg in the previous year, though similar mildly exotic terms—*alla Polacca, all'Ongarese,* and *alla Turca*—were by no means uncommon in Viennese music of the time. More significant are the leaping chordal basses and dotted-rhythm figuration which characterize this and many other of Hummel's last movements, since it is precisely this type of writing which reappears, marvellously transfigured, in the finale of Beethoven's 'Archduke' Trio.

3 The Grand Sonata Style: Beethoven and Schubert

I T was no doubt partly in emulation of his teacher Haydn and partly as a means of emphasizing that his powers as a composer of concerted chamber music at least equalled his skill as a pianist and improviser, that Beethoven specially cultivated the piano trio in Vienna during the 1790s, eventually issuing three examples as his Opus I. But equally it is clear that, with the publication of these works, Beethoven sought to fulfil an ambition which he had nursed since his earliest days in Bonn. It was there, in 1785, at the age of 14, that he produced his three early piano quartets, remarkably enough in the same year as, and possibly slightly before, Mozart's first essays in the medium; and it was there also that, before leaving for Vienna in November 1792, he completed two apprentice works for the trio medium, a set of fourteen variations on a severely unmelodic theme, which was issued eventually in 1804 as his Op. 44, and a three-movement piano trio in E flat (WoO 38) which remained unpublished during his lifetime. None of these earliest compositions has much artistic value, but as a group they provide interesting evidence of the composer's first attempts to achieve an effective synthesis between Haydn's vivid keyboard style and the subtly integrated piano and string textures characteristic of Mozart.

The circumstances surrounding the composition, initial performance, and later publication of the Op. 1 trios have been the subject of much speculation, and some attempt here to separate the facts from the theories may not be inappropriate. All that is known for certain is that the works were issued by the Viennese publisher Artaria, in two separate stages—one early in July 1795 for the benefit of the subscribers,[1] who included Prince Lichnowsky, Count Apponyi, and the Countess Thun, and the other

---

[1] A. W. Thayer, *The Life of Ludwig van Beethoven*, rev. and ed. Elliott Forbes (Princeton, NJ, 1964), 175.

on 21 October of the same year for the general public. But exactly
how long before this the works were begun, and how precisely
they reached their finalized state remains unclear. Thayer believed
that Beethoven had made some considerable progress with the
trios before he left Bonn in 1792, basing his conclusion on a
statement contained in Anton Gräffer's manuscript catalogue of
the composer's works that the early E flat trio (WoO 38) was
'composed *anno* 1791, and originally intended for the three trios
Op. 1, but omitted by Beethoven as too weak'.[2] From this Thayer
inferred that the Op. 1 project was already firmly in the composer's mind during 1791 and that, despite an abortive first
attempt, he continued to make progress with it during the
following year.[3] On the other hand, Nottebohm, on quite
different grounds, believed that the G major trio (No. 2 in the set)
was not fully completed until 1794;[4] while Schindler, Beethoven's
devoted friend, asserted that the C minor work (No. 3) was the
first to be written, without however specifying a precise date.[5]

Special importance attaches to a performance of all three Op. 1
trios which is said to have taken place in Haydn's presence at the
end of 1793 or very early in the following year;[6] the venue for the
concert was Prince Lichnowsky's residence in Vienna, and
Beethoven himself was the pianist with Ignaz Schuppanzigh
(violin) and Nikolaus Kraft (cello) as the distinguished string
players. The account of the event originated with Beethoven's
pupil Ferdinand Ries, and it has to be acknowledged that
Schindler was doubtful about its accuracy. However, the report
seems too detailed to have been pure invention and there is
probably no reason to suppose that the substance of it is anything
other than true. It remains, however, decidedly uncertain
whether Haydn was actually present at the performance. According to Ries's account it was on this occasion that the older
composer offended Beethoven by advising against the publication
of the C minor trio, despite its obvious claims to be the finest of

---

[2] Thayer–Forbes, *Beethoven*, 123. Anton Gräffer was an employee of the publisher
Artaria, who appears to have prepared the catalogue of Beethoven's musical *Nachlass* for
an auction in Nov. 1827: see D. Johnson, 'The Artaria Collection of Beethoven
Manuscripts: a New Source', A. Tyson (ed.), *Beethoven Studies* (London, 1974), 177–8.

[3] Thayer–Forbes, *Beethoven*, 165.

[4] Ibid. 148.

[5] J. S. Shedlock, 'Beethoven's Sketch Books', *Musical Times* 33 (1892), 395.

[6] Thayer–Forbes, *Beethoven*, 164–5.

the set; but there are nowadays grounds for believing that Haydn's remark may not have been made until his return from his second London visit, in August 1795, and thus after the subscribers' copies had already been issued.

Whether or not accurate in every detail Ries's account gave rise to two later assumptions which call for comment. One is that there was a continuing rift between Beethoven and Haydn as a result of the offensive remark that the latter is alleged to have made; and the other that, because of the large time-gap between the putative performance date in 1793 and the eventual date of publication, the works must have been subjected to substantial revisions before being passed to the publisher. The question of a rift between the two composers need not be taken too seriously. Beethoven may well have been puzzled by Haydn's advice, whenever it was given, and he had a tendency to allow puzzlement to erupt into short-lived rages; but there is no reason to think that the older man's comment was passed for other than the soundest of reasons. Trios at the time were still designed mainly for the enjoyment of amateurs, and a work with three of its four movements in a minor key might well have been expected to encounter some sales resistance, from both publishers and potential performers. None of Mozart's trios was in a minor key, and those relatively few of Haydn's that were tended to compensate with major-key finales of considerable exuberance. It is difficult therefore to believe that Beethoven did not soon recognize that a helpful intention lay behind Haydn's advice. Also, it is hardly reasonable to suppose that it was out of pique that he discarded Haydn as a teacher in 1794 and turned to Albrechtsberger, since he must have known well in advance that the older composer had planned a long absence in London. Indeed, it seems quite likely that it was Haydn who recommended Albrechtsberger to him.

The matter of the revision of the trios demands more detailed consideration since, if it was as substantial as has been suggested, it implies the original existence of two somewhat different versions of the works: a performance version of 1793 and a published version of 1795. The basis for supposing that there were major revisions (or, as some have claimed, the substitution of new movements) is a large bound collection of Beethoven sketches now in the British Library (Add. MS 29.801, fos.39–162), commonly called the *Kafka* sketchbook after a previous owner.[7] This volume is of particular interest because it contains sketches from Beethoven's earliest Bonn period up to 1800, including a significant number for the Op. 1 trios, together with ones relating to the Op. 5 cello sonatas, the Op. 10 and Op. 14 piano sonatas, the Op. 11 clarinet trio, the first two piano concertos, the first symphony, and numerous other works of the time. Particularly important is the fact that several of the trio sketches appear on pages containing fugal exercises worked by Beethoven during his period of study with Albrechtsberger between January 1794 and March 1795. From this it has proved a small, but by no means conclusive, step to infer that the sketches also belong to this later period and provide evidence that major work was done on the trios after their initial performance at the Lichnowsky soirée in 1793.

It will be seen that a great deal hinges on the dating of the sketches. If they were written at Bonn and brought to Vienna by Beethoven, and their sheets used considerably later for jotting down counterpoint exercises, then there is no reason to suppose that the published version of the trios differed greatly from the 1793 version, apart from such minor revisions as the change of time signature from 4/4 to 2/4 in the finale of the G major work, apparently recommended by the cellist Kraft.[8] But if, on the other hand, some or all of the sketches do really date from 1794–5, during the time of Beethoven's studies with Albrechtsberger, as Nottebohm appears to have believed, then it is difficult to deny that the composer may well have engaged in some considerable reworking of the trios.[9] However, in the continued absence of any earlier versions of the works the idea of a substantial revision must remain purely hypothetical.

Already, in his Op. 1 trios, Beethoven began to move beyond the range of his predecessors towards a more expansive conception of the genre. Although Haydn's influence is evident enough in the piano writing, there also creeps in a new element of flamboyancy, derived no doubt from Clementi, Dussek, and other composer-virtuosi of the period. The resultant piano parts,

[7] J. Kerman, *Ludwig van Beethoven: Autograph Miscellany from circa 1786 to 1799. Brit. Lib. Add. MS. 29801, ff. 39–162 (the 'Kafka' Sketchbook)* (London, 1970). See vol. 1, fos. 69[r+v] and 86[r+v], 116[v], 126[r+v], and 139[v] for the piano trio sketches; and vol. 2, p. 276, for further consideration of the genesis of the Op. 1 trios; see also Shedlock, 'Sketch Books'. 394–7.

[8] Thayer–Forbes, *Beethoven*, 165, 171.

[9] Ibid. 165.

with frequent octave doublings and strong chordal writing, appear somewhat overpowering; but there is little reason to suppose that, against the light-toned pianos of the period, the strings would have had any difficulty in asserting themselves. The string parts, modelled on mature Mozart, are consistently independent and eventful, involving substantial melodic contributions, particularly in the slow movements, and using thematic interchange with the keyboard and integrated accompaniment figuration as a means of shaping the sonata structures. One development of special importance was the addition to the earlier Haydn/Mozart pattern of a fourth movement—a scherzo or minuet, placed third—through which the trio achieved grander dimensions and, increasingly, a status equivalent to that of the string quartet. The added movement, in quick 3/4 time, is hardly a dance movement (despite its designation in the C minor trio as a 'minuet'), but a lively and often whimsical piece, with irregular phrasing and sudden modulations, of the type which Haydn in his string quartets had already tended to call 'scherzo'. Similar movements are found also in Beethoven's first published piano sonatas, the Op. 2 set of 1796, and in his earliest attempt at a piano trio, the E flat work (WoO 38) of 1791, mentioned above. This latter composition, curiously, lacks a slow movement—an example, presumably, of incompleteness rather than structural innovation.[10]

Despite their early place in Beethoven's output the Op. 1 trios show an assured approach to the medium and an impressive command of musical structure. The first movements are conceived on a broad scale, exceeding in size, with their spacious developments and expanded recapitulations, even the grandest of his early piano sonatas. To some extent this expansive character results from the special scope which the trio medium affords for varied repetition. In many instances, after a principal idea has been stated, there is an immediate repeat in which interest and variety are preserved by means of new decorative detail and altered scoring. The process is one which Beethoven was to employ with

[10] The *Kafka* Sketchbook (see note 7) contains on fo. 129[r+v] a fully scored sketch of an [Alle]gretto in E flat for piano trio which, so the handwriting suggests, may date from 1790–2. It is possible that this was associated in some way with WoO 38; but the fact that it shares the work's principal tonic key makes it unlikely to have been intended as its slow movement.

greater subtlety in his later works, but even within the relatively simple style of the Op. 1 trios it contributes an impressive effect of breadth. Equally, long-range repetition is used in a bold and original manner. One notable example is to be found in the first movement of Op. 1 No. 1 where, by providing after the end of the recapitulation a return to the second subject group in the tonic, effectively as a partial recapitulation repeat, a lengthy coda is devised which, with elements of the first subject interwoven and the original closing theme of the exposition reserved to the very end, extends to no less than forty-seven bars. Very striking, too, is the grand slow introduction with which the G major trio opens; though it contributes mainly scene-setting melodic and harmonic formulas, it provides also, like the introductions to many of Haydn's later symphonies, significant allusions to the main theme of the ensuing Allegro. The idea of incorporating a slow introduction was adopted again by Beethoven, with fine effect, for his E flat trio, Op. 70 No. 2; but relatively few examples are to be found in the works of later trio composers.

In the slow movements of the E flat and G major trios it is the beauty of the melodic ideas and the variety of the scoring which create the strongest impression. Both movements start, conventionally enough, with eight-bar themes stated by the piano alone and then repeated by the full ensemble; but they soon develop in wholly individual ways, with new harmonic colouring and finely turned textures, the slow tempi involved providing scope for some lyrical solos by both stringed instruments. Most engaging, in the G major trio, is the cello's high-pitched restatement of the movement's principal theme, from the eighth bar of the reprise, in support of which the violin supplies calm interior figuration and the piano rising demisemiquavers in each hand, alternately.

The scherzos (so named in the first two trios only) appear to have been among the first of their kind for the medium, and destined therefore to serve as models for numerous later trio composers. In a delightfully capricious vein the composer starts each of them with a single stringed instrument—violin in No. 1 and cello in No. 2—and in the case of the E flat work provides a main theme of curious rhythmic and melodic ambiguity. Starting obliquely in C minor, he writes a complete eight-bar phrase, but deceives the ear by making the whole first bar sound like an upbeat pattern. As a result the principal phrase appears repeatedly to be short by one bar, in a witty and pointed manner one can only describe as Haydnesque (see Ex. 16). Some interesting points of comparison exist between the first two of the Op. 1 trios and certain of Haydn's late trios. For instance, during the final movement of the E flat work, in a remarkable expansion of the recapitulation of the second subject group, there is a sudden deviation to E (= F flat) major for a Neapolitan return of the second main theme, which corresponds exactly to the similar move (mentioned in Chapter 2) in the finale of Haydn's late E flat trio, Hob. XV. 22. And secondly, in the slow movement of Op. 1 No. 2 in G major, the choice of the remote key of E major (the major submediant) parallels precisely the key selected in the same context in Haydn's G major trio, Hob. XV. 25. If we discount simple coincidence (much more probable in the second case than the first) there remain two likely explanations. One is that Beethoven was simply following his mentor's example, as a modest form of tribute—something which would have been feasible only if he had had access to the Haydn works in manuscript form, since neither of them was published until 1795.

Ex. 16

And the other is that Haydn may have been the 'borrower'; that, when he left for London in 1794, the impression he took with him of the Beethoven trios was so strong that, consciously or not, he transferred ideas from them to his own work. More importantly, however, the linked passages suggest that Haydn and his pupil may have devoted considerable time to the study and analysis of each other's trios during the period of their closest relationship, in 1793.

The third of the 'Lichnowsky' trios, the one in C minor, is certainly the finest of the set. Its thematic ideas are more individual than those in the other trios, and they are treated with exceptional resource. It is more tautly structured, its key-schemes are more precisely balanced, and its string writing is bolder and more idiomatic. The subdued opening of the first movement, with its clear-cut motifs, evokes a remarkable sense of coiled energy waiting to be released, an effect only enhanced by the tiny violin cadenza in bars 9 and 10, a forerunner of many similar rhetorical strokes in his later minor-key works (notably the oboe cadenza in the fifth symphony, at the start of the first movement's recapitulation). In its seriousness of mood and directness of expression the movement reflects the spirit more of Mozart than of Haydn, particularly the former's C minor piano sonata, K457. Both the inner movements differ structurally from their counter-parts in the earlier trios. In the slow movement the variation technique which the composer had tested out earlier in his Op. 44 variations, is applied to a calm rocking theme of 32 bars (including repeats) with charming results. A special sense of symmetry is imparted to the five variations by allotting the principal role in each alternately to the piano and the strings; and many colourful touches of scoring are incorporated, such as the pizzicato string accompaniment maintained throughout variation 3 and the quasi-vocal duet between cello and violin in variation 4. The minor-key Menuetto, marked 'Quasi Allegro' but never achieving a true scherzo character, is constructed largely from developments of its initial four-note pattern and maintains a severe, rather close-fisted intensity. By contrast, the 'trio' section, in the major mode, is wide in range and characterized by unequal phrase-lengths and some extremely rapid descending scale passages (eventually in octaves), which may have been intended to be played glissando on the light-actioned pianos of the time. Most arresting of all, however, is the last movement, which seems to proclaim a fresh stage in Beethoven's thinking. Gone is the simple prettiness of the previous trio finales, and in its place there is a new urgency of expression with defiant C minor gestures, typically in upward-rushing arpeggios, and a new air of drama. Unexpected, and strikingly original in the context, is the subdued ending in the major key, a finely judged expression of calm after the storm has passed. It is as well that Haydn's advice about the publication of the trio, however helpfully intended, was not taken. It is those very expressive features which at the time may have seemed damaging to its prospects, that have most endeared it to later connoisseurs, both amateur and professional, as the crowning point of the whole set. Following the publication of the Op. 1 trios it was thirteen years before Beethoven again turned to the standard piano trio. During the intervening period his only related contribution was a trio for clarinet, cello, and piano composed in 1798, probably at the request of the renowned clarinettist, Joseph Beer (1744–1812). A powerful work, it employs some rather obvious thematic ideas to excellent effect, not least in the lively set of variations on the operatic trio 'Pria ch'io l'impegno' from Joseph Weigl's *L'Amor marinaro* which serves as a finale.[11] Though hardly representative of Beethoven at his most sophisticated, the work provides a valuable link, in a sparse repertoire, between Mozart's clarinet trio, K498, and Brahms's trio for clarinet, cello, and piano, Op. 114, of 1891. Beethoven made one further venture with the clarinet trio ensemble in 1805, when he published a trio version of his famous Septet in E flat, Op. 20, the work which probably brought him most fame during the early part of the century.[12]

The practice of transcribing newly published compositions of particular distinction for alternative media was commonly ap-

---

[11] Thayer–Forbes, *Beethoven*, 214. Joseph Weigl (1766–1846), son of the principal cellist in Haydn's orchestra at Esterháza, was well known in Vienna at the turn of the nineteenth century for his popular German and Italian operas. His earliest theatrical success was *La Principessa d'Amalfi* (1794) which Haydn, his godfather, described as 'novel in conception, noble, expressive—in short a masterpiece'. *L'Amor marinaro* (1797), the first of his operas to gain widespread acclaim, was played in many of the principal European theatres. The theme from it used by Beethoven in his clarinet trio is the closing section of the terzetto, 'Pria ch'io l'impegno' (No. 12). According to Thayer, the elder Artaria reported that Beethoven was unaware of the origin of the theme and decidedly annoyed when he discovered the truth about it.

[12] Ibid. 265–6.

plied at the time to both orchestral and chamber works, and served as an effective method of disseminating knowledge of the latest music. Very often these arrangements were made, not by the composer himself, but by professional transcribers, or students who were in the pay of publishers. In Beethoven's case, more often than not, it was the loyal Ferdinand Ries who undertook such work. His transcriptions include piano-trio and piano-quartet versions, respectively, of the second and third symphonies, and arrangements for piano trio of the Op. 9 string trios and the Op. 18 quartets undertaken, according to Thayer, 'without Beethoven's knowledge or consent'. An interesting and amusing episode is recorded by Thayer concerning the C minor trio from the Op. 1 set. In 1817 Beethoven was presented, by an unnamed musician,[13] with an arrangement he had made of the trio for string quintet (with two violas), a transcription, it seems, of somewhat modest merits. Instead of flying into a rage, as might reasonably have been expected, Beethoven apparently took a lively interest in the production, substantially revised it, and eventually, in 1819, allowed its publication by Artaria as his Op. 104. His manuscript score of the retranscription bears the heading: 'Arrangement of a Terzett as a | 3-voiced Quintet | by Mr Goodwill | and from appearing to be in 5 voices | brought to the light of day in 5 real voices | and lifted from the most abject *Miserabilität* | to moderate respectability | by Mr Wellwisher | 1817 | August 14 | N.B. The original 3-voiced Quintet has been sacrificed as a burnt offering to the gods of the Underworld.'[14]

In the meantime, some ten years earlier, Beethoven had returned to the orthodox piano trio with a pair of works in D major and E flat major, which were published in 1809 as Op. 70 Nos. 1 and 2. The trios were probably written, or at least completed, while the composer was staying at Heiligenstadt during the summer of 1808. His residence in Vienna at the time was the house of his close friend the Countess Marie von Erdödy, and it was to her that the trios were dedicated—though not, unhappily enough, without the friction that so often beset Beethoven's personal relationships. As the Lichnowskys could

---

[13] Later identified as a 'Herr Kaufmann' in a letter (Anderson No. 801) written by Beethoven to the publisher Steiner in Aug. 1817.

[14] Quoted in Thayer–Forbes, *Beethoven*, 678: see also Alan Tyson, 'The Authors of the Op. 104 String Quintet', in Tyson (ed.), *Beethoven Studies*, 158.

testify, Beethoven was not the easiest of house-guests to accommodate, and during his stay with the countess a quarrel of
unknown cause developed.[15] As a result we find the composer
writing to Breitkopf and Härtel in May 1809 asking for her name
to be struck out of the dedication and that of the Archduke
Rudolph substituted. Fortunately the trouble was patched up in
time for the original dedication to be restored, and posterity was
spared the problem of having to distinguish between three
'Archduke' trios.

The linking together of large-scale compositions under a single
opus number was a common enough practice for Beethoven in
the early part of his career; but by 1809 it had become sufficiently
rare to have acquired a special significance. Beethoven adopted
the practice on only one later occasion, for his two cello sonatas,
Op. 102; and of his main successors only Schumann with his three
string quartets, Op. 41, and Brahms with his first two quartets
and his clarinet sonatas provided similar connections. Perhaps, for
Beethoven, the intention to dedicate two similar works to a single
patron was sufficient incentive, though this, curiously, does not
apply in the case of the late cello sonatas. However another, and
more interesting, possibility is that he wished, by juxtaposing
contrasted works within a single framework, to stress the scope
offered by the medium involved for vivid differences of expression. Certainly, in the case of the Op. 70 trios, the contrasts are
obvious enough, both in their broad features and in their details.
The first of them, the so-called 'Geister' Trio, in three movements, is highly concentrated, tense and energetic, mysterious and
humorous by turns, whereas the second, in four movements, is
lyrical and relaxed, warm in expression, jocular at times, and full
of subtle musical surprises. It is regrettable that neither individually nor as a pair have the works received the full recognition they
deserve, having been overshadowed three years later—and consistently thereafter—by the 'Archduke' Trio.

The 'Erdödy' trios (as they might reasonably be called) belong
to the midpoint of Beethoven's second period, to the year which
also saw the production of the fifth and sixth symphonies and the
Choral Fantasia. With their larger, more closely integrated

---

[15] Thayer–Forbes, *Beethoven*, 450–1.

structures and richer sonorities they are as different from the Op. 1 trios as the 'Rasumovsky' quartets (of 1806–7) are from the Op. 18 set. One important contributory factor to their increased grandeur was, of course, the more highly developed piano of the period, with its additional tonal strength, greater responsiveness, and, particularly, enlarged compass. Details of compass and tessitura will be considered in more detail in the next chapter, but it will be appropriate here to outline some of the more general ways in which Beethoven benefited from the wider keyboard spacing and stronger treble and bass sonorities of the contemporary instruments. A fine example of the magisterial manner made possible is provided by the opening bars of Op. 70 No. 1, with the pianist's hands three octaves apart and the strings occupying the two intervening octaves, all playing fortissimo (see Ex. 17 below). Yet it is not solely from the increased power of the later pianos that he gains, but also from the scope they afford for an altogether wider range of dynamics: more very soft tonal shades as well as very loud ones, more expressive use of crescendo and diminuendo, more sudden sforzandos and pianissimos. And alongside these such quasi-orchestral effects as keyboard tremolandi, sustained high or low trills, and prolonged octave rolls deep in the bass, all of which are used to impart colour of special significance to the grimly picturesque slow movement of the D major trio.

Vivid instrumental characterization of this type is combined in the D major trio with a strongly integrated structure in which motivic development, subtle key distribution, and counterpoint all feature significantly. In the outer movements particular stress is laid on two distantly related keys—the flat submediant (B flat major) and the flat mediant (F major). The intention to explore these key areas is announced at the opening of the work (in bar 5) where, after the initial D major scalic flourish has ended unexpectedly on an F natural (sustained by the cello), the piano left hand introduces a soft octave B flat, implying an incomplete B flat triad; this immediately falls a semitone to A, providing a VI♭/V 6/4 progression which ushers in the second segment of the principal theme (See Ex. 17). The harmonic procedure is similar to that used in the 'Emperor' Concerto to link the slow movement to the finale, where the bass falls from B (= C flat) on the bassoons to B flat (dominant of E flat) on the horns; in that case, however, the chordal implication, though perfectly clear, is left entirely to the

Ex. 17

listener's imagination. Later in the trio's first movement, preceding the start of the second subject group, F major (the flat mediant) is emphasized in a powerful eight-bar passage based on the second segment of the principal theme. Matching this, after the start of the recapitulation, there is a new minor version of the opening scalic flourish, out of which the equivocal F natural emerges simply as the dominant of B flat, and introduces in that key some entirely new developments, decorating the main theme's second phrase. Thus a symmetrical pattern is established whereby each appearance of the second subject group is prefaced by a passage bearing a flat submediant relationship to its key (F major preceding A major in the exposition, and B flat major preceding D major in the recapitulation), and whereby the contrasted key-colours, in both exposition and recapitulation, are related to episodes exploring a single theme-segment in a process of continuous development and expansion. The development section proper is long and elaborate, and significantly keeps well clear, apart from one short passage, of keys on the flat side of D major. Both segments of the principal theme are involved, and from the halfway point wrestle together in some tough, uncompromising contrapuntal writing which, were we unaware of the work's date of origin, might readily suggest a 'third-period' style (see Ex. 18). Rather surprisingly, for so late a work, Beethoven marks both halves of the first movement to be repeated. The only other middle period works which similarly have double repeats in

Ex. 18

their first movements are the second 'Rasumovsky' quartet and the piano sonatas Op. 78 in F sharp major and Op. 79 in G major. The very rarity of the practice points to the likelihood that Beethoven may have had some special reason for employing it. Perhaps, not unreasonably, he may have wished to provide a second chance for the complexities of his development to be properly appreciated. However, it is usual in performance nowadays for the short first half to be repeated and for the second repeat to be ignored—possibly in the mistaken belief that in this way a better 'balance' between the two halves can be achieved.

The work's mysterious slow movement, from which it has gained its 'Geister' (ghost) sobriquet, is as remarkable for its key scheme as for its novelties of scoring. Set in D minor (and thus preserving a single tonic throughout the whole work) it is based on two tiny melodic ideas, stated consecutively in opening bars, the first a three-note pattern in bare octaves on the strings and the second an undulating figure, with chordal accompaniment, on the piano. Both motifs are frequently presented in new scoring but, interestingly, never occur in sequence in the same instrumental part (see Ex. 19).

Structurally the movement is organized on fairly normal sonata lines, except that the second subject 'area' (with virtually no trace of a subsidiary melodic idea) is set in the strikingly irregular key of C major, the flat leading-note in relation to the basic tonic. This is maintained until the end of the exposition where a wandering chromatic bass (prophetic of the first movement coda in the Choral Symphony) contrives to impart a thoroughly sinister character to a simple cadence point. After an eight-bar transition (or miniature development?) there is a full-length recapitulation in which the original second subject 'area' is simply raised a whole tone in pitch to D minor; and to end, an impressive coda, with rapid descending chromatic scales and drumming note-repetitions on the strings which convey a sense of ruin and dissolution. Apart from these drumming figures there is little which is unusual about the string writing; it is left to the piano to underline the prevailing air of gloom and mystery, partly by emphasizing the lowest part of its register and partly by cultivating a texture with unusually wide spacing between the hands. The Gothic effects—shuddering diminished sevenths and rumbling figures deep in the bass (pointing forward to Weber's

Ex. 19

Der Freischütz)—are sufficiently unusual in Beethoven to suggest that he may have been attempting to portray some specific dramatic or pictorial scene. It is known that in 1807/8 he was considering writing an opera on the subject of Macbeth, using as a libretto a play by Heinrich Joseph von Collin, based on Shakespeare.[16] Indeed, before abandoning the idea as 'too gloomy' he had already made some preliminary sketches which are said to relate to the witches' incantation and Macbeth's first entry. These, according to Nottebohm, not only occupy part of the pages used for sketches of the Largo of the 'Geister' Trio, but also share the same, D minor, tonality. It seems therefore very possible that the famous slow movement may have been associated in some way with the Macbeth project. Whether in its final form the movement relates best to the weird sisters, the midnight murder of Duncan, the appearance of Banquo's ghost, or none of these, the listener must decide for himself.

[16] G. Nottebohm, *Zweite Beethoveniana* (Leipzig, 1887), 225–7: see also Emily Anderson, 'Beethoven's Operatic Plans', *Proceedings of the Royal Musical Association* 88 (1961–2), 66–7.

Hardly less Shakespearian in manner, though not in intent, is the humorous, quirky, eccentric even, finale to the trio, which releases the tension engendered by its predecessor much as the appearance of the bibulous porter does after the murder scene in Macbeth. Often criticized as trifling or excessively lightweight, the movement is one which seems to invite misunderstanding, or at least a strong conflict of opinions. In a spirited defence Joseph Kerman describes it as 'Beethoven's *Musikalischer Spass* without Mozart's malice', an observation which sums up aptly enough its admirable compound of high spirits, wit, and occasional rustic good humour.[17] Its opening phrase, which leads to an abrupt halt on the dominant of the submediant (an F sharp major chord) and then returns to the tonic with no intervening 'resolution', points directly forward to another *locus classicus* of Beethovenian Olympian humour—the scherzo (in E major) of the C sharp minor quartet, Op. 131, the initial idea of which reproduces, at a much faster speed, exactly the same progression. And, similarly, the strange passage in the final coda (at bar 378), involving high pizzicatos and a distant (B flat minor) tonality, recalls the spirit at least of the bizarre pizzicato sections which characterize the end of the same quartet movement. Serving both as a scherzo and a sonata-form finale, the last movement provides a key scheme which ingeniously mirrors that of the first movement. Again it is the keys of F major and B flat major which are emphasized, in D major or A major contexts, twice each during the exposition and recapitulation. As in the first movement they are used partly to provide an oblique approach to the second subject group and partly to enrich each section with additional developments. Among scoring details of particular note there may be mentioned the very low piano bass-line in bars 28 to 35; the widely spaced writing for piano and strings in three octaves (as in the first movement) from bar 119, expanding to four octaves from bar 124; and the wonderfully humorous division of the main theme, a bar at a time, between the two stringed instruments during the final coda. Beethoven, it is said, completed this movement, and indeed the whole D major trio, with unusual speed and fluency. Certainly the finale shows every sign of having sprung from a

[17] J. Kerman, 'Tändelnde Lazzi: On Beethoven's Trio in D major, Op. 70 No. 1', in M. H. Brown and R. J. Wiley (eds.), *Slavonic and Western Music: Essays for Gerald Abraham* (Oxford, 1985), 109.

single impetus, as if it had entered his mind whole and unified from the start—though this did not eliminate, as the surviving sketches show, the customary need for much revision and recasting of detail.[18]

In the case of the second 'Erdödy' trio very few sketches have survived, so that the successive stages of its composition cannot readily be traced. It is, however, a complex work and there is reason to suppose, with Riemann, that it may well have cost the composer more painstaking effort than its fellow trio.[19] The slow introduction to the first movement is of special interest. Like the equivalent section in the second of the Op. 1 trios it is linked melodically to the ensuing Allegro, but linked to the second subject group, not the first. Also, it recurs briefly at the end of the movement (in the manner of Haydn's 'Drumroll' Symphony) to provide a structurally significant point of repose during the final coda. Delicately scored, the introduction starts with the cello alone (another unusual feature, paralleled in the A major cello sonata, Op. 69, of the same period) and proceeds in four-part imitative counterpoint involving all three instruments, before breaking into pianistic flourishes, over dominant harmony, which presage the coming Allegro. On its return at the end of the movement Beethoven takes the somewhat unusual step of altering the original scoring and aiming towards a rather fuller texture. This he achieves partly by a reordering of the parts—involving the transfer of the solo cello opening to the piano and the original bass-line to the cello an octave lower—and partly by adding a new chordal enrichment from the end of the third bar.

In the Allegro the composer embarks on some strange harmonic adventures which involve the approach to crucial preparatory dominants from the flat side of the key, so that they are nearly—but never entirely—robbed of their dominant character. The first instance, a relatively simple one, occurs at the start of the second subject group where the cello, with a long-held B flat initiates a short passage based on the introduction, which moves quite rapidly towards G flat major before being pulled back abruptly to the dominant of B flat for the new principal theme in

[18] See D. Weise (ed.) *Beethoven: Ein Skizzenbuch zur Pastoralsymphonie Op. 68 und zu den Trios Op. 70 Nos. 1 und 2*, 2 vols. (Bonn, 1961).

[19] A. Tyson, 'Stages in the Composition of Beethoven's Piano Trio, Op. 70 No. 1', *Proceedings of the Royal Musical Association* 97 (1970–1), 4.

that key. More complex, both to the eye and the ear, is the key sequence furnished by the development section, and the altogether startling method of returning home at the point of recapitulation. In bar 13 of the development, following a series of diminished sevenths, the tonality settles temporarily in A flat major and then starts to move progressively flatwise through A flat minor, C flat (= B) major and F flat (= E) major, the associated chords supporting brief melodic elements from the second subject group. Then, using F flat (= E) major as the Neapolitan chord in E flat minor, the harmony gradually sideslips to the dominant of D flat as the point of recapitulation is reached. Beethoven's way out of the apparent impasse he has created involves a notable piece of musical sleight of hand, described by Tovey as 'perhaps the most unexpected return in all music'.[20] In a remarkable three-bar passage he piles up overlapping versions of the principal thematic idea in three different, and necessarily conflicting, keys—D flat on the cello, F minor on the violin, and finally E flat on the piano, the crucial move to F minor (the supertonic in the home key) being achieved by means of an intervening diminished seventh. In practice, however, it is the 6/4–5/3 progression in the fourth bar of Example 20 which provides the extreme 'gravitational' pull necessary to restore E flat fully as the basic key centre. Harmonic twists of a similar, though somewhat more playful, nature are to be found in the third movement (Allegretto) of the trio. One of these occurs in bar 24, where a long, flowing principal melody in A flat major is brought to a sudden halt on VI♭/V♭ chord over a bass D, which sounds, in its immediate tonal surroundings, like a supertonic chromatic seventh; however, after a bar's hesitation, the music proceeds as though from a plain dominant seventh, its harmonic direction having been switched by a gentle type of musical pun. A second instance arises in bar 37, where after a full close (with plagal extension) in E flat there occurs a strange four-bar link for the piano right hand alone, leading to a return of the principal theme in the home tonic. What might well, in the context, have been a straightforward diatonic progression is transformed by the introduction of B naturals, B double-flats, and D naturals into a curiously enigmatic phrase, part humorous and part mysterious

---

[20] D. F. Tovey, *Beethoven* (London, 1944), 101.

Ex. 20

(see Ex. 21). Details of this sort are the more arresting because of the otherwise relaxed character of the Allegretto, which, with its attractively lyrical theme, has the air somewhat of a 'contrasting trio' section to a preceding—but in this case non-existent—scherzo. In its actual middle section four-bar phrases are set antiphonally between the strings and the piano, the former briefly simulating a string trio by the use of consistent double stops in the violin part. Also, there is a charmingly Schubertian passage with modulations which pass rapidly through G sharp (= A flat) minor to F flat (= E) major, as a Neapolitan chord in E flat, in a manner which closely, and possibly intentionally, recalls the harmonic events in the first movement development, outlined above.

Expansion of tonality is carried to even further limits in the finale, a sonata-form movement of outstanding liveliness and originality. As in the D major trio, it is the third-related (chromatic mediant and submediant) key-areas which are explored, and not simply as localized patches of key 'colour', but as principal tonalities for entire sections. Thus, the whole of the

Ex. 21 [Allegretto ma non troppo]

second subject group is set in G major in the exposition, and in C major in the recapitulation, the contrasted key in each case being approached by a designedly abrupt and angular transition. Against the background of E flat, the major mediant (G major) sounds bright and joyous, and to match this Beethoven provides a second subject group of notable energy and exuberance in which the extremes of register of all three instruments are fully exploited. The corresponding passage in the recapitulation biases the overall tonality so heavily in favour of C major that the composer takes the unusual step of repeating the entire second subject group once again, this time in the original tonic key. And even then it takes a further twenty-three bars over a tonic pedal at the end fully to restore the tonal balance of the movement.

The second movement of the work stands resolutely aside from all these modulatory adventures. Based on two themes, respectively in C major and C minor, it provides decorative variations on each in turn, following the 'double-variation' pattern favoured by Haydn, and at the same time remains contentedly within the tiny orbit of keys closely related to each tonic. The resultant tonal stability, coupled with a pervading air of gentle whimsicality, imparts a classical serenity to the movement and renders it a perfect foil to its more unbridled neighbours. It is strange that this powerful and original work—'an exquisite study in chamber-music writing from beginning to end', as Gerald Abraham calls it—is relatively neglected nowadays.[21] Perhaps the most likely explanation is that various of its principal melodic ideas, being designed with deeper structural purposes in mind, lack some of the immediate surface charm which is most likely to attract popular admiration to the work as a whole.

No such difficulty has affected the last of Beethoven's full-length trios, the 'Archduke', Op. 97 in B flat, composed in 1811. Widely acclaimed in the composer's lifetime for the grandeur of its conception and the quality of its ideas, it has held its place ever since as one of the finest achievements in the trio form and, indeed, in classical chamber music generally. The principal themes of the work attract immediate attention for their supple-ness and cantabile character; it is noteworthy that each is stated initially at a soft dynamic level and in most cases with the term 'dolce' appended. Also, many of the themes are linked together by a strong family likeness and thus engender a powerful sense of unity in the work as a whole. Thematic allusions between movements, at a conscious level, are not very common in Beethoven, and there is no reason to suppose that this trio provides a special exception. But it is not unusual to find that a basic thematic 'mould', relevant to an entire work, has formed in the composer's mind, possibly without his full awareness, which serves as a crucible from which interrelated melodic ideas emerge in the normal process of composition. The unusual extent to which this appears to have occurred in the 'Archduke' Trio, and its effect upon the shaping of the entire work, may be judged from the brief instances given in Example 22. The matter is significant because of the insight it provides into the 'wholeness' of the work—the strong sense of inevitability by which a composition of such large dimensions attains unity.

Some relatively minor features apart, the trio's forms and key schemes are unexceptional. Beethoven again adopts a four-

---

[21] G. Abraham, *The Concise Oxford History of Music* (London, 1979), 622.

Ex. 22

movement pattern, but for the first time in one of his trios places the slow movement third, after the scherzo. This enables him to link the Andante to the rondo finale, using a simple chord change whereby, at the final cadence, the slow movement's key-note D is transformed, above a new dominant seventh, into the leading-note in E flat and thus prepares the way for the rondo theme gradually to restore the home tonic. The method is somewhat similar to that used to connect the slow movement to the scherzo in two other of his main chamber works of the period, the F minor string quartet, Op. 95, and the G major violin sonata, Op. 96. In the trio the effect of joining two already very long movements is to produce continuous—and, indeed, continuously captivating—music for the ensemble over an exceptionally large time-span.

Third relationships are again a feature of the key scheme, but are used in a less radical way than in the Op. 70 trios. The second subject group in the first movement, for example, is set with beautiful effect in the major submediant (G major), but it is recapitulated quite conventionally in the tonic; and the choice of D major for the slow movement, after two extended movements in B flat, provides a wholly Haydnesque type of contrast as a means of establishing a mood of warmth and serenity for the radiant set of variations.

The unusually long rondo finale contains several structural features of particular interest. The principal theme, though fundamentally in B flat major, starts repeatedly on a dominant seventh in E flat and maintains that key, the subdominant, for four bars before turning to its real tonic. It is thus a particular type of modulating theme, similar to those found in the rondo finales of the second 'Rasumovsky' quartet and the fourth piano concerto, both of which start in C major before moving to their main keys of E minor and G major, respectively. In the case of the trio a special problem arises because the rondo theme, starting as it does on the dominant of the subdominant (over a dominant seventh), cannot be approached for the purpose of reprise by means of a normal preparatory dominant. Beethoven's ingenious solution to the problem is to establish well in advance, and in numerous imaginative ways, the actual dominant harmony (complete with dominant seventh) over which the theme is to enter; and to rely on its strong melodic profile, rather than any shift of harmony, to characterize the point of its return. There is, however, one exception, and a particularly fascinating one. At the end of the recapitulation, the return of the rondo theme is approached by the same method as before, but at the last moment shifting harmonies and a sudden enharmonic side-step bring the music to rest on a dominant seventh in A major. Logically, if the former harmonic pattern were to be preserved, the return should proceed at this point in E major; but Beethoven, for the first time, suddenly treats his dominant seventh as a *real* preparatory chord, shifts into A major, and provides in that key a new version of the rondo theme, now presto and in 6/8 time, with G natural subtly removed from its melody and harmony so that no trace remains of the original subdominant harmonic characteristics. The use of the 'foreign' key area of A major is remarkable mainly because it is maintained at such length; no less than thirty-one bars elapse before a further return of the rondo theme at last restores the original tonic. Elsewhere in Beethoven, such 'wrong-key' returns tend to be more short-lived. A lovely early example occurs in the finale of the E flat piano sonata, Op. 7, of 1796, where a magical reprise of the rondo theme in the key of E major is preserved for only five bars before slipping back into the original tonic key. In

Op. 97, so disruptive is the effect of the long A major passage that it requires a coda of exceptional spaciousness, much of it over a tonic pedal, to provide an effective counterbalance.

The large and significant role allotted to the piano in Op. 97 is allied to string writing of a rather subdued character. No doubt the demanding, though not unduly showy, style of the piano writing reflects to some extent Beethoven's wish to please the work's dedicatee, the Archduke Rudolph, who is known to have been an accomplished amateur pianist. But it would be a mistake to suppose that the strings are restrained simply in order to allow greater scope for the pianist. Although the scoring appears to give the piano part undue prominence, in practice the string contributions are so telling, and so much concerned with important motifs and countermelodies, that the balance of interest within the ensemble is never seriously imperilled. What is unarguable, however, is the unusually low pitch of the string parts, and of the violin part in particular. The explanation for this probably lies in the expressive character of the music. In this work, more than any of his other trios, Beethoven sought to achieve a strongly unified sound complex, one in which, for example, antiphonal elements and others involving vivid contrast are curbed in favour of a consistency of texture and mellowness of sonority more akin to a string quartet or quintet. Thus, an important function of the strings is to supply inner parts which combine with and supplement the piano's overtones in order to create a special sense of fullness and warmth. One result of this is to impart emphasis to such occasional high-pitched string passages as do occur. A memorable example is the strikingly beautiful violin entry in bar 43 of the first movement's development section which takes the second segment of the opening theme, in G major, up to g'''.

A further notable feature is the extensive use of pizzicato. The device was employed by Beethoven as early as Op. 1 No. 1 (at the end of the slow movement), and consistently in his later trios; but never previously with such freedom and richness of effect as in the 'Archduke'. Two particular examples stand out: the thirty-three-bar passage at the end of the first movement's development section where, at a consistent *pp* dynamic until the final crescendo, descending piano arpeggios are outlined with trills against rising string scales in thirds and tenths, played pizzicato with magical effect; and secondly, the fifteen-bar accompaniment pattern, from bar 25 of the scherzo, where pizzicato strings add a wonderful delicacy and verve to the piano's version of the second half of the main theme.

According to Thayer, the 'Archduke' Trio received its first public performance at a concert in aid of a military charity, held on Monday, 11 April 1814, at the Hotel zum Romischen Kaiser in Vienna. Louis Spohr, who was present, reported movingly about the efforts of the deaf composer to make sense of the piano part, on what was apparently a badly out-of-tune instrument. 'In the *forte* passages', he recalled, 'the poor deaf man pounded on the keys until the strings jangled, and in *piano* he played so softly that whole groups of notes were omitted . . . I was deeply saddened at so hard a fate.'[22]

The evidence is rather meagre to suggest that Beethoven planned any large-scale trios after the 'Archduke'. Thayer records part of a letter published in London in *The Harmonicon* for January 1824, in which the writer reported having visited Beethoven in Baden in September 1823. 'I heard a MS. trio of his for the pianoforte, violin and violoncello', he wrote, 'which I thought very beautiful; and it is, I understand, to appear shortly in London.'[23] Thayer mistakenly identifies the letter-writer as 'an Englishman, Edward Schulz'; but, as Alan Tyson has shown, his name was actually J. R. (probably Johann Reinhold) Schultz, though nothing further seems to be known about him.[24] The 'MS. trio' that he heard is unlikely to have been the 'Archduke' since by 1823 it had already been published for seven years. Thayer, interestingly, mentions the existence of some sketches dated 1815 for a trio in F minor, but naturally discounts these since the composition they foreshadowed seems never to have materialized.[25] The remaining possibility is that what the traveller heard was the set of variations for piano trio on the aria 'Ich bin der Schneider Kakadu' from Wenzel Müller's opera *Die Schwestern von Prag*, which Beethoven published in Vienna in May 1824 as his Op. 121. No date of composition is known, but its style suggests that it belongs to the composer's middle period, possibly

[22] Thayer–Forbes, *Beethoven*, 577–8.
[23] Ibid. 870–1.
[24] See Tyson, 'Stages in the Composition of Beethoven's Piano Trio Op. 70 No. 1', 2.
[25] The references to the performance of a manuscript trio, and to the sketches for a projected trio in F minor, are included only in Krehbiel's English edition of Thayer's *Life of Beethoven* (repr. London, 1960) iii, 134–5.

around 1815; certainly 1823 would be improbably late.[26] It is a substantial and delightful work, but adds little of importance to our understanding of Beethoven's treatment of the genre. Thayer's brief reference to the F minor trio sketches remains, therefore, the sole indication that the composer may have had later plans for a full-length trio.

After the 'Archduke' Trio it was some sixteen years before the next major examples of the genre appeared: Schubert's great piano trios in B flat (D 898) and E flat (D 929). For reasons which will become clear, it is not easy to arrive at precise datings for these works; but the likelihood is that they were both written about a year before the composer's death, during a two- or three-month period between October 1827 and January 1828. The E flat trio presents the lesser problems of chronology. The autograph manuscript of the work indicates clearly that it was begun in November 1827; and there is documentary evidence to show that it was performed by Joseph Boehm (violin), Joseph Lincke (cello), and Carl Maria von Bocklet (piano) at Schubert's only public concert of his works, in a room provided by the Gesellschaft der Musikfreunde, on 26 March 1828.[27] Furthermore, it was published (one of the very few large-scale works by Schubert to receive such recognition in his lifetime) by Probst of Leipzig in October 1828, and became at the end of his life probably the single most widely recognized of his instrumental compositions. The B flat trio seems, on the other hand, to have fared less happily. Not only is there no surviving autograph MS to fix its date of composition but also it was left unpublished until 1836, eight years after the composer's death. Furthermore, there appears to have been no public performance of the work during Schubert's lifetime, though it was almost certainly played privately in

[26] See Thayer–Forbes, *Beethoven*, 659, where the variations are listed under 'works composed in 1816'. Thayer comments, however, that, in a letter to Gottfried Härtel of 19 July 1816, Beethoven referred to the work as 'composed earlier, but nevertheless not to be rejected'. Wenzel Müller (1767–1835), whose career as a theatre conductor in Vienna and Prague spanned nearly half a century, was the composer of numerous Singspiels, parodies, and other dramatic works, including *Kaspar der Fagottist, oder die Zauberzither* (1791), based on a text drawn from the same literary source—Wieland's *Djinnistan* collection (1786)—as Mozart's *Die Zauberflöte*. The aria from his opera, *Die Schwestern von Prag* (1794), which Beethoven used for his trio variations, originally had the text 'Ich bin der Schneider wez, wez, wez'. At what point the word 'Kakadu' (cockatoo) was substituted remains unclear.

[27] See O. E. Deutsch, *Schubert: Thematic Catalogue of all his Works in Chronological Order* (London, 1951) 452–3; also J. Reed, *Schubert*, (London, 1987), 178–9.

his presence at Joseph von Spaun's house towards the end of January 1828. Another possibility is that it was performed by Schuppanzigh, Lincke, and Bocklet at a concert known to have taken place at the Musikverein on 26 December 1827, though there are conflicting claims that it was in fact the E flat trio that was played on that occasion.[28] It will be seen therefore that the question of precedence in the dating of the trios remains unclear. Nowadays it is customary (and perfectly reasonable) to accept the order of composition indicated by Otto Deutsch in his Schubert catalogue, which places the B flat work as the earlier of the two, though his numberings—D 898 and D 929—seem to indicate too large a time-gap between the works, even when allowance has been made for Schubert's extraordinary fecundity.

The two trios form an admirably contrasted partnership. Together they provide vivid witness to the richness and diversity of Schubert's musical thought during the final year of his life, a luxuriance evident equally in his C major string quintet, and his three final piano sonatas from the same period. So fittingly do the two works represent complementary facets of Schubert's musical personality—'active, masculine, dramatic' for the E flat trio and 'passive, feminine, lyrical' for the B flat, according to Schumann's rather over-simplified view[29]—that it is hardly possible, let alone desirable, to regard either of them as superior to the other. Nevertheless, it is worth observing that in the early nineteenth century the E flat work gained particular regard at the expense of its partner, no doubt because of its earlier date of publication; and that subsequently the pendulum swung somewhat in the opposite direction, with the result that the E flat trio, for all its strength and beauty, has not in more recent times received all the recognition it deserves.

Schubert's handling of the medium is equally masterly in both works. In particular his treatment of the piano in relation to the strings shows a remarkable freedom and assurance, of a type not always apparent in his works for piano solo. Very characteristic is his emphasis on the instrument's topmost register, with both of the pianist's hands at a higher pitch than the strings, providing, in

---

[28] See E. Badura-Skoda, 'The Chronology of Schubert's Piano Trios', in E. Badura-Skoda and P. Branscombe (eds.), *Schubert Studies: Problems of Style and Chronology* (Cambridge, 1982) 277–95: see also Reed, *Schubert*, 179.

[29] A. Einstein, *Schubert* (London, 1951), 311.

piano duet terms, a primo part to their secondo. Also, Schubert
avails himself of frequent opportunities for full chordal writing,
though invariably in such a way as to avoid needless doubling of
the strings. But, despite the richness of his instrumental palette,
the composer never allows his piano part to dominate the others;
indeed, in these trios more perhaps than in those of any earlier
composers, Beethoven not excepted, a genuine three-sided partnership—an artistic triple alliance—is achieved. The string writing is equally individual. Particularly noteworthy are the many
instances where strong, penetrating lines are created by setting the
strings in octaves against the piano, and where high-pitched,
technically demanding contributions from the cello generate life
and colour within the texture.

In both trios Schubert adopts the 'grand sonata' style of
Beethoven, employing expansive four-movement structures on
the lines of the 'Archduke' Trio, but with the scherzo in each case
placed third. Superficially, the two works appear to be cast in
much the same mould; but on closer examination it becomes clear
that there is nothing fixed about their formal designs, the
corresponding movements in each displaying much variety of
treatment. Schubert's approach to large-scale sonata form is
plainly different from Beethoven's. Altogether less concerned
with tightly knit motivic development, he relies upon spaced
repetitions (often with delicate variations incorporated), vivid key
contrasts, and the power of melodic and rhythmic drive to
provide his structures with the necessary strength and cohesion. A
clearer idea of his methods, and of the degree of variety he
achieves, may be gained from a comparison of parallel movements in the trios. In the two opening movements it is the
number and disposition of the themes, and their treatment in the
development, which provide the most striking difference. The B
flat trio is the more 'regular' of the two, by reason of its clear-cut
first and second themes, set in tonic and dominant respectively;
these are elaborated in turn, and sometimes in combination,
during a fairly short, but tonally wide-ranging development
section, which includes a move to E major (the most 'distant'
tonality from B flat) and to G flat for a carefully planned 'false'
reprise immediately before the recapitulation proper. The E flat
trio, on the other hand, has six short themes in its exposition, the
third of which astonishes by arriving in B (=C flat) minor,

approached through an enharmonic change dramatically disguised by a rapid ascending chromatic scale in octaves on the
piano. In order to re-establish the tonal equilibrium a strong
affirmation of the dominant is required in the fifth and sixth
themes, beginning at bars 116 and 140, respectively. The development is concerned solely with the last of the exposition ideas, a
tiny codetta theme of great beauty, scored in four parts with a
quartet-like suavity of expression (see Ex. 23). In a notably
extensive section (198 bars as compared to only 99 in the B flat
trio) this melodic fragment, accompanied repeatedly by descending triplet figuration in the piano right hand (recalling the A flat
Impromptu from D 899), forms the basis of three spacious
terraces of sound, each following the same modulatory pattern,
but from different starting-points. The following outline shows
the overall scheme, but omits, for simplicity's sake, numerous
incidental modulations which precede the end of each 'terrace';
these are well worth following through in the score:

Terrace 1: B major and minor, D major and minor, F major . . . to
the dominant of F sharp.
Terrace 2: F sharp major and minor, A major and minor, C major
. . . to the dominant of C sharp (= D flat).
Terrace 3: D flat (= C sharp) major and minor, E major and
minor, G major . . . via a changed progression to the dominant
of E flat major.

By the emphasis he throws on thematic variety in the exposition,
and the restricted melodic focus he provides in the very long
development, Schubert creates an impression of remarkable
expansiveness and structural majesty. The difference in style and
expression from the gentler, more song-like manner of the B flat
trio's equivalent movement could hardly be more marked.

Equally striking are the contrasts in form and expression
between the two slow movements. That in the B flat trio
comprises an extended ternary structure in E flat major, which
opens in a warm, reposeful mood, its lyricism enhanced by the use
of dissonant suspensions, expressive leanings on the flattened sixth
degree of the scale, and an unusually high-lying cello part. After
an eloquent middle section in the relative minor, with high, finely
scored keyboard figuration, the reprise, somewhat shortened,
begins in the subdominant (A flat major) and proceeds thereafter,

Ex. 23

through some heart-stopping modulations, both to and from E (= F flat) major, to a coda of infinite gentleness. It is not unlikely that the separate slow movement in E flat (D 897), published in 1844 as a *Notturno* for piano trio, was originally intended for this trio, but was discarded by the composer as unsuitable. Certainly it contains attractive music and would not have been entirely inappropriate. But by comparison with the exalted mood and finely controlled shades of expression of the movement which now stands in the trio, it remains earthbound, simply as a charming type of parlour music. The slow movement of the other trio (D 929), a modified sonata rondo in C minor of solemn character, begins with a twenty-bar theme of exceptional beauty, stated initially by the cello alone, with a marching chordal accompaniment on the piano. According to an old tradition passed down by Leopold von Sonnleithner,[30] Schubert based this

[30] See A. Fareanu, 'Leopold von Sonnleithners Erinnerungen an Franz Schubert', *Zeitschrift für Musikwissenschaft* 1 (1919), 466.

theme on a Swedish song which he heard sung by Isak Berg in November 1827 at the Fröhlich sisters' house in the Spielgasse.[31] Recently the song, entitled 'Se solen sjunker' (the sun has set), has been traced and again made available, and it has to be said that, apart from sharing the same key (C minor) and a similar marching rhythm, it bears only a very marginal resemblance to Schubert's superb theme.[32] In addition to the grace and power of this melody, two other particularly impressive features of the movement stand out: one is its stormy central episode (bars 104 to 128) centred on F sharp minor, where a wild despair seems to overtake the music, foreshadowing the similarly turbulent mood expressed in the slow movements of the late A major piano sonata (D 959) and C major string quintet (D 956); and the other, the seventeen-bar coda in which finely judged alternations of major and minor harmony provide exquisite colouring in support of elegantly varied fragments of the main theme. It is interesting to note, in passing, that both slow movements start in an 'unclassical' manner with two preparatory bars before the entry of the main theme, and thereby set a precedent which was to be followed by numerous trio composers later in the nineteenth century.

Less significant differences separate the two scherzos. Both are in triple time, both have central 'trios', and both show a delightful urge towards contrapuntal elaboration. In the B flat trio, for example, an ingenious quasi-fugal effect is achieved at the opening where (from bar 3) a two-bar phrase on the piano is answered in imitation at the fifth above by the violin and then, similarly, at the seventh below by the cello—a device which is echoed at various focal points later in the movement. And in the E flat scherzo (from D 929), a canon at the octave is preserved throughout, the *dux* and *comes* being allotted separately to the strings and piano, sometimes with the order of entry reversed. The method recalls that found in some of the gay dance movements of Haydn's earliest string quartets, or in more sombre mood, in the so-called 'Witches' minuet from his D minor quartet, Op. 76

[31] O. E. Deutsch, *Schubert Catalogue*, entry 887 on pp. 429–30, notes that the slow movement theme of the G major string quartet (D 887), of June 1826, was 'said by Anna Fröhlich to have been taken from a Swedish folk-song (or rather a song by Isaac Albert Berg)'. If this is so, Schubert is likely to have been acquainted with Berg and his Swedish repertoire some time before the singer's reported recital in 1827.

[32] See Manfred Willfort, 'Das Urbild des Andantes aus Schuberts Klaviertrio, D. 929' *Österreichische Musikzeitschrift* 33 (1978) 277–83: also Reed, *Schubert*, 180–1.

No. 2. Schubert, with his customary skill, manages to embrace some colourful key changes within his canonic scheme, and combines them with felicities of scoring to produce trio writing of great delicacy (see Ex. 24). In a letter to his publisher Probst in May 1828, Schubert asked him particularly to ensure that this movement was played 'at a moderate pace and *piano* throughout; the trio, on the other hand, vigorous, except where p and pp are marked'.

The final movements again reveal marked contrasts of style. While the finale of the B flat work is dance-like in character, and displays much formal subtlety, together with a remarkable economy of material, its counterpart in the E flat trio is boldly assertive in manner, diffuse in form, and often extravagantly virtuosic in a fashion which is somewhat surprising in a mature Schubert chamber work. Effective finales are notoriously difficult to write, and it is likely that Schubert may at times have found them particularly troublesome. Certainly there is considerable

Ex. 24

evidence, in the form of fragmentary and unfinished work from earlier in his career, to suggest that he overcame the associated problems only rather gradually. In his later works these movements not infrequently display rondo characteristics, though the forms are usually handled with considerable freedom; and in some notable instances moto perpetuo elements are also incorporated, often involving rapid figuration in 6/8 time, suggestive of the tarantella—for example, in the final movements of the string quartets in D minor, D 810 ('Death and the Maiden'), and G major, D 887, and in the C minor piano sonata, D 958.

In the finale of the B flat trio it is the limited range of the ideas employed, and the ingenious ways in which they are treated, which are particularly intriguing. Schubert calls the movement a rondo, but departs from orthodoxy in numerous structural details, relying upon an instinct for natural continuity and a clearcut system of spaced repetitions to provide cohesion. The form of the movement is so unusual, and so full of interesting detail, that it may be helpful here to set out its overall plan in tabular form (see Table 1).

The economy of material is remarkable. Virtually everything in the movement is based on the two themes Ⓐ and Ⓑ (including the three 'themes' marked Ⓒ, Ⓓ, and Ⓔ, which are simply variants); and the single most prominent feature is the four-bar phrase marked Ⓑ(i), which is used repeatedly as a main idea, a countertheme, or as a means of achieving modulations (see Ex. 25).

It will be seen that the movement falls into two more or less equal halves (bars 1–280 and 281–654), with an overall key scheme which observes, with numerous modulatory digressions, the normal tonic–dominant/tonic–tonic pattern. There are, however, in the second half, some significant additions which contribute extra substance and variety. One is the subdominant reprise (at bar 281), which provides the effect of a 'false' recapitulation, and another the remarkable developmental 'digression' in G minor and 3/2 time (at bar 370, see Ex. 25) which follows the tonic key return of Ⓐ (i) at bar 345. This latter passage is a 'digression' only in the sense that it appears to spring from its context in a sudden flash of inspiration, to dance its way airily through a succession of related keys on its way back to Ⓑ (i); thematically it is as closely related as everything else in the

TABLE 1.   *Fourth movement of Schubert's trio in B flat, D 898*

Bars	Theme	Section	Key pattern
1–26	Ⓐ	Rondo theme (i)	B♭–B♭
26–52		Rondo theme (ii)	F–B♭
52–75	Ⓑ	Second subject (i)	B♭–G min.
		Second subject (ii) and varied repeat	G min.–F
76–88		Link based on Ⓑ(i)	
88–116	Ⓒ	Third subject derived from Ⓑ(i)	A♭–F min.
116–39	Ⓑ	Second subject (ii)	F min.–E♭
			C min.–B♭
			G min.–F
140–51		Link based on Ⓑ(i)	
152–76	Ⓒ	Third subject derived from Ⓑ(i)	F–F
176–250	Ⓓ	Development of Ⓑ(i) and Ⓐ(i)	F–F
250–80	Ⓔ	'Dance' section on rhythm of Ⓐ(i) and on Ⓑ(i)	D♭–G
281–344	Ⓐ	Rondo theme (i) and (ii) and extension	E♭–B♭
345–70	Ⓐ	Rondo theme (i) only	B♭–B♭
370–84		Developmental 'digression' in 3/2 based on Ⓑ(i) and end of Ⓐ(i)	G min.–B♭
385–408	Ⓑ	Second subject (i) and (ii)	B♭–G min.–B♭
409–21		Link based on Ⓑ(i)	
421–49	Ⓒ	Third subject derived from Ⓑ(i)	D♭–B♭ min.
449–72	Ⓑ	Second subject (ii)	B♭ min.–A♭
			F min.–E♭
			C min.–B♭
473–84		Link based on Ⓑ(i)	
485–509	Ⓒ	Third subject derived from Ⓑ(i)	B♭–B♭
509–82	Ⓓ	Development of Ⓑ(i) and A (i)	B♭–B♭
583–610	Ⓔ	'Dance' section on rhythm of Ⓐ(i) and on Ⓑ(i)	G♭–B♭
611–54		Coda: Presto based on 'theme' Ⓓ	B♭–B♭

Ex. 25

movement to the principal subject matter, with Ⓑ (i) on the violin and the final bars of Ⓐ (i) and (ii), in the minor, on the cello. It is interesting to note also how the composer introduces strikingly scored structural 'pillars' (marked Ⓔ), once again in 3/2 time and dance style, just before the end of each half of the movement. These explore the third-related keys of D flat and G flat, both of them flat submediants in relation to their surrounding tonalities, and thus temporarily interrupt the expected progress to the dominant and tonic 'home' keys at these points. So marked is the radiant style of these episodes that they tend to sound newly minted in context; but, as is shown in Example 25, their main features are all drawn straightforwardly enough from the movement's basic ideas.

There is no reason to argue with Schubert's use of the term 'rondo'. Although an orthodox second return of the rondo theme is lacking, there is sufficient spaced repetition of important melodic elements to provide an overall rondo-like effect. Indeed, the impression created is of a group of circling dancers, continually rotating, and each returning to centre stage, in the manner of a round. There is no central development section of a formal type; development, in the sense of elegant variation and thematic expansion, goes on continuously. But, as nearly always in Schubert, key symmetry is precisely maintained.

The finale to the other trio, D 929, is more problematic.

Indeed, it is this movement which in recent times has most strongly attracted adverse criticism to the work as a whole. Organized very sectionally, in loosely connected paragraphs, it is long and discursive, and relies heavily for its effect upon the character of its principal themes which, in the first two sections particularly, are not of the first order. After hearing the work performed in public in March 1828, Schubert decided to shorten the last movement by a total of ninety-nine bars, and gave careful instructions to Probst, his publisher, that 'the cuts are to be strictly observed in the first edition'. Comparison of the first edition with the autograph shows that, in addition to the removal of a repeat sign, two sections each of about fifty bars were deleted, one of them apparently involving 'a unique combination of the cello theme from the slow movement with the *l'istesso tempo* subject [as first at bar 73) of the finale.[33] As a result the movement's general unwieldiness was considerably modified, though its basic problem—its structural diffuseness—still to some extent remained. However, despite such difficulties, the composer secures, throughout the movement, effects of great breadth and splendour, notably in the 'second subject' paragraphs, in 6/8 time, which contain some of the most brilliant and exciting piano trio writing in the repertoire. Also, he achieves an outstandingly imaginative stroke by his reintroduction in the finale of the 'Swedish' theme from the slow movement, using a type of transference which is decidedly unusual in his chamber music. The melody first recurs at the centrepoint of the movement, in B minor, a remote key usage which may well be intended to recall the startling $B(=C$ flat) minor episode at the beginning of the first movement. On this occasion, as also at its final appearance in the tonic minor at the end of the work, the theme is accompanied by descending piano figuration, consisting of paired quavers in cross-rhythm, which is derived from the keyboard part (from bar 139) of the brilliant 6/8 section referred to above; and thus it is unobtrusively melded into the natural flow of the music. The finale is incontestably a difficult movement to bring off in performance, particularly when Schubert's demand for 'a continual uniformity of tempo at the changes of time signature' is strictly observed. But when presented with authority and

---

[33] See Badura-Skoda, 'Chronology of Schubert's Trios', 294.

panache, and preferably with a rather light-toned piano, it can generate its own wholly convincing cohesion, and provide a vivid and characterful ending to the entire work.

Schumann, with his usual insight, and his penchant for vivid analogy, described the E flat trio as having 'passed across the face of the musical world like some angry portent in the sky';[34] and when one compares its untrammelled energy and rugged scoring with the homelier eloquence of the B flat work, his meaning is not hard to discern. Among Schubert's later works such 'portents' are increasingly found: in the first movement of the C major ('Reliquie') piano sonata, D 840, for example; in the slow movements of the G major string quartet, D 887 and the A major piano sonata, D 959, and in the last Heine settings—'Die Stadt', 'Am Meer', and 'Der Doppelgänger'—from the *Schwanengesang* cycle, D 957, all of which reveal a similar fierce intensity of expression that comes near to breaking the aesthetic and technical norms of the period. What was portended, at least in the short term, was the inevitable conflict between form and content which, in the wake of Viennese classicism, a loosening of structural bonds, a freer approach to chromaticism, and the expansion of tonality were bound to create.

[34] Einstein, *Schubert*, 311.

4 Interlude: Some Aspects of Technique

DURING its lengthy evolution the piano trio has come to be regarded, not altogether unjustly, as a taxing medium to control for both composers and performers. According to one commentator, it is 'one of the most difficult forms to manipulate' and one which is 'seldom satisfactory in balance'.[1] It will, therefore, be appropriate, before proceeding further with our survey, to consider briefly some of the basic technical problems which surround trio composition, especially those related to the nature of the instruments involved, and the methods of scoring for them.

Despite its intimacy of style and expression the trio genre has tended, throughout its development, to reflect microcosmically major aspects of other forms of music: initially, as we have seen, the classical sonata, the symphony, the concerto, the string quartet, and opera; and subsequently, after about 1830, the keyboard miniature, the solo song, the grand romantic concerto, and a variety of other instrumental forms of a dramatic, lyrical, or virtuosic character. Thus, it is hardly possible to identify a single set of techniques which is uniformly applicable to the genre. Before 1830, during the high days of Viennese classicism, technique functioned principally in support of structural logic, textural integrity, and the attainment of a democratic spread of interest among the parts, as much in the piano trio as in all other forms of chamber composition. But later stylistic changes brought about a weakening of the traditional aims, and the former technical criteria were gradually modified. One obvious source of difficulty was the inescapably fixed nature of the classical chamber media. Unlike the orchestra, or even the choral group, which could readily be expanded or contracted to accommodate changes in style, the piano trio and its fellow chamber ensembles, designed originally for music in the late eighteenth-century style, necessarily lacked any such scope for adaptability. Thus in face of

[1] T. Dunhill, *Chamber Music: A Treatise for Students* (London, 1925), 186.

the demand to embrace instrumental writing of ever greater richness and complexity, the inflexible media were compelled to accept radical stylistic changes in which purity of line was frequently sacrificed for colour and textural homogeneity for an increased element of individual display. Only at the earliest period of the trio's history, when for a time continuing developments in its participating instruments brought about a parallel growth between medium and genre, did a harmonious interaction between stylistic and technical requirements become possible.

Of particular importance in the initial stages were the advances made in piano construction. The delicate Stein and Walter pianos, which Haydn and Mozart so greatly admired and wrote for so exquisitely, soon proved inadequate to meet the needs of Beethoven and his contemporaries. Although the piano would undoubtedly have developed anyway at the time, it is clear that Beethoven accelerated the process very considerably. Not only did he write keyboard passages which appear in logic to require a larger compass than was currently available[2] but he also demanded by his grander textures and more dramatic style, both of writing and playing, instruments of larger tone and more robust construction. His friend and colleague, Anton Reicha, recalled in his memoirs how, in his early days at Bonn, the young Beethoven had fared in the performance of a Mozart concerto. 'All the time', he wrote, 'the strings kept snapping and jumping in the air, while the hammers got entangled in the broken strings. Beethoven, wishing to finish the piece at all costs, begged me to disentangle the hammers and remove the broken strings whenever he paused in playing.'[3] It is probable that the instrument was neither very new nor very strong, and that Beethoven's treatment of it was not a model of delicacy. Nevertheless, the whole episode suggests clearly enough how unready many of the instruments of the period were to meet the needs of the rising generation of composers and performers.

The piano makers responded with instruments of wider compass, with tougher frames, sturdier hammers with harder felt coverings, tauter and stronger strings, a heavier touch, and richer tone. Amongst the leading makers involved, in succession to Stein, Walter, and Wenzel Schantz of the late eighteenth century,

---

[2] For example, in the first movement of the piano sonata Op. 10 No. 3, at bar 104.
[3] E. Closson, *A History of the Piano* (London, 1947), 93.

were J. A. Streicher, Sébastien Erard, John Broadwood, and Conrad Graf, examples of whose instruments were all at various times owned by Beethoven;[4] and Ignaz and Camille Pleyel whose pianos were especially favoured by Chopin, Liszt, and Anton Rubinstein.[5] One development of particular importance was the double-escapement mechanism introduced by Sébastien Erard during the 1820s, which provided additional scope for the clean and rapid repetition of notes; and another, the use of iron frames to give added strength, a common practice with American makers from early in the century, including Hawkins, Chickering, and Steinway, the last of whom brought out, in 1856, the first grand piano with a single-piece iron frame, instead of one bolted together in sections.[6]

Inevitably, as pianos became stronger in tone and construction, they provided increasing competition for the strings in chamber ensembles; and although the violin family had already attained a high degree of perfection with the products of the great Cremonese makers over a century earlier, various significant changes were introduced to meet the new musical requirements of the time. These included the raising of the height of the bridge to increase the resistance of the strings to bow pressure, the use of a backward-sloping and longer neck to facilitate fingering, the adoption of the modern 'Tourte' bow with its tighter, more even bow-hairs, and eventually the introduction of metal, or metal coverings, for at least the two lowest strings on the various instruments. In this way a new type of balance was created within chamber ensembles, in which the bigger, more rounded tone of the later pianos was matched by a quality of string sound which was not only fuller but also more penetrating. And the piano trio, in consequence, soon acquired the overall increase in power and sonority necessary to accommodate the grander styles and richer textures of the later types of music being written for it.

Among the most important first contributions to the trio's growth was the enlargement of the piano's compass, a development which can be clearly traced through the succession of the Beethoven trios. For the first three published works, the 'Lich-

---

[4] Closson, *History*, 93, n. 1. It is interesting to note that a piano made in 1839 by Conrad Graf was presented to Clara Wieck on the occasion of her marriage to Robert Schumann, and that it eventually came into the possession of Brahms.

[5] Closson, *History*, 98–9.

[6] Ibid.

nowsky' Trios, a five-octave compass (FF to f'''), such as was available on the pianos of Mozart's time, is sufficient. Beethoven makes considerable use of the topmost note, as did Mozart also, but writes no passages which 'presuppose' a higher register. Adapted to the same bass range is the first of the Op. 70 trios, though it requires an additional fifth at the top (up to c''''), such as was available on some Sébastien Erard and John Broadwood instruments of the period. The absence of a top c'''' sharp seems to be indicated by a downward octave leap in the piano's right-hand passage in bars 215 to 218 of the finale (see Ex. 26(i)). The second trio of Op. 70, however, is rather more problematic. Clearly Beethoven is working within the same bass range, down to FF, though he gives signs of chafing at its restrictions, in such passages as bars 14 to 16 of the Allegretto (see Ex. 26(ii)). But the upper limit, though restricted in the first three movements to c'''' (like the D major trio), is suddenly lifted to f'''' at two places in the finale, at bars 67 and 329–31, increasing the total range to six octaves. It is possible, of course, that the two Op. 70 trios were conceived for different-sized pianos; but a more likely explanation is that the 'rogue' sections in the finale of the E flat work represent a Beethovenian pressure towards an ideal which was barely realizable at the time. Both the problem passages can be taken an octave lower without technical difficulty, though with some inevitable loss of musical effect. Three years later, however, in the 'Archduke' Trio, a still further extension of the piano

Ex. 26

compass is indicated, downwards to EE flat and upwards to e''''
flat, suggesting the need for a six-and-a-half-octave piano (CC to
g'''') such as the one by Johann Streicher which Beethoven had
specially made for himself a few years later, in 1816. From this
point onwards the compass of six and a half octaves became
normal for a considerable period, proving sufficient for virtually
all the early Romantic repertoire, including the works of Schubert, Chopin, Mendelssohn, and Schumann.

The upward extension of the piano's compass was not immediately paralleled by any corresponding increase in the violin's
range. There is, for example, nothing in Beethoven's later piano
trios to match in altitude the many high-pitched first violin
passages found in the 'Rasumovsky' quartets. One needs to look
considerably further forward in history, to the end of the
nineteenth century and beyond, to find in piano trios violin
writing of consistently higher tessitura. One reason is that, unlike
the string quartet, where the violin's place on the surface (at least
in classical contexts) is only rather rarely overturned, the piano
trio has no natural pitch hierarchy, so that the individual instruments stand out in the texture by virtue more of their tonal
qualities than their relative pitch positions. The point is well
illustrated by the passage at bar 107 in the first movement of the
'Archduke' Trio, where imitative entries between the cello (at the
top), the violin (in the middle), and the piano left hand (at the
bottom) are 'covered' by a continuous triplet pattern, high up in
the piano right hand. The effect is pure piano trio writing, not
realizable in precisely the same way by any other chamber
medium (see Ex. 27).

In the case of the cello the increased tonal power of the piano
posed some rather special problems, by limiting its ability to
provide an independent bass-line to the ensemble. With the
softer-toned, earlier pianos it was frequently possible for the cello
by itself to provide an effective bass below the keyboard part; and
this, indeed, remained the case with more powerful pianos,
provided the style of the writing was sufficiently light in texture
and dynamics—typically in sprightly scherzos, where the cello
line might be played saltato, or even pizzicato. But increasingly,
the principal provision of a firm bass-line fell to the piano, leaving
the cello either to double ineffectively, in a manner alien to an
advanced chamber style, or to move to the tenor range and to the

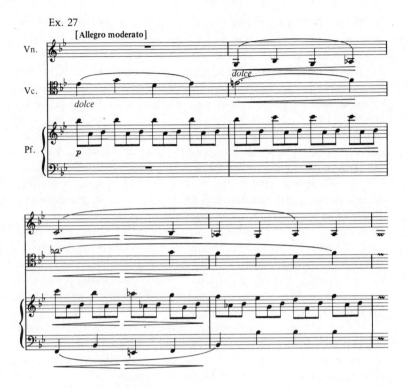

presentation of interior counterthemes or cantabile melodic passages. As a result the overall sonority of the trio combination began to change, the high-pitched cello parts imparting a richly emotive character to the scoring which, if not treated carefully, led rather too easily to turgid or sentimental modes of expression.

The independence of the cello, perhaps the most decisive step in the progress towards the true piano trio, is achieved in Mozart's mature works at the cost of many extended rests in the part. These help to emphasize the concertante nature of the piano writing, particularly when the violin is also temporarily silent, and at the same time contribute towards a light and open texture in which new entries are thrown into sharp relief. Beethoven, in the Op. 1 trios, adopts much the same principle, though he provides rather more straightforward doubling between the cello and the piano bass, no doubt to ensure a firm foundation for his weightier keyboard writing. In the later Beethoven trios, however, as also in those of Schubert and Brahms, with the advent of more powerful pianos doublings of the bass disappear almost entirely, being retained only for such special purposes as the sustaining of a pedal bass or the highlighting of an important bass melody—as for example in bars 216 to 220 of the first movement of Brahms's C minor trio, Op. 101. It is characteristic of Schubert that he creates a sharp polarization between the strings and piano, and indulges more freely than Beethoven in strong octave or double-octave writing between the strings. After his death, however, progress with string independence was not consistently maintained; in general the early Romantic composers, including Mendelssohn and Schumann, show less concern to preserve the integrity of the parts, in some cases allowing the violin and cello simply to double the top and bottom of the piano texture. And even Dvořák, for all his eager emulation of Beethoven, Schubert, and Brahms, occasionally ties his cello parts to the piano bass, though usually in a cleverly disguised manner, as in the passage in Example 28, which shows bars 70 to 74 of the first movement of his F minor trio, Op. 65.

With its progressive emancipation the cello began also to take a larger share of important solo passages.[7] Although the motivic sonata style of Mozart and Beethoven rarely allowed for more than quite short solo interpolations, and those mainly in slow movements, some striking instances are to be found in Beethoven where he uses the cello alone at the start of movements—in the scherzos of Op. 1 No. 2 and the 'Archduke', for example, and at the very beginning of Op. 70 No. 2. But it is noteworthy that in the slow movement of the 'Archduke', with all its supreme lyricism, the cello is never allotted more than fragments of the main theme and makes no extended solo contribution. Later in the nineteenth century, however, lengthy, and often very lyrical, cello solos are to be found: at the start of the slow movements of all Dvořák's trios, for instance, and in the second movements of the Tchaikovsky and second Rachmaninov trios (in the sixth and fifth variations, respectively), where an element of individual display is introduced which represents a marked departure from traditional stylistic norms.

[7] Beethoven's early recognition of the solo capabilities of the cello in chamber music is shown clearly by his two cello sonatas, Op. 5, of 1797, which were the first major works of their type in the classical sonata style.

Ex. 28

The violin, as the normal 'principal voice' in chamber music, is able usually to fulfil its solo role, even in quite extended melodic passages, without acquiring any of the special 'expressive aura' which tends to surround solo cello contributions of any length. Only when it is left entirely unaccompanied does it convey, in context, a somewhat more exotic impression, as for example at the opening of Smetana's G minor trio, Op. 15 (see Ex. 50 (i) in ch. 6). And the piano, despite being self-sufficient in the provision of melody and harmony, is customarily restricted, at least in the classical style, to quite short solo passages, so as to avoid over-stressing its inevitably somewhat dominant role in the ensemble. Nevertheless, by the end of the century both instruments are given concerto-like passages of a thoroughly flamboyant charac-ter, particularly in the virtuoso-style trios of the Russian pianist-composers of the period.

As the length and prominence of solo sections for all three instruments increased during the nineteenth century, so also did the problems involved in providing appropriate forms of accompaniment. In classical practice the difficulties were minimized by the use of short themes, often passed to and fro between the instruments, and by the introduction of distinctive counterthemes to ensure as equitable a distribution of interest as possible. The most telling examples are rather too long for quotation here, but the two bars in Example 29 from the first movement of Schubert's B flat trio adequately summarize the method. In later times, however, trio movements not infrequently started with principal themes of heroic style and proportions, presented by one or both of the strings, which demanded a background piano accompaniment concerned mainly with the simple provision of harmony. One of the earlier examples is the opening of Mendelssohn's D minor trio, Op. 49, where the piano quietly supports the initial cello (and later violin) melody with a swiftly moving pattern of off-beat chords; the method is effective enough, but strictly non-classical in the degree of subordination it imposes on the accompaniment. Early in the present century, even more extreme examples were produced, particularly by minor French composers. One such is the opening of Guy Ropartz's A minor trio (1919), where for the first thirty bars the piano accompanies the strings uninterruptedly with rippling arpeggio figures, in both hands and in contrary motion, which provide the essential harmony but little else of structural significance. And another is the slow movement of Albéric Magnard's F minor trio (1906) in which, for no less than sixty-six bars (from bar 102), the piano supplies a limpid background of leaping octaves entirely confined to the note F at varying pitches.

Ex. 29

Accompaniments provided by the strings are usually valuable in inverse proportion to their length. Some of the most effective usages are to be found in the Mozart trios, where such simple devices as held or repeated notes and chords and finely shaped figuration, based on the original accompanied sonata principles, are turned to new artistic purposes. Invariably very attractive are the places where the piano part 'leans' gracefully against a chordal background on the strings, as in bars 124 to 135 of the first movement of K 542 in E major. And equally successful is the 'etching' of accompaniment figuration by means of short rests, clear-cut rhythms, and pointed phrasing, in order to give character and vitality to the subsidiary part. A delightful example of the latter occurs at the start of the development in the first movement of the B flat trio, K 502, where the violin's elegant pattern strikingly invigorates what might otherwise have been somewhat pedestrian scoring (see Ex. 30).

These Mozartian methods, developed in a host of new ways, became the recognized model for many later trio composers. But problems tended to arise in contexts where composers felt impelled to provide systematic string accompaniments to extended keyboard themes. Not infrequently the long, repetitive, and largely symmetrical melodies favoured by late romantic composers would attract accompaniments of a similar nature; and these, when allotted to the strings, often exhibited orchestral rather than chamber characteristics. Rudimentary scoring of this type occurs throughout the first section of the finale of Smetana's G minor trio written in the middle of the century, a lapse from his usually high standards which is almost certainly attributable to the

Ex. 30

music's origins as part of a solo piano sonata. Later and more sophisticated, but equally remote from a strict chamber style, is the lengthy accompanimental passage from bar 20 of the first movement of Tchaikovsky's piano trio, Op. 50, where the cello supplies an extended pattern of repeated sextuplet semiquavers and the violin some disjunct thematic fragments, all in support of the work's principal melody stated molto espressivo on the piano. In this latter case it has to be allowed that the style of the writing is in perfect accord with the overall nature of the work, which in general makes a virtue out of its undisguisedly orchestral conception.

Less frequently encountered, but also of much interest, are passages where the two stringed instruments play as a duet without piano accompaniment. The rarity of this type of scoring, particularly among the earlier trios, is probably attributable to the limited ability of the two unaccompanied strings to produce triadic harmony. The problem is, of course, easily enough surmounted by the use of double-stopping, but this device has necessarily to be restricted if the essential character of the trio medium is not to be destroyed. Fullness of harmony, it may be noted in passing, seems to have been consistently less valued than clarity of texture, otherwise piano quartets would surely have greatly outnumbered trios. One or two notable instances are to be found where the two unaccompanied strings are used to provide complete harmony, but only for relatively short periods. One is the 'trio' section of the third movement of Beethoven's Op. 70 No. 2 where, in a series of four-bar phrases in antiphony with the piano, the violin uses consistent double-stoppings, supported by the cello, to produce the purest of three-part writing; and another is the third variation in the slow movement of Brahms's C major trio, Op. 87, in which both strings employ triple-stopped chords to great effect, with a resultant body of sound which easily matches in power and sonority the loud answering chords on the piano. Less usual still is plain two-strand unaccompanied writing for strings, which occurs mainly in more modern contexts, such as the passage from figure 8 at the end of the *Passacaille* in Ravel's trio in A minor; in this case, by concentrating on bare fourths and fifths between the instrumental lines, the composer succeeds in creating a cold, mysterious, rather mournful atmosphere. By contrast, Brahms, in the slow movement of his C minor trio, is careful to involve only imperfect consonances at all the essential points between the string parts, so that the third of the chord, in the implied harmony, is at all times either present or strongly inferred. The result is a passage of warmth and colour which is sufficiently sonorous to provide a fitting complement to the piano's answering phrases.

The question of blend requires particularly careful judgement in passages of what may be called 'tutti' scoring, where all three instruments move together in step and often in full harmony. The classical practice in such contexts is to reduce the amount of doubling to the minimum, so as to avoid any mismatch between string and piano tone. In Mozart and early Beethoven it is not unusual to find the cello doubling the piano's bottom line, presumably in compensation for any weakness of bass tone in the instruments of the period; but both composers are careful to avoid any treatment of the melodic surface which involves the combination of violin and piano in unison. Subsequently, in later Beethoven and Schubert, doublings of any sort are eliminated and a beautifully sonorous effect is achieved by the conjunction of uncluttered string and piano lines. Example 31, from the slow movement of the 'Archduke' Trio, shows how faithfully Beethoven preserves the integrity of each thread in his texture. The effectiveness of this type of scoring is so apparent that it is astonishing to observe how many composers later in the nineteenth century neglected to employ it. Without discernible logic a coarser style of scoring appears to have been regarded as complementary to the freer structural procedures cultivated at the time. The new approach is already evident in the first movement of Mendelssohn's D minor trio, from bar 25, and is maintained in his second trio throughout the *maggiore* section at the centre of the scherzo, where a 'rocking' semiquaver pattern in the piano right hand succeeds ingeniously in doubling both the violin and cello parts at the unison. Even more relentless is the doubling found in Schumann's trios. Repeatedly, in fully harmonized passages, the top and bottom of the piano part are needlessly reinforced by string tone, suggesting a makeshift instrumental arrangement rather than finely conceived scoring. Eventually, with Brahms and Dvořák, a restoration of classical structural ideals brought with it a return to the older method of scoring. Brahms is outstanding for the degree of independence he achieves in all the

Ex. 31

contributory lines, even in his most massively scored passages; and Dvořák is only slightly less scrupulous.

Many of the basic features of technique summarized above in relation to eighteenth- and nineteenth-century trios apply with equal force to twentieth-century works in the form, though changes in style have necessarily produced differences of emphasis. Significantly, the problems of overweight keyboard writing, quasi-orchestral scoring, and the inequitable distribution of interest in the parts, typical of the grand trios of the late-nineteenth century, have tended to lessen considerably in face of the trend towards neo-classicism which has emerged in many countries since the 1920s. The increasingly contrapuntal style which this has encouraged, together with lean piano writing, open textures well 'aired' by rests, and a strong rhythmic dichotomy between strings and keyboard, have led to trio scoring of great sophistication, in which many of the fundamental classical criteria have been restored. However, there have also been important innovations.

For example, the present century's fascination with colourful instrumental effects has led to the use of a whole range of special string devices, such as the 'snap' pizzicato, the glissando, quarter-tone and three-quarter-tone writing, extended passages in harmonics, scordatura tuning, and col legno bowing; and a more frequent use of passages for unaccompanied strings has laid greater emphasis than formerly on tonal contrast within the ensemble rather than on blend. But of the changes introduced none has so radically altered the basic concepts underlying trio composition as the new orientation which has been given in some recent works to the piano's role. This has involved a replacement of the traditional opposition between piano and strings by a new process of equalisation, in which the keyboard renounces much of its normal independence and self-sufficiency and becomes, virtually, an additional stringed instrument of wider compass, contributing only single thematic lines and isolated groups of

notes or chords to the texture, with an extensive use of rests. A recent work which demonstrates the procedure is Jonathan Harvey's only piano trio, of 1971, in which additional severity of style is supplied by the use of wide octave displacements in the melodic line (see Ex. 32, which shows the end of the second movement). More than many other apparently radical new departures this technique has struck tellingly at the basis of traditional piano trio writing, removing much of the differentiation between the separate tonal planes in the ensemble which has, historically, been central to its character. It remains to be seen whether such innovations will lead eventually to a new concept of the genre, equal in style and eloquence to its predecessor.

5 The German Romantics

THE repertoire gained by the piano trio during the Viennese classical period up to the death of Schubert, though high in quality, is relatively modest in size. As a result largely of the genre's delayed origins, no more than two dozen first-rate trios were produced (half of them Haydn's last works in the form) as compared to nearly a hundred string quartets of comparable calibre from the same period. After the late 1830s, however, this situation began to change as a growing number of composers, attracted by the increased tonal power, range, and singing qualities of the piano, together with its proved effectiveness in combination with solo strings, were drawn to make new contributions to the genre. Naturally enough, it was the Germans, Mendelssohn, Schumann, and Brahms, who, as the most direct inheritors of the classical tradition, provided the lead; but elsewhere in Europe also composers of distinction added significantly to the repertoire with works which, despite some inescapable Teutonic traits, showed many distinctive features of a local or nationalist character. Their contribution will be considered in more detail in the next chapter.

The growing interest in the trio form at this time was not accompanied, unfortunately, by any matching expansion, or even maintenance, of the cherished ideals of classical chamber composition. On the contrary, the new spirit of the times, with its emphasis on melodic charm and harmonic colour at the expense of formal logic, and its concentration on miniature forms and song-like modes of expression, proved detrimental to all types of chamber composition, causing a serious weakening of the structural imperatives which provided its traditional basis. It would hardly have been surprising, in fact, if, in face of the new wave of romanticism, chamber music had lost contact entirely with the grand sonata designs of the past and degenerated into suite-style compilations of colourful descriptive miniatures. That this did not happen is due largely to the efforts of the most prominent traditionalist composers of the time. Conscious of the sovereign value of their heritage, they strove to find effective ways of reconciling the richness of the new musical expression with the constraints inherent in the classical sonata style. Naturally it was the composers with the highest creative 'profiles', in all branches of composition, who made the strongest impact; but their lesser contemporaries should not be underrated. Some of these were leading musicians whose main interests lay in fields other than chamber music, such as the opera composers Marschner (1795–1861) and Goetz (1840–76), the symphonists Berwald (1796–1868) and Raff (1822–82), and the piano virtuosi Anton Rubinstein (1829–94) and Xaver Scharwenka (1850–1924); others again were minor composers of professional competence in many branches of the art, such as Woldemar Bargiel (1828–97) and Heinrich von Herzogenberg (1843–1900), who enjoyed much local acclaim, but were relatively little known internationally. Each of them produced at least one piano trio, and some of these, even nowadays, remain of considerable interest—and not solely to historians.

By 1828, the year of Schubert's death, the young Mendelssohn, who was nearly as remarkable a child prodigy as Mozart, had already produced a substantial series of chamber works. These include (in addition to two very early unpublished works—a C minor trio for violin, viola, and piano, and a piano quartet in D minor) the three piano quartets, issued as Op. 1–3, a violin sonata, a sextet for piano, violin, two violas, cello, and double-bass, and the astonishingly accomplished octet for strings Op. 20, all completed before his seventeenth birthday. In these earliest compositions it is already possible to discern the main strengths and weaknesses which were to mark his later output in all branches of music. On the one hand, a gift for lyrical melody, deft craftsmanship, and a convincing management of large-scale structures; and on the other, limited thematic and harmonic resource, a tendency towards mechanical repetition and a restricted emotional range. The most classical of romantic composers, Mendelssohn appears to have turned intuitively during his boyhood to those models who could most directly guide him towards the development of a personal style—J. S. Bach and Handel for counterpoint and rhythmic poise, and Mozart, particularly, for clarity of structure. And already by 1825, the year of the octet, he had attained virtually all the technique necessary for his purpose, together with a thoroughly individual mode of expression. Greatly impressed though he clearly was by Beethoven, he seems to have recognized instinctively that he lacked the depth of musical personality to follow his example very closely; he therefore used his finely honed technique and lively imagination to evolve a cooler, more 'rational' chamber style, which counterbalanced by its classical grace what it lacked in profundity of expression.

It was no doubt a recognition of this which prompted Schumann to the characteristically thoughtful observation, 'Mendelssohn is the Mozart of the nineteenth century, the most illuminating of musicians, who sees through the contradictions of our era, and is the first to reconcile them.' The 'contradictions' were those between literary-based Lied forms and classical sonata structures; between the virtuoso style and the more intimate, introspective approach of the romantic miniaturist; and between the technical disciplines inherited from J. S. Bach and the Viennese classics and the wayward creative urges typical of the post-Beethovenian age. Mendelssohn's 'reconciliation' was made possible through such innate personal characteristics as delicacy of taste, refinement of thought, and a certain aristocratic reserve. But it was also these facets of his personality which placed beyond his reach the heady excitement, imaginative daring, and indeed sublimity to which so many other composers of his time eagerly aspired. Schumann, on the other hand, though equally troubled by the 'contradictions', seems to have been temperamentally less suited to the efficient artistic solution, achieved through self-denial and simple technical expertise. But despite risking, and in some cases incurring, failure, he not infrequently got closer to the heart of the problem than his senior colleague, and provided deeper and more disturbing emotional insights.

A gap of nearly six years separates the dates of composition of Mendelssohn's two mature piano trios. The first, Op. 49 in D minor, was completed in 1839, an initial version appearing on 18 July, and a further, considerably altered one (evidence of the composer's customary obsession with revisions) on 13 September. And the second, Op. 66 in C minor, was finished in April 1845 and published about a year later, with a dedication to Louis Spohr. Despite the considerable period of time which separates them, the two works show many features in common, not only technical traits but also more general shades of mood and expression. Both are in four movements, with a characteristic 'fairy' scherzo placed third in succession to a Lied-style slow movement; both reveal a similarly individual handling of sonata and rondo forms in their outer movements; and both share a special brand of minor-key seriousness, typical of many of the composer's large-scale works, and valuable for the scope it provides for clear-cut contrasts of tonal darkness and light. This uniformity of design contributes to the broadly 'classical' image created by the works as a pair; but it also compares rather unfavourably with the arresting contrasts of style and expression evident, for example, between the two Op. 70 trios of Beethoven or the late Schubert trios, from which a decidedly more 'romantic' bias results. The impression created is that, since Mendelssohn conceived his structures more as fixed patterns than as living forms, he saw no reason not to readopt for the second trio much the same arrangement as had served him well for the first. The nature of the plan was such as to accommodate a wide range of powerfully expressive ideas in an ordered and symmetrical way, with deftly controlled variations of tempo, texture, and dynamics, and largely predictable peaks and troughs of emotional pressure. As a result, it becomes the expressive character of the themes, and the scope they afford for sequential repetition and ingenious schemes of modulation, rather than any more intensive method of treatment through logical expansion and development, that provides the dominant structural factor in the sonata-style movements—and not solely in Mendelssohn's works, but in those also of many lesser composers of the period.

Some insight into Mendelssohn's approach can be gained by comparing the first movements of the two trios. At the beginning of the D minor work a powerful cantabile theme is initiated by the cello, with chordal piano accompaniment, and continued by the violin from bar 17, rather in the manner of a vocal duet. Constructed in eight-bar phrases the theme follows a perfectly regular pattern, with cadential points of repose occurring on the seventh and eighth bars of each phrase. At bar 39, however, the anticipated moment of relaxation is displaced by a sudden upward arpeggio on the piano, leading to a new dotted-rhythm figure (see Ex. 33(i)). This disrupts the phrasing, breaks the song-like continuity, and gives immediate promise of a new sonata-style continuation. In a simple way the passage epitomizes the problem of using song-like material for principal sonata themes, and shows one of the many ingenious solutions which Mendelssohn was able to offer. Schumann was sufficiently impressed by the idea to adopt the substance of it for his own D minor trio, Op. 63, written eight years later.[1] In his case a sudden upward arpeggio on the piano is introduced in bar 14 of his first movement, and leads in a very similar way to disruptive dotted rhythms (see Ex. 33(ii)). But because it totally displaces the natural accents, his procedure is even more dynamic than Mendelssohn's, breaking the melodic flow and creating a sonata-style momentum just at the point where its need is most urgently felt.

The beginning of Mendelssohn's second trio involves a somewhat different, but equally convincing, process. The opening eight-bar phrase, a soft, largely conjunct melody stated initially by the piano, is interrupted in bar 8 by abrupt, forte chords which proceed to a half-close on the dominant. Then, following a restatement of the opening theme, a different idea, still in the tonic, is introduced by the strings in turn, against a new semiquaver pattern on the piano, apparently derived freely, in diminution, from elements of the original theme; and this leads, through various repetitions and sequences, to a further return of the opening idea in bar 42. The whole passage is remarkably expansive, and achieves its sonata-style effect by the momentum it acquires through its vivid juxtaposition of contrasted themes and gradual accumulation of rapid accompaniment patterns. Strikingly enough, no relaxation occurs before the start of the second subject group, which arrives as the culmination of the opening paragraph—as a joyful, climactic release of the energy previously accumulated.

Mendelssohn's second subjects in both trios tend, interestingly, to follow a common pattern. Set initially in the major mode, they are invariably lyrical in character, with strong diatonic profiles and precise rhythms. But, in seeking to achieve structural balance, after his expansive opening paragraphs, the composer is forced to restrain their natural lyrical impulses in a way which tends to impart a curiously epigrammatic quality to them. His standard procedure in individual movements is to fashion a four-bar phrase

---

[1] See A. Molnar, 'Die beide Klaviertrios in D moll von Schumann (Op 63) und Mendelssohn (Op. 49)', *Sammelbände der Robert Schumann Gesellschaft*, i (Leipzig, 1961), 79.

Ex. 33

over tonic-to-dominant harmony, and then isolate it by an immediate repetition, before proceeding to an answering continuation and a return to the original tonic. Later, the 'isolated' fragment is invariably given an important role in the development section as a means of cementing disparate elements and providing thematic significance to extended modulatory, and often sequential, passages. It is worth noting, in this context, that the themes always start from the dominant degree of the scale, so that they can be slotted readily into almost any later passage, major or minor. And also that many of them, from both trios, have a strong family resemblance, as can be seen in Example 34.

In the final movements of both works a distinctive type of rondo is used, based on three principal themes. The first two are presented in a regular sonata fashion, the second in both cases in the relative major. But to a quite unusual extent they are allowed to permeate the movement throughout its course, contributing melodic segments of varying length in numerous different scorings and contrapuntal combinations, and in a variety of related keys, in a way which severely limits the impact of the normal structural reprises natural to the rondo form. One important result of this is to throw special emphasis onto the third principal theme. This, in both finales, is situated at the centre of the movement in the key of the submediant, and denied any part in the development process, later returning in the tonic major in order to provide a warmly expressive (in Op. 49) or majestic (in

Ex. 34

Op. 66) climax, just before the coda. In the C minor trio this third theme resembles a chorale melody, specifically that commonly associated with Luther's 'Gelobet seist du, Jesu Christ', though it is by no means an exact quotation (see Ex. 35). It is presented initially in five short phrases, interspersed by fragments of the movement's opening theme, providing in the process a curious distant echo of the *meno mosso*, central section of Chopin's C sharp minor scherzo, Op. 39, of 1838. On its return at the end of the movement, Mendelssohn subjects the theme to a quasi-orchestral type of scoring, with multiple stoppings for the strings and rolling octaves in the piano bass, all of which is effective enough in context, but comes near to overstepping the normal restraints of the chamber style.

Apart from this last instance and some examples of needless doubling, mentioned earlier, Mendelssohn's scoring is notable for its precision. In keeping with the spirit of his times he occasionally writes passages involving brilliant display for the piano which,

because of their unsuitability for 'exchange' with the strings, are somewhat suspect by classical criteria. A typical example is the passage from bar 163 of the first movement of Op. 49 marked agitato, where the piano provides a rippling surface of very rapid triplets in support of somewhat staid crotchet patterns on the strings. It should be remembered, however, that in such cases—as also in the scherzo of the D minor trio, where the piano has a part of concerto-like virtuosity—the effect would have been a great deal less overpowering on a light-toned piano of Mendelssohn's time than on a present-day concert grand. Moreover, it is interesting to observe that, in his later trio, the composer restricts the piano's role quite considerably in his search for a more homogeneous texture. In particular the use of strings alone at the start of the scherzo sounds like a gesture of abnegation—or repentance, even.

For Schumann, writing in 1839, Mendelssohn's Op. 49 was 'the master trio of the present era, just as, in their times, were the B flat and D major trios of Beethoven, and that of Schubert in E flat. It is a beautiful composition that years from now will delight our grandchildren and great-grandchildren.'[2] One can hardly disagree with this verdict, particularly in light of the general standard of chamber composition in the late 1830s. Among the better products of the period are the seven trios of Heinrich Marschner, particularly the one in G minor, Op. 111, which Schumann is known to have admired;[3] and among the feebler specimens is the Op. 3 trio by Ambroise Thomas (of *Mignon* fame) dating from c.1835, a decidedly uninspiring affair which Schumann mockingly described as 'a salon trio, which permits one to peer about through his lorgnette without entirely losing the thread'.[4] But since Schumann's day the Mendelssohn trios have had a somewhat mixed reception. P. H. Láng, for example, asserted in 1941 that 'the great pathos of the Beethoven mood ... is almost reached in the two magnificent piano trios',[5] while Gerald Abraham declared in 1938 that the 'D minor trio far too often

[2] L. B. Plantinga, *Schumann as Critic* (New Haven, Conn., 1967), 267.

[3] Not only did Schumann write a particularly favourable review of Marschner's G minor trio in the *Neue Zeitschrift für Musik*, but he also apparently took its scherzo as a model for the equivalent movement in his own A minor string quartet, Op. 41 No.1, of 1841.

[4] Plantinga, *Schumann*, 189.

[5] P. H. Láng, *Music in Western Civilization* (New York, 1941), 822.

suggests a brilliant piano solo with not particularly obbligato string parts';[6] and more recently, in 1957, Andrew Porter commented 'what was deft in the Octet has in the D minor trio become glib; what was romantic has turned sentimental. Invention sparks freely, but at a low voltage.'[7] The more one compares Mendelssohn's works with those of his great Viennese predecessors, the more mechanical his structures and techniques of development tend to appear. But it is questionable whether such comparisons are entirely just. The classical style, with all its formidable implications, was too recently past in Mendelssohn's day for him to attempt to adopt its criteria wholesale and still retain his individuality. Thus it was the force of history, as much as his personal artistic attributes, which pressed upon him willy-nilly the role of a cautious originator rather than a major consolidator.

Schumann's rather hesitant first attempt at a piano trio was made in 1842, the year which also saw the creation of two of his most important chamber works, the piano quintet in E flat, Op. 44, and the piano quartet in E flat, Op. 47. Possibly because of his strenuous preoccupation with these major compositions, he designed the trio on a somewhat modest scale, with four miniature movements in the style of character pieces, and only published it, after much revision, eight years later, under the title *Vier Fantasiestücke*, Op. 88. His other three piano trios are all full-scale works, the first two of which—Op. 63 in D minor and Op. 80 in F major—date from 1847 and the third—Op. 110 in G minor—from 1851. As we have seen earlier Schumann's admiration for the first of the Mendelssohn trios is reflected in various surface details of his own D minor trio, even down to the choice of its basic key. But at a deeper level of thought and feeling the similarities are much less positive. Where Mendelssohn presses his music forward in vigorous strides, full of self-confidence, Schumann seems to hover nervously and uncertainly in the half-shadows; and where Mendelssohn provides straightforward melodic ideas and handles them with fine craftsmanship, Schumann is often more wayward, displaying an attractive element of fantasy and unpredictability, but less security of technique.

[6] G. Abraham, *A Hundred Years of Music*, 4th edn. (London, 1938), 68.

[7] A. Porter, 'Felix Mendelssohn (1809–1847)', in A. Robertson (ed.), *Chamber Music*, (London, 1957), 180–1.

Nevertheless, over the whole range of his trios, Schumann can be regarded as at least Mendelssohn's equal. His melodic and harmonic palette is richer, his rhythms are more flexible, and he is a more imaginative contrapuntist. His sonata structures, though less obviously effective than Mendelssohn's, are more varied and inventive; furthermore, he is less showy and he strikes deeper, provoking in the listener a more intense response. Like his predecessor, Schumann tends to overscore for the piano, but usually by providing excessive doubling of the string parts rather than bravura passage-work in competition with them. And his middle movements, though conceived as a regular 'song and dance' pairing, are less stereotyped than Mendelssohn's; in particular his scherzos (a term he never actually uses) tend to convey an unusually quiet, introspective mood—reflecting more of the Eusebius than the Florestan side to his complex nature.

The D minor trio is typically uneven in quality. Its scherzo is burdened with an excess of dotted rhythms and has a decidedly bland 'trio'; while the finale, though adventurous enough in structure, contains too many weak transitions to be wholly convincing. But the first and third movements are exceptionally fine, with arresting ideas and an impressive formal grasp. The composer's desire to achieve rhythmic flexibility is immediately evident at the start of the first movement, where the violin introduces the principal theme on a tied crotchet upbeat, before the entry of the piano accompaniment; and again, at bar 14, where the sudden change of accent described earlier (see Ex. 33) leads to a short passage in which the basic bar-rhythms are almost totally obscured (see Ex. 36). A similar pliancy is apparent in several of the melodic shapes. The opening theme, for example, appears in three slightly different versions during the first fourteen bars, each of which takes a new direction from its third whole bar.

Ex. 36

And the haunting subsidiary phrase in bars 7 and 8 is subjected to considerable later variation, in both length and interval structure, but always without impairing its distinctive character.

In the exposition to the first movement there is repeated evidence of Schumann's naturally contrapuntal approach. From the start fragments of the violin's principal theme are echoed in free imitation by the cello which, in the process, temporarily abandons its doubling of the piano bass to provide a warm inner part; and in the first restatement of the second theme (from bar 30) the violin and cello engage in a canon, two octaves apart and at half a bar's distance, which persists for a further four bars. Moreover, towards the end of the exposition, an unexpected recurrence of the first theme, in F major on the cello, is combined with fragments of the second subject, before broadening out into a more freely designed duet. It is surprising to find counterpoint, a technical resource more commonly associated with development sections, employed so early in the movement. Perhaps it is possible to detect here a first move towards the process of 'continuous development' which was to gain increasing acceptance later in the century. Certainly, by his liberal use of the technique, Schumann is able to impart a special richness and sense of unity to his texture. Curiously enough, the middle section itself, which is unusually long, contains little real development in the classical manner and no very obviously contrapuntal approach, the composer relying instead on spaced repetitions of ` elements of the original themes in a variety of keys. One main reason for the section's exceptional size is its inclusion, from bar 90, of an entirely new melodic idea, which with several repetitions occupies thirty-five bars. The notion of introducing new thematic material during the development was not, of course, new; but in this case it is given special prominence by virtue of its distinctive melodic character, its positioning in the movement, and, particularly, its very unusual scoring. Placed high in the piano's range, the new theme is presented in very soft (*ppp*) triplet-quaver chords, with the accompanying string parts marked '*am Steg*' (*sul ponticello*). The effect is startling, not to say bizarre, and suggests that some special, secret message is being conveyed, a not too improbable assumption in view of the composer's known fondness for cryptograms (see Ex. 37). Later, at the end of the movement, the 'cryptic' theme's initial phrase

Ex. 37

returns in the piano part, at a slower tempo and in even more
hushed tones, at first in D major and then, mysteriously, in B flat,
as if to reinforce its special significance.

It is surprising that a composer as sensitive as Schumann in so
many other respects should have scored so crudely for the piano
trio. All too often in the first movement, the music sounds as
though it had been arranged somewhat casually for the medium
rather than composed specifically in terms of the rich resources it
has to offer. For some reason Schumann seems to have felt
impelled to write consistently for this middle range of the piano's
compass (the high placing of the 'cryptic' theme is quite exceptional). Indeed, it is only a few stray notes in the bass which
extend his piano parts beyond the five-octave compass of
Mozart's time. Furthermore, he is inclined to keep the strings at a
generally low pitch, and to provide very few rests in their parts.
In the D minor trio's first movement, for example, the violin has
only three whole bars of rest and the cello only four; and as a
result the texture is frequently opaque, with many undesirable

unison passages between the violin part and the piano's topmost line.

In the meditative slow movement of Op. 63, however, the composer seems to have experienced altogether fewer problems of scoring and structure. Marked '*mit inniger Empfindung*' (with heartfelt emotion), and related in style to both late Beethoven and J. S. Bach (of the organ chorale preludes), the movement shows Schumann's trio writing at its most concentrated and deeply expressive. The piano part, marked una corda in the two outer sections of the ternary structure, provides a sustained background of rich, often chromatic harmonies, deployed in a freely contrapuntal manner; and against this the strings in turn present extended melodic paragraphs which are free in rhythm and phrasing, and apparently improvisatory in character. The structure is none the less tightly organized, a high degree of unity being created by the use of specific intervals and fragmentary motifs, woven into the texture at spaced intervals. One instance is the violin's B flat arpeggio figure in bar 8 (see Ex. 38(i)) which occurs six times at different pitches, partly to mark section endings, but mainly to provide continuity of thought and mood throughout the central part of the movement; and another is the seven-note figure allocated to the cello in bars 11 and 12 (see Ex. 38(ii)) which returns at bar 20 as the leading idea of the middle section and later reappears three times in varied forms (see Ex. 38(iii)). From the scoring point of view it is noteworthy that, apart from one short passage at the end of the middle section, the

Ex. 38

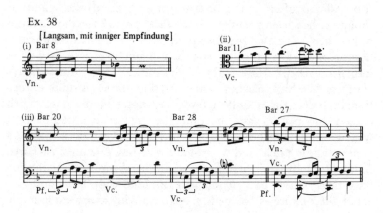

cello operates quite independently of the piano bass, often in its
tenor register; and that doublings between violin and piano occur
only when both instruments are subservient to a principal melody
on the cello. Though all the instruments occupy the central pitch
range in Schumann's customary manner, rests are used more
freely than usual to reduce congestion in the texture.

Following Beethoven's example in the 'Archduke' Trio, Schumann places his slow movement third, after the scherzo, and adds
a short transition on the piano which leads directly into the finale.
This is a vigorous rondo of a highly sectionalized type, which
includes recurrences of the principal theme in an unusual variety
of keys—F, G, and C majors as well as the home tonic—more
suggestive of a concerto grosso movement with ritornello returns
than a classical sonata rondo. The main rondo theme bears some
resemblance to the first theme of the opening movement of the
work, and is sometimes cited as an intentional transformation of
it. To some extent this is true also of the slow movement which
seems to share with the first movement a number of significantly
placed intervals and melodic fragments. However, in the comparatively rare cases where Schumann uses theme transference
between movements, as for example between the first and last
movements of the piano quintet, he does so normally in a clear,
unambiguous manner. Recondite cross-references of the type
implied here are likely to have occurred less by deliberate design
than through the unconscious workings of the mind in the process
of creation—but they are not, for that reason, any less interesting.

The second of the Schumann trios, Op. 80 in F major, also
completed in 1847, is more compact and more direct in expression than its predecessor. The first movement in 6/8 time is full of
bustling energy, with clear-cut themes and some effective imitative counterpoint, particularly in the development. But its scoring
is typically overloaded with superfluous doublings between piano
and strings, so that neither 'side' attains any real independence. As
with his earlier trio it is the slow movement which particularly
stands out for the richness and originality of its ideas. Set in D flat
major and song-like in character, it is closer than its predecessor in
Op. 63 to Mendelssohn's standard 'Song without Words' type of
slow movement, but considerably more complex in structure and
texture. Immediately striking is the opening paragraph where the
violin's principal theme, with a chordal accompaniment in triplets

for the piano right hand, is underpinned by a canonic line shared between the cello and the piano bass. The canon, which is at the fifth below, is maintained exactly (apart from a halving of the time interval between the *dux* and *comes* in bar 2) for a full five bars, and subsequently preserved more freely to the end of the section. The resultant harmonic scheme is outstandingly colourful, and the canonic artifice, though far from obtrusive, is powerfully integrative. An outline of the opening (without the piano's right hand chords) is shown in Example 39. The movement's overall structure is an unusual blend of ternary and rondo forms, highly sectionalized but with smooth transitional links; and there is an unorthodox, but perfectly effective key-scheme, involving a large number of enharmonic changes. In broad outline the structural pattern is as shown in Table 2.

Schumann's fondness for canonic writing is again evident in the third movement, a gentle intermezzo in B flat minor (though not so described by the composer) which points forward, stylistically, towards Brahms. Over a triple-time, dotted-rhythm chordal pattern in the piano left hand, a graceful melodic line is built up, consisting entirely of two-part canons—at either the octave or the unison, and at a whole bar's distance—allocated in a variety of pairings to the violin, cello, and piano right hand. And in order to provide a balanced structure, the whole ingenious complex is fitted skilfully within an overall ternary scheme, with a middle section in the relative major (during part of which the canon briefly ceases), a modified reprise, and an extended coda. It is possible that the movement was to some extent prompted by the example of the canonic scherzo in Schubert's E flat trio (D929), a work which Schumann is known greatly to have admired. But it is likely also that he enjoyed the problem-solving involved, as

Ex. 39

TABLE 2. *Second movement of Schumann's trio in F major, Op. 80*

Bars	Theme	Key	Tempo	Features
1–13	(A)	D♭ major	♩ = 58	Main theme with canonic accompaniment.
14–17		C♯ minor		Link: based on (A).
18–19	(B)	A major		First subsidiary theme: imitative.
20–3	(C)	E major		Chordal transition with arpeggios.
24–32	(D)	C♯ minor		Second subsidiary theme: violin arpeggios and chordal piano accompaniment.
33–5	(B′)	A♭ major	*Lebhaft*	First subsidiary theme: as before.
36–43	(A′)	A♭ major		'Rondo' return of (A) in the dominant, with a new countertheme.
44–5		A♭ minor		Link: a new chordal passage.
46–7	(B″)	B major		First subsidiary theme: as before.
48–51	(C′)	F♯ major		Chordal transition: as before.
52–62	(D′)	E♭ minor		Second subsidiary: as before, and expanded.
63–72	(B‴)	E♭ major	*Lebhaft*	First subsidiary theme: with an expansion.
73–84	(A″)	D♭ major		'Rondo' return of (A), with a new accompaniment.
85–9	(C″)	A♭ major		Chordal transition, as before: a new double-dotted figure on strings, based on original accompaniment to (A).
90–6		D♭ major		Coda, based on the double-dotted figure from the previous section, against repeated triplets.

well as appreciating the undoubted spur to a logical flow of musical ideas which, in certain contexts, canonic procedures can valuably supply.

The finale returns to the energetic style of the first movement, and reveals much the same strengths and weaknesses: on the one hand powerful contrapuntal writing, particularly in the development section, and on the other an excessive amount of doubling between piano and strings. It is noticeable, as much in this work as in the D minor trio, that the amount of doubling is altogether greater in the outer movements than in the inner ones. It is as if the composer was happy to cultivate a relatively lighter style in his more lyrical central movements, with greater independence for the strings, but felt impelled to provide impressive, heavy-weight scoring in his sonata-style movements so as to give them special substance and authority. If he had wished to seek guidance in the matter, he could hardly have done better than to have studied the G minor piano trio by his wife, Clara, which had appeared as her Op. 17 in the previous year. This is a substantial, four-movement work which, though clearly influenced by Mendelssohn, has strongly profiled melodic ideas and a resourceful harmonic style. What it lacks in originality it amply offsets by the excellence of its technical command, and in particular the high skill with which it is scored. It would not have been surprising if Clara, as a distinguished concert pianist, had been tempted to overload the piano's role at the expense of the strings; but in fact she shows admirable judgement, achieving a fine balance of interest in the ensemble with little or no trace of superfluous doublings.

It is not unlikely that Schumann may have received some friendly advice (or even severe criticism) about the nature of the scoring in his F major trio from those involved in its first performance at the Leipzig Gewandhaus in February 1850: Ferdinand David (violin), Julius Rietz (cello), and Clara Schumann, all three renowned at the time not only as performers but also as composers of considerable merit. It is difficult, however, to detect any very marked change of approach in the last of his trios, Op. 110 in G minor, which was completed in the following year. Only in the first two movements is the general concept somewhat different, the strings being allocated a more soloistic role than usual, and the piano a correspondingly greater amount of purely accompanimental writing. The G minor trio is usually regarded as the weakest of Schumann's essays in the form, and not without some justification; but there are many redeeming features, especially in the first two movements. In particular attention may be drawn to the hauntingly beautiful second theme in the first movement, and the adept way in which it is combined (in bars 36 and 40) with the main transitional motif from the preceding paragraph; and to the splendidly scored *fugato* passage at bar 112 during the development in the first movement (perhaps inspired by Clara's *fugato* at the equivalent place in the finale of her trio), with one of its principal ideas taken pizzicato by the strings in turn. Also very effective is the charmingly paced ending to the first movement, where the principal ideas gradually disintegrate, fading to a pianissimo close, again with prominent pizzicato scoring.

The slow movement which follows is powerfully emotional in style, with the two strings, at the start, providing a 'vocal', almost operatic, type of duet against off-beat piano chords. Its middle section, in contrast, introduces dramatic, and heavily scored, chordal gestures which seem to point forward prophetically towards the style of Brahms. But the rest of the trio is sadly disappointing. The third movement, in a fast 2/4 metre, begins with an idea reminiscent of the composer's fourth symphony (the principal theme of the first movement), but its treatment is dull and lifeless, and even the interpolation of two contrasting 'trios' does little to remedy the position. The second of the 'trio' sections introduces dotted rhythms and triplets in a march-like manner suggestive of Schubert (of the B flat trio), but lacks much of the grace and vitality of the earlier composer's approach. The themes in this section are confined largely to the strings, and if Schumann had only exploited the upper register of the piano in the accompaniment, a much more buoyant effect, in Schubertian style, could readily have been achieved. The finale suggests a composer dogged by a desperate weariness. Set out as a simple type of rondo, it is grotesquely repetitive and over-sectionalized. The principal theme has some affinity with the main first movement idea of the piano quintet, but it lacks purpose and continuity, and by the end of the movement, after its thirteenth repetition, has long outstayed its welcome. The composer marks the movement '*Kräftig, mit Humor*'; but in light of what we know of his total mental breakdown three years later, the 'humour' can hardly seem other than black indeed.[8]

Despite their obvious shortcomings the Schumann trios command admiration on many counts; for their originality, their strongly characterized, often very beautiful, melodic ideas, their richness of harmony, their subtle treatment of rhythm and phrasing, and their skilful use of counterpoint. But against these undoubted virtues there have to be weighed the basic weaknesses they reveal in structure and scoring. It seems almost as if his technical facility was at times insufficient to bear the weight of his originality; as if he remained to some extent the victim of the somewhat sketchy technical training he received in his youth. But more discipline, it has to be acknowledged, might well have meant less fantasy and caprice, and the sacrifice of one or more essential facets of his musical personality.

During his lifetime, as a result very largely of his own and Mendelssohn's influence, trio composition continued to make fruitful progress, both inside and outside Germany. Among the German composers most directly inspired by Schumann's example were the long-lived Carl Reinecke (1824–1910), who produced seven trios, and Woldemar Bargiel, the step-brother of Clara Schumann, who published three. The earliest of Bargiel's trios, Op. 6 in F major, appeared (with a respectful dedication to his brother-in-law) in 1856, the year of Schumann's death. Its most curious feature is its introductory Adagio, a thirty-bar contrapuntal movement, largely in G minor, which seems to bear no relationship, either in key, style, or thematic content, to any other part of the work; and its most Schumannesque element the scherzo, which proceeds in almost continuous dactylic, dotted rhythms, interrupted only by a charming central section with lyrical string contributions against piano arpeggio figuration. Also published in 1856 was the trio in G minor, Op. 1, by Hans von Bronsart (1830–1913) which was described by Liszt in a letter to Joachim Raff of February 1857 as 'a successful and very respectable work'; and two further compositions of some note are the trios of the Saxon composer, Robert Volkmann (1815–83), both written in the mid 1840s. The first of them, Op. 8 in F

---

[8] It was in February 1854 that Schumann's mental disorder drove him to attempt suicide by throwing himself into the Rhine. The remaining two years of his life were spent in a private asylum.

major, is a somewhat lightweight affair, but its successor, Op. 5 in B flat minor, is a stormy and passionate work which gained the approval not only of Liszt, to whom it was dedicated, but also of Hans von Bulow and Wagner, despite its conventional harmonic style and lack of genuine melodic interest. It is worth observing that the approval expressed by Liszt of the works by Bronsart and Volkmann can hardly be taken to indicate that either or both of them were necessarily sympathetic to the aims of the so-called 'New German' school centred around Liszt at Weimar. Indeed, Volkmann (together with the arch conservatives Reinecke and Bargiel) was among those who were invited to give active support to Joachim, Grimm, Max Bruch, and the young Brahms in their ill-conceived public protest of March 1860 against the alleged excesses of the Liszt circle.[9]

Far more enterprising, however, than any of the works just mentioned is the trio in B major, Op. 8, by the twenty-year-old Brahms. This, his first published chamber work, was begun in the summer of 1853, shortly after his first meeting with Schumann, and completed early in the following year. Brahms at the time was under considerable psychological pressure because of the exaggerated reputation that had been wished on him by Schumann. After their initial encounter in 1853, the older composer had acclaimed him (with extraordinary insight, considering the paucity of evidence available to him at the time) as the great saviour of German music for whom he had waited so long and so eagerly. 'I felt certain', he had declared in an article in the *Neue Zeitschrift für Musik*, 'that ... an individual would suddenly appear, fated to give expression to the times in the highest and most ideal manner, who would achieve mastery, not step by step, but all at once, springing like Minerva fully armed from the head of Jove. And now here he is, a young man at whose cradle graces and heroes stood watch.'[10] Such was the authority of Schumann's word that great things were anticipated throughout Germany from the young composer, who had still to publish his first opus. 'The open praise which you bestowed on me', he wrote to Schumann in November, 'has excited public expectations to such a degree that I do not see how I can come near to fulfilling them.' Understandably, he was extremely anxious to make the right choice of works with which to go into print, deciding eventually on his three piano sonatas (Op. 1 in C, Op. 2 in F sharp minor, and Op. 5 in F minor), a group of songs (Op. 3), and the E flat minor scherzo for piano (Op. 4). Significantly, in the same letter to Schumann he also wrote 'I contemplate issuing none of my trios', suggesting that he had already made several attempts at the genre,[11] and implying furthermore that he may even at this stage have had serious doubts about publishing the B major work on which he was currently engaged. However, the completion of the trio early in the following year, its first performance, and the warmth of its initial reception seem, at least temporarily, to have allayed the composer's fears, since in May 1854 he submitted it for publication to the Leipzig firm of Breitkopf and Härtel. And in the process he sent on its way into the world one of the very few of his published works which had not entirely measured up to his stringent, self-imposed standards. In fact Brahms was not alone in feeling some doubts about the work; Clara Schumann, secretly recording in her diary for 26 March her impressions of the trio's first performance, wrote: 'I could only wish for another first movement, as the existing one does not satisfy me, although I admit that the beginning of it is fine. The other three movements are quite worthy of the gifted artist.'

The weaknesses of the B major trio result from the natural shortcomings of a young composer at the start of his career. Each of the four movements begins with a boldly imaginative idea; but each, with the exception of the scherzo, fails to sustain its impetus convincingly as the music proceeds. The resultant diffuseness of structure (equally apparent in the early piano sonatas) is not untypical of much sonata-style writing of the period, and is conspicuous mainly by comparison with what Brahms was to achieve later. But, for the composer, the fact of having issued a work with such manifest weaknesses remained a source of nagging discontent, only relieved some thirty-five years later when, at the height of his powers, he undertook a complete

---

[11] An unidentified piano trio in A major, brought to public notice by Ernst Bücken of Cologne University in 1924, is believed by some to be an early work by Brahms. The ascription is based on stylistic evidence only, but this is quite strong. Certain features of style suggest that, if it is genuine, it may date from the same period as the B major trio, Op. 8. See R. Fellinger, 'Ist das Klaviertrio in A dur ein Jugendwerk von Johannes Brahms?', *Die Musik* 24 (1941–2), 197.

revision of it, issuing the new version in 1891.[12] Even for the mightily self-critical Brahms this was a surprising step to take, and one without many parallels in musical history—the nearest being, perhaps, Hindemith's revision of his *Marienleben* song-cycle, which he completed some twenty-five years after publishing the original version. [13] Brahms's continued designation of the 'new' trio as Op. 8 innocently created some misleading evidence about the roots of his chamber style, even providing some illusory support for Schumann's 'fully-armed Minerva' observation. The original work remained, of course, in circulation, but it was inevitably overshadowed by the revision, and is rarely if ever heard nowadays in performance.

The effect of the revision was to produce a tauter, more cogent work, which was barely two-thirds the length of the original; and this was achieved without any undue sacrifice of the trio's original youthful exuberance. Apart from the scherzo, of which only the coda was modified, each movement underwent radical changes. These were concentrated in two main areas: the major reworking of second-subject sections in order to sharpen their melodic and harmonic orientation and give them a stronger sense of sonata-style inevitability; and the elimination of certain romantic 'excesses', such as the developmental *fugato* in the recapitulation of the first movement, and the imperfectly integrated allegro section originally incorporated into the slow movement—a device later employed with greater success in the F major string quintet and the A major violin sonata. Also removed from the slow movement, to the composer's considerable relief, was the original second theme, the strong similarity of which to Schubert's song 'Am Meer' from the *Schwanengesang* cycle had escaped his notice before publication is 1854, and rankled not a little thereafter. In its place he fitted an undulating cello melody in G sharp minor of great eloquence which provides an admirable foil to the hymn-like solemnity of the movement's opening theme. And in the

---

[12] Useful comparisons between the two versions are to be found in H. Gál., *Johannes Brahms*, tr. K. J. Stein (London, 1963), and in I. Keys, *Brahms Chamber Music* (London, 1974), 38. See also J. E. P. Greenwood, 'Brahms's trio Op. 8: the two versions of the first movement', Univ. of London diss. 1983.

[13] Originally composed in 1922–3, the fifteen songs were thoroughly revised between 1936 and 1948 in line with the composer's later theory of harmony and tonality, as set out in his treatise, *Unterweisung im Tonsatz* (Mainz, 1937 and 1939); English edn., *The Craft of Musical Composition* (London and New York, 1942).

recapitulation, with mature skill, he combined the essence of this new theme with the string phrases which form part of the movement's original first subject (see Ex. 40). Such a major recasting of the work must have involved Brahms in immense labour, particularly in view of the need to achieve a convincing reconciliation of his early and late styles. Indeed, it is hard to think of any other front-rank composer who would have been willing, let alone able, to undertake so complex a task. The fact that the revision works so well is testimony to Brahms's skill; but it is also indicative of the somewhat narrow range of his overall stylistic development. As Schumann's prescient observation suggested, Brahms never had a really 'early' manner, so that the style-gap between 1854 and 1891 was not so wide as to be unbridgeable.

A particularly difficult problem was posed, one suspects, by the extended lyrical theme at the start of the first movement which is markedly mid-century in style, a warmly romantic 'gesture' of the type favoured by the Mendelssohn/Schumann circle. It is significant that this opening idea was singled out for appreciative comment by Clara Schumann in her diary entry, mentioned above, particularly since she herself had created a first theme of similar breadth and lyricism in her G minor trio of 1846. The difficulty with such themes, as we have seen earlier, is to make them participate convincingly in the motivic style of development and dramatic thrust of ideas peculiar to fully organized sonata schemes. Interestingly enough, Brahms allowed this theme to stand in the revision, partly no doubt because its removal would have involved too great a denial of his youthful inspiration, and partly because, simply as a theme, it has such splendid

Ex. 40

power and direction. After allowing it to run its full course of over fifty bars, he disrupts its continuity by a vividly active transition, including much quaver triplet figuration, which immediately gives a foretaste of later developmental tactics. The substituted second subject, in the relative minor, preserves a simple relationship with the opening theme by again proceeding largely in even crotchets, but creates variety through its emphasis on descending arpeggio patterns in contrast to the grand arch shapes of the earlier melody. Triplets recur in the brief codetta before the first-time bar, and prepare the way for a complex, richly scored development, during which only fragmentary references are made to the main theme, set against motivically significant keyboard passages with flowing, off-beat chordal writing. In order to recapitulate the first theme without sacrificing entirely the tension generated, Brahms starts it obliquely in the relative minor, reduces its length by over a half, and accompanies it consistently by the triplet patterns already exploited so effectively during the development. Only in the coda, marked 'tranquillo', does he fully re-establish the relaxed lyrical mood of the opening of the movement; and by expanding motifs from both principal themes, over an arpeggiated accompaniment in slow harmonic rhythm, achieves a remarkable sense of balance and proportion.

It was during the long time-gap which separated the two versions of the B major trio that the bulk of Brahms's chamber music was composed. After 1891, during his final phase, there remained to be written only the wonderful clarinet works (including the A minor clarinet trio, to be considered later), inspired by the playing of Richard Mühlfeld. Earlier, it was the decade after 1880 which proved particularly fruitful, the period of the three violin sonatas, the second cello sonata, the two string quintets, and the two mature piano trios, Op. 87 in C and Op. 101 in C minor, each of which powerfully exemplifies the composer's very personal form of romantic classicism attained through intensive study and stringent self-discipline. Increasingly important in his management of sonata structures was his cultivation of variation writing, aspects of which he had developed from early in his career, notably in his piano variations on themes by Schumann, Handel, and Paganini, and his orchestral 'St Anthony' Variations. By his use of sophisticated methods of variation, related as much to underlying details of harmony, rhythm, and structure as to melody, he was able to infuse the sonata style with various strikingly new techniques, by which profound structural logic and motivic development of classical precision could co-exist with warmly romantic emotional expression. Though lacking the inspired dynamism of Beethoven's most finely honed thematic arguments, his methods combine subtlety of form with variety of expression in a wholly convincing way; and in the process far exceed the stiffly repetitious style which had disfigured the large-scale works of his immediate predecessors. It was very largely the novelty of Brahms's approach to thematic development and the flexibility of his means of motivic integration which prompted Schoenberg to describe him, in *Style and Idea*, by the significant term 'progressive'.[14]

A relentless process of selection and rejection remained for Brahms a continuing element in his creative approach; even as late as 1880 he is found discarding works which had failed to satisfy his exacting criteria. In that year he showed two first movements for piano trio, one in C major and the other in E flat, to Clara Schumann and his surgeon friend Theodor Billroth for their critical opinions. Both samples apparently received warm approval from his associates, but despite this he abandoned work on the E flat work and proceeded only with the C major one, completing it at Ischl in the summer of 1882, and publishing it as his Op. 87.[15] Possibly Brahms intended the C major and E flat trios to form a matching or contrasting pair of works, on the pattern of Beethoven's Op. 70 trios or the late Schubert works. Couplings of this type can be found among his other chamber works, the two piano quartets of 1863, for example, the C minor and A minor string quartets of 1873, and the two clarinet sonatas of 1895. If this was his plan, however, it had necessarily to be abandoned when the E flat trio failed to turn out to his satisfaction. It was not, therefore, until the summer of 1886 at Hofstetten, near Thun, that he produced in the C minor piano trio, Op. 101, a worthy companion work for Op. 87. Since these two trios are so closely related in their technical mastery, and at the same time so

---

[14] A. Schoenberg, *Style and Idea* (New York, 1950). For a discussion of Schoenberg's views see: T. L. Carpenter, 'Brahms: Progressive or Regressive? An Analysis of the Piano Trio in C minor from other Schoenbergian Perspectives', Univ. of London diss., 1983.

[15] See Gál, *Brahms*, 161.

well contrasted in emotional expression, it will be appropriate to regard them as a genuine 'pair' and consider them in parallel. The two opening movements epitomize the contrasts of expression involved. In Op. 87 the writing is warm and expansive, providing a remarkable compound of intellectual strength and emotional fervour in which complex technical procedures pass virtually unnoticed in the compelling flow of lyrical ideas; while in Op. 101 the style is taut and dramatic, with strongly contrasted themes and tightly reined transitions and developments. A prominent role is played in both movements by the use of basic motifs which, when transmuted and developed, form a constant source of logical growth. In Op. 87 two simple intervals—an octave (rising or descending) and an ascending semitone—are of particular importance. The octave, used not only melodically but also as a feature of the string scoring, contributes greatly to the openness of the texture and the basic vigour of the music; while the recurrent semitone, in addition to its melodic role, often promotes minor key or chromatic colouring and thus gives added richness to the harmony. In Op. 101 a similar significance attaches to the four-note figure B (natural or flat), C, D, E flat, first evident in the left hand of the piano part, below the main theme, in the opening bar (see Ex. 41(i)). Subsequently, this appears inverted above the main theme in bar 22, transformed into the opening idea of the second subject group in bar 38 (see Ex. 41(ii)), and augmented, in combination with the first theme, at the start of the development in bar 81 (see Ex. 41(iii)). Much of the expansiveness of the opening movement of the C major work results from the abundance of melodic ideas contained in its second subject group, each of which flows from its predecessor with a Schubertian grace and spontaneity. In the C minor trio, on the other hand, there is much less scope for lyrical expression, the second theme leading simply to a variation of itself and then to a terse closing idea, providing an exposition of only 43 bars. In order to compensate for what may at first have seemed like excessive compression, Brahms originally marked his exposition to be repeated in the traditional way; but later he discarded the idea, presumably because he recognized that an increase in length could be achieved only at the cost of some of the movement's concentrated energy.

The two slow movements are very different in structure. That

Ex. 41

in Op. 87 (placed second, before the scherzo) consists of a set of five variations on a twenty-seven-bar theme of folk-song-like character in A minor. The strings and piano strike out from the start on independent lines, the former, two octaves apart, presenting the principal melodic idea with its 'snap' rhythms suggestive of Hungarian influence, and the latter accompanying with a series of off-beat chords. However, both 'halves' of the ensemble turn out to be providing elements of equal significance for the subsequent variation treatment. In variation 1, for instance, the piano leads with a new version of its original accompanying material, while the strings simply repeat, at low pitch and rather morosely, the first phrase of their opening melody. And in variation 2, both the basic thematic elements are ingeniously combined into a single texture, presented initially on the piano alone and later with fragmentary string interjections. Rich chordal writing and powerful antiphony characterize the third variation, the full string sonorities of which point forward to the Double Concerto of 1888; while in contrast the fourth variation, in the major, is gently lyrical, giving a charming new slant to the piano's original syncopated chordal idea and weaving from it a continuous rocking pattern in 6/8 time. The last variation, also in 6/8, allots the opening string melody refashioned as a plaintive serenade to cello and violin, at first individually and then as an expressive duet. The innocuous-looking accompaniment in semiquaver sextuplets turns out on closer inspection to be reproducing exactly, in an arpeggiated form, the keyboard's original chordal progression. A touch of charming subtlety in the main 'folk' theme is shown in the structure of its final phrase, in which the melodic pattern of the last four bars provides an exact inversion of that in the preceding three, with a central overlap. This feature, in different guises, is faithfully reproduced at the end of each of the variations and thus contributes discreetly to the total integration of the movement.

For Op. 101, in contrast, Brahms provided one of the shortest and least complex of his slow movements. Placed third, after the scherzo, and set in the tonic major key, it unfolds on simple ternary lines, with a move to the relative minor for the middle section representing the only significant modulatory feature. However, by the use of irregular bar-lengths and some unusual scoring, a movement of much individuality results. The rhythmic scheme adopted provides for one bar of 3/4 time followed by two of 2/4 time (originally sketched by the composer as 7/4), and is somewhat similar to the pattern found in the 'Hungarian Song' on which Brahms, in 1853, based a set of piano variations, as part of his Op. 21. There is no suggestion that the trio theme is an actual Hungarian melody; merely that in it Brahms's thinking was coloured, as in many other instances, by elements of Hungarian origin. The scoring is characterized by clear-cut antiphonal writing throughout much of the movement, in which piano and strings (as an unaccompanied duo) answer each other's phrases in accordance with their separate instrumental capacities. Towards the end of the movement, where the answering phrases are particularly closely spaced, much ingenuity is expended on the string parts, in the way of held notes and double stops, to help them match the sustaining power of the piano as nearly as possible.

The sovereign nature of Brahms's technique at this period is particularly apparent in the two scherzos. Both in C minor, they share a similar, somewhat eerie, character, expressed in Op. 87 by rustling piano figuration and soft, mainly low-pitched, string-writing, and in Op. 101 by a sparse texture, the continuous use of mutes, and some highly effective pizzicato writing. And yet they differ quite markedly in structure. Whereas the Op. 87 movement is worked on largely classical lines, with a central, warmly melodic 'trio' section in C major and at a slower tempo, the movement in the later trio is conceived without strong contrasts, as a precisely fashioned ternary structure, with a centrepiece which also involves a simple ABA pattern. The result is a setting of remarkable symmetry, which is as notable for its uniformity of mood and tempo as for its formal coherence. It was this section of the later trio which aroused the particular enthusiasm of Clara Schumann: 'No other work of Johannes', she wrote in her diary for June 1887, 'has so entirely transported me; so tender is the flow of the second movement, which is wonderfully poetic. I am happier tonight than I have been for a long time.'

In the final movement of the C major trio, an allegro in rondo form marked 'giocoso', a playful manner, is evident immediately in the emphatic F sharp which obtrudes repeatedly in the principal theme as the only 'foreign' element in an otherwise wholly diatonic melody. Charmingly harmonized as part of a diminished seventh, the F sharp procures, in the opening bar, a chord sequence similar to that used in a very different expressive context at the start of the third symphony, of 1883. In both cases the progression provides the springboard for music of outstanding vitality. Equally striking is the trio movement's second main theme; starting in E minor (at bar 23) it has a delightfully varied continuation which, following excursions to B flat major and G minor, settles in the dominant only after some remarkable chromatic adventures, involving a series of augmented sixths, each of which appears anxious to deflect it from its natural progression homewards (see Ex. 42). Concealed artistry in counterpoint, and economy in the use of thematic material, results in a lithe, strongly sculpted movement. Only in the very long dominant preparation (from bar 97) which leads to the recapitulation does the momentum seem temporarily to flag.

The finale of Op. 101 is more enigmatic. Its opening theme—in 6/8 time and, following Brahms's frequent practice, still in the minor mode—creates a sense of agitation which contrasts well with the tranquillity established in the preceding slow movement. But subsequently rhythmic dislocations, such as the cross-accented duplets in bars 11 and 15, and a slackening of the tempo for the second group at bar 50, introduce a curious effect of brusqueness and unease. Towards the end of a short, rather

Ex. 42

skeletal development, there is an abrupt leap to an apparent climax in C major, but this proves to be a piece of Beethovenian tragic irony and is soon clouded over by darker minor harmony for a return of the opening theme. Eventually, however, the major tonic is firmly established for an extensive coda of 66 bars, in which both main themes return transformed and lead through a *crescendo e stringendo* to a final page of remarkable exuberance.

With the C major and C minor trios Brahms brought the genre, in its classical-romantic form, to a splendid culmination in the late nineteenth century. Many successors and imitators sought to achieve a comparable excellence in their work, but none showed the same capacity for combining profuse melodic invention with a seemingly effortless mastery of technique. Moving outside the orthodox ensemble, he further enriched the trio repertoire by the works he produced in which a wind instrument replaces one of the strings; the horn trio in E flat of 1868, and the clarinet trio in A minor, 1892. In these he set himself the difficult technical problem of absorbing a wind instrument into the ensemble without either exaggerating or minimizing its natural attributes as a soloist. By restricting himself in the horn trio to a natural instrument, and thus to a limited melodic range, he succeeded in creating a work of remarkable refinement, the themes of which, while particularly idiomatic for the horn, are transferable with equally good effect to the other instruments in the ensemble. Sensing that special problems were likely to arise in sustaining interest and variety throughout a large structure, he discarded the customary sonata-style opening, replacing it (perhaps on the pattern of Mozart's clarinet trio) with a more manageable sectional form—a lyrical Andante, with *più animato* interludes. Only in the finale does the 'hunting-horn' style of the music favour the wind instrument somewhat at the expense of its partners, and of the violin in particular, but in a manner wholly justified by the spirited effects which result. In the other trio, so eloquent is the combination of the clarinet and the cello that for once it is the piano that is in danger of being overshadowed. But even in the beautiful slow movement, where the risk is greatest, Brahms's accompaniments are shaped with such variety and inventiveness that the crucial parity of interest between the instruments is never seriously endangered. Clarinet trios were also produced by two of Brahms's colleagues in Vienna, Alexander von Zemlinsky and Robert Kahn, the former's work in 1895 as his Op. 3, and the latter's in 1906. Zemlinsky, whose later reputation rests mainly on his operas, is noted particularly for having taught Schoenberg counterpoint during the 1890s. His trio, though heavily indebted in style to Brahms, is a substantial, well-crafted work, with a particularly striking slow movement in which the clarinet and cello assume the character of high and low voices in a mock-operatic duet. Brahms was sufficiently enthusiastic about the work to have made special efforts to secure its publication.

Most significant among the Austro-Germans who wrote piano trios of the regular type in succession to Brahms are Hans Pfitzner, Max Reger, and Joseph Marx. Pfitzner, who is known principally for his works for the stage and particularly for his opera *Palestrina*, was active in chamber composition sporadically throughout his life, though his output is relatively small: in addition to the trio it includes a cello sonata, a piano quintet, and three string quartets. His F major trio, Op. 8, written in 1896 when he was 27, is a large, four-movement work of some distinction, which displays resourceful scoring and considerable skill in its handling of post-Brahmsian harmony. However, with the exception of the scherzo, a delightfully deft piece of instrumental fantasy, the movements tend to be rather self-indulgently long, with more repetition than their melodic ideas can reasonably be expected to bear. Also at times a Lisztian element of bombast invades the piano writing, and in the last movement particularly shifts the general sonority towards, if not over, the accepted limits of the chamber style. A Brahmsian feature worth noticing is the use of the tonic minor for the finale of this major key work, perhaps suggested by the older composer's third symphony, which was first performed in 1883.

Rather more significant is Max Reger's E minor trio, Op. 102, a mature work, published in 1908, and belonging to the same period as his orchestral *Variations on a Theme of Hiller*, Op. 100. Grandly designed, in four substantial movements, the work well demonstrates the strengths and weaknesses of Reger's chamber style; on the one hand, skilled craftsmanship, firm structural control, and precise and detailed scoring; and on the other, overindulgent chromaticism, a self-defeating degree of complexity, and an almost total lack of melodic distinction. As with much chamber music of the period it is the outer movements which are the most impressive and the inner ones which are the most engaging. Particularly striking is the scherzo (placed second), a type of *danse macabre* in C minor, distinguished by flashes of sardonic humour in the manner of Mahler. At its centre, in what seems to be an intentionally 'shocking' contrast, there is a 'trio' in Ländler style in E major, in which the strings ruminate together in strict canon at the octave while the piano supplies exaggeratedly romantic harmony and keyboard figuration in a mock-Brahmsian style.

The other trio composer, Joseph Marx (1882–1964), an Austrian, is renowned chiefly as a song-writer. His output of chamber music is not large, but includes a piano quartet, a violin sonata, and a cello sonata, all written before the first world war. His *Trio-Phantasie* (as he calls it), which dates from 1910 when he was 28, is of interest particularly for its structure, which involves the linking of five sonata sections into a single continuous movement, and the use of thematic metamorphosis and recall. The five sections, of which the first involves a broad sonata form and the last two the recall and expansion of themes from the opening, are marked in sequence as follows: (1) *Schwungvoll, aber nicht zu schnell*; (2) Adagietto; (3) Scherzando; (4) Intermezzo; (5) *Tanz finale*. No great economy of length or style results from the unification process, and much of the scoring, particularly for the piano, is decidedly ponderous. The structural system involved clearly owes a good deal to the basic example of Liszt, and specifically in piano trio terms, to the works of Berwald and Novák, which we shall consider later. But it is interesting also to notice how closely related in conception the work is to the British single-movement chamber works of the Phantasy type (to be discussed in Chapter 7) which W. W. Cobbett commissioned, or prompted by his prize awards, from such composers as Frank Bridge, Ralph Vaughan Williams, and John Ireland during the early decades of the twentieth century. By a strange twist of fate two lines of historical development seem fleetingly to have intersected: that of the great German romantic tradition in a state, at least as far as piano trios were concerned, of terminal decline; and that of chamber music in Britain at what to all appearances seemed to be its long awaited moment of regeneration.

6 The Nationalists

OUTSIDE Germany and Austria little of significance was achieved in modern chamber music before the middle of the nineteenth century; and even after 1850 most non-German composers, lacking native traditions on which to build, made only sparse and isolated contributions, often finding readier scope for nationalist expression in opera and orchestral music. By the end of the century, however, as a result of pioneer work in many parts of Europe, a body of new chamber music of considerable size and quality had been created, which was important not only in its own right, but also as a secure basis for crucial later developments.

The role played by the piano trio in this general evolutionary process was small but by no means negligible. Increasingly, during the second half of the nineteenth century, characterful additions were made to the repertoire, particularly by French, Czech, and Russian composers, which tended to differ stylistically as much from each other as from the products of the central Austro-Germans of the period. And as a result, the artistic scope of the genre was significantly enriched. Although many of the composers involved revealed in their music distinctively national traits of style and 'language', it was only the Czechs who were sufficiently numerous, and sufficiently linked in technique and expression, to form anything resembling a national school—one which, starting with Smetana (whose trio is dated 1855), proceeded in a reasonably coherent line of descent, despite their varying abilities, through Fibich, Dvořák, Suk, and Förster, to Vituslav Novák in the early twentieth century. Moreover, it was the Czechs who at this time contributed the interesting idea of using the piano trio as an elegiac medium, a concept later adopted, as a way of paying homage to recently deceased colleagues, by a number of Russian composers.

The means of attaining national identity show a considerable diversity of approach. In Russia and Bohemia individuality was often imparted to the music, consciously or unconsciously, by the use of folk idioms. In some cases a nationalist 'imprint' was achieved by the adoption of specific dance-rhythms and folk, or folk-inspired, melodies; but more commonly it resulted simply from innate or acquired modes of expression, the product of the composers' birth, upbringing, and environment. Elsewhere in Europe, however, the nationalist threads are not always so readily disentangled from the central Teutonic pattern. In France, under the influence of César Franck, a markedly Wagnerian slant overlaid the emergence of a distinctively Gallic style, until Fauré, one of the greatest chamber composers of the period, began to prepare the nation, in George Auric's words, 'for the great revelation brought about by Debussy'.[1] While in Britain, at the same period, the efforts of Parry and Stanford to restore dignity to the nation's music leant rather too heavily on a Brahmsian musical language to allow a truly individual style to emerge, before the folk-song revival and renewal of interest in early British music, at the start of the new century, created a fresh awareness of the country's musical potential.

Because of its many diverse strands the overall pattern of nineteenth-century development, confusing enough in terms of chamber music generally, is particularly unclear for the piano trio. The difficulty lies partly in the relative sparsity of trio examples over the whole period, partly in their irregular spread over many different countries, and partly in the 'abnormality' which many of the works display—by their exceptionally early or late appearance in their composer's career, or their lack of any obvious relationship to his other compositions. For this reason, in the present survey, both geographical and chronological approaches will be pursued, and emphasis will be placed mainly on the composers with the highest creative profiles in a wide range of compositional fields. Also, in cases where the natural scope of a particular development clearly embraces works of a later date, no undue importance will be attached to the close of the century as a firm terminal point.

An early nationalist work, standing in splendid historical isolation, is the delightful G minor piano trio, Op. 8, by the seventeen-year-old Chopin, which was composed in 1827/8, almost exactly at the time that Schubert was completing his two

---

[1] In *La Revue musicale* (Dec. 1924).

late trios. Written before the young composer left Warsaw for Paris, and at about the same period as the famous 'Là ci darem la mano' variations, Op. 2, which Schumann hailed with such enthusiasm, the piano trio is an accomplished work of classical proportions, laid out in four movements with the scherzo placed before the slow movement. Originally designed for the rather strange combination of viola, cello, and piano, and later rescored for the standard trio ensemble, it has a somewhat low-lying violin part; and as a result the string lines tend to lie closer together than is normal and provide the medium with an interior sonority of unusual warmth. The piano part, not surprisingly, is elaborate and brilliantly effective. But the trio is no mere showpiece for a virtuoso pianist with largely superfluous accompanying strings; indeed, the strings play a markedly constructive part in the composition as a whole, contributing elegant colouring to the scoring and taking a substantial share in the presentation of melodic material. As might be expected from a composer who was later to produce a fine cello sonata (one of his last compositions, dated 1847), the lower stringed instrument has a particularly distinctive role to play, not only as a soloist but also as a contributor to many finely judged contrapuntal textures. Most obviously Polish in character is the dance-like finale, which has a main theme somewhat akin to that in the last movement of the composer's F minor piano concerto, Op. 21, and a short, repetitive second idea with a strong rhythmic profile of unmistakably Slavonic cast (see Ex. 43). Ingenious use is made of both melodies, especially in the coda where they are combined on the strings with a splendidly climactic effect. The fluency and apparent spontaneity of Chopin's trio writing suggest that he may well have performed regularly with an ensemble of his own in Warsaw. Certainly, during his later career in Paris, he is known often to have played trios at the Salle Pleyel, usually beginning his programmes with a work he particularly admired, Mozart's E major trio, K542. Chopin, however, was an isolated phenomenon in Polish music. The foundations he laid for the creation later in the century of a truly nationalist style came to little, mainly because of the political and cultural domination of his homeland by neighbouring Russia and Germany. Of later native Polish composers the most influential were Moniuszko (1819–72) and Zelenski (1837–1921), who concentrated their efforts largely on

Ex. 43

opera and on artistic Polish songs of a somewhat homely character. Chamber music played only a restricted role in the musical life of the country, and few new works of significance were composed before the twentieth century. The chief piano trio to emerge was one in E flat, Op. 22, by Zelenski, a somewhat conventional piece which aims at little beyond a heightened salon-music style.

Almost equally isolated were the English and Scandinavian trio composers of the time. In England sporadic attempts at trio composition were made by Sterndale Bennett in 1839, and by his pupil Edward Bache in c.1851, after which a gap of more than thirty years intervened before the appearance of the trios, three each, of Parry and Stanford. These works, though much indebted to Continental models—the earlier ones to Mendelssohn and the later to Brahms—all display English characteristics typical of their respective periods: competent workmanship, a certain directness of melodic style, and a touch of salon sentimentality. Sterndale Bennett's 'Chamber Trio in A', as he calls it, published as his Op. 26, appears to have enjoyed considerable popularity in its day, but its themes are too colourless, and their treatment too limited technically, to make much of an impression nowadays.[2] His most enterprising idea occurs in the second movement, where the 'serenade' concept of its title is neatly captured by a *cantando* theme in 2/4 time in the piano right hand, accompanied by quavers in 6/8 time on the strings, and broken chords suggestive of a strumming guitar in the piano left hand. More impressive is Bache's D minor trio, Op. 25, which he wrote while studying with Sterndale Bennett between 1849 and 1852. The shadow of

[2] Modern edn., ed. G. Bush, in *Musica Britannica* 37 (London, 1972).

Mendelssohn hangs a little heavily over the work, but it is expertly written for the ensemble and there are many moments of striking individuality, particularly in the purposeful way the work's strongly shaped melodic ideas are developed. Unhappily, Bache died of tuberculosis before his twenty-fifth birthday, and a talent of notable promise was lost.

A marked predilection for Germanic modes of expression is again evident in the work of Niels Gade (1817–90), the foremost Danish composer of the period. In 1843, some seven years later than Sterndale Bennett, he too was drawn to Leipzig, where he enjoyed the friendship and generous professional support of both Mendelssohn and Schumann. His F major piano trio, Op. 42, which was published in 1864, owes a good deal stylistically to the influence of his German colleagues, though it retains, particularly in its melodic ideas, some slight traces of his national origins. In general Gade controls his structure well and, apart from some rather clumsy doublings in the Schumann manner, shows good craftsmanship; but his music provides more for charm than strength, and conveys too bland an impression to sustain interest over large-scale formal designs. Decidedly more individuality is apparent in the piano trios of the Swedish composer Franz Berwald (1796–1868), which were written between 1849 and 1859.[3] In these works as also in his four symphonies, Berwald employs a novel approach to structure, which involves the interlinking and interweaving of normal classical movements, or sections of movements, in such a way as to form extended works of unbroken continuity. The method is analogous to that used by Schubert in such large-scale keyboard works as the *Wanderer Fantasia* and the F minor Fantasia for piano duet; and it reflects, *pari passu*, the formal practices which Liszt was developing in his symphonic poems at this period, though there is nothing to indicate any particular link between the two composers. Berwald's system is well exemplified by the F minor trio, of 1851, the overall structure of which can be seen in Table 3. Similarly spacious designs, involving three closely integrated 'movements',

---

[3] The trios published in Berwald's lifetime were those in E flat (1851), F minor (1852), and D minor (c. 1854). A fourth trio in C major, issued posthumously in 1896, is a reworking of a much earlier one in the same key dating from 1845. All five works are now available, together with sketches and fragments, in vol. 12 of *F. Berwald: Sämtliche Werke*, ed. N. Castegren, H. Blomsted, F. Lindberg, B. Hammar, E. Lomnäs, *et al.*, *Monumenta Musicae Svecicae*, 2nd ser. (Kassel 1966–).

TABLE 3.   *Berwald's trio No. 2 in F minor*

Movement	Tempo mark	Time	Key and structure
I	Introduction	C	F minor: 4 bars, with cadenzas for violin and cello in turn
	Allegro Molto	C	F minor: abbreviated sonata form: three principal themes
	(leading to)		
II	Larghetto	3/4	F major: ternary form, with a reprise in D major
	(leading to)		
III	Scherzo (molto allegro)	3/4	F minor: in free rondo form
	Introduction (reprise)	C	B♭ minor: 4 bars, with the original string cadenzas in reverse order
	Allegro molto (partial reprise)	C	B♭ minor: the original second subject featured prominently
	Coda	C	F minor

are to be found in the other Berwald trios (see n. 3). Particularly characteristic, in each of these works, is the cultivation of swerving chromatic harmonies, delicate cadenzas (for strings as well as piano), and some improbable-looking, but invariably perfectly effective touches of scoring. Notable specimens of adventurous harmony and scoring can be seen in the larghetto section of the F minor trio: in the setting of the beautiful opening theme in F major, with its charming approach to the dominant by way of E major harmony, the chromatic mediant in the new key; and in the finely judged texture of the middle section, where widely spaced piano writing, with trills in the right hand and 'drum–tap' patterns in the left, encloses a tightly-knit canon at the octave between violin and cello, all at a soft dynamic level (see Ex. 44). No doubt because of their unorthodox features Berwald's works appear to have received little recognition during his lifetime, even from his own countrymen; but in more recent times his inventiveness and originality have been more fully appreciated and have gained him high regard, particularly for his four symphonies. It remains the case, however, that his substantial output of chamber music, which includes in addition to the piano trios many fine works for strings alone, is still relatively unexplored.

Valuable though Berwald's achievement was, it stimulated little enough activity in chamber composition amongst his fellow Scandinavians in the years following his death. Indeed, during the last quarter of the century, apart from a few, not fully characteris-

Ex. 44

tic contributions by Grieg,[4] virtually no new work of significance appeared from any part of Scandinavia. By contrast, in other parts of Europe, it was at this period that chamber music began to enjoy its most marked revival. In France, for example, following the end of the Franco-Prussian War in 1871, there began an upsurge of creative activity in abstract instrumental music generally, which was to provide a new impetus of special importance for the various chamber genres. This renaissance was particularly encouraged by the establishment at this time of the Société Nationale de Musique under the guidance of Saint-Saens and Romain Bussine, with Franck, Duparc, and Lalo as active supporters. This new organization took a powerfully nationalist line (as its motto 'Ars Gallica' proclaimed) and sought by its encouragement of native composers to hold back the tide of German, and especially Wagnerian, influence. Of great importance was the part played by César Franck, not only through his compositions but also through his teaching at the Paris Conservatoire. Among his pupils were several who were to take a major role in developing French chamber music at the turn of the century, including Vincent d'Indy, Chausson, Ropartz, and Lekeu, each of whom contributed at least one piano trio.

One needs, however, to look back some thirty years before the founding of the Société Nationale to trace the beginnings of the new French chamber style. It was then, in 1841, that César Franck, as a precocious youngster of 19, produced three remarkable essays in the trio form and published them as his Op. 1, under the title *Trois trios concertans*. Of these the first in F sharp minor is certainly the most enterprising. Though clearly an apprentice work, and by no means free from crudities of structure and scoring, it provides some remarkable anticipations of the composer's later development not only in its melodic and harmonic resource, but also in its handling of thematic transformation and simple cyclic organization. Too early to have been inspired by Liszt its structural innovations are probably indebted mainly to Schubert, of the keyboard fantasias. And influence of a more specific kind is traceable to Mendelssohn, whose scherzo from his early B minor piano quartet, written over fifteen years earlier,

---

[4] Grieg's only contribution to the piano trio genre is an *Andante con moto* composed in 1878 and published posthumously.

almost certainly served as a model for the equivalent movement in Franck's F sharp minor trio.

In creating the first trio of the set the composer's overriding concern seems to have been with its structure; and to this end he was clearly happy to work with only the simplest kind of thematic material, designed largely, if not solely, with its potential for metamorphosis and clear cyclic recall in mind. The stark opening of the work, a remarkable conception for its period, serves to underline this. The piano, left hand alone, presents an eight-bar ostinato theme in soft octaves (ⓐ in Example 45) which is typically Franckian in the way it circles obsessively around a single note. Then, at bar 9 the cello adds a countermelody (ⓑ in Example 45) above the ostinato bass, completing the thematic 'pair' which is to act as a 'motto' idea for the whole work; and at bar 17 the violin contributes yet another strand to the complex. In all there are four statements of the ground bass at the start before a freer type of writing begins to emerge. The movement is arranged in four large sections, alternately in tonic minor and major, and there is little to suggest a normal sonata structure, with contrasted key areas. The second main theme (ⓒ in Example 45) is presented each time unchanged in the major-key sections, and has a similar utter simplicity of outline to the opening idea. It, too, is plainly designed for easy recognition when it recurs in later movements.

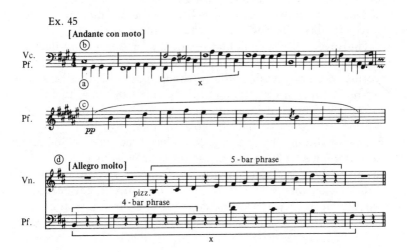

Ex. 45

Each of the two succeeding movements, a scherzo in B minor and an allegro finale in F sharp major, has its own independent thematic material, and each also incorporates significant elements drawn from the motto themes of the first movement. The exactness with which the principal theme of the 'Mendelssohnian' scherzo combines with motto theme ⓓ indicates careful pre-planning by the composer; and since the scherzo has, of the two, the more precise melodic and rhythmic character it may well have been the first to be conceived, and thus have exerted some influence on the motto theme's original, definitive shape. Considerable cunning is involved in the combination, since a 'fit' is possible only from halfway through the third bar of motto theme ⓓ ; and this, reinterpreted in terms of the scherzo's 3/4 metric scheme, means that the two phrases involved have to be pitched against each other asymmetrically over an extended paragraph (see ⓓ in Example 45). The scherzo's two 'trio' sections, each with different music, are both set in the movement's tonic major key, and thus mirror the second-theme sections of the first movement; and they are both derivative. The first takes up, in the major, the opening bars of the second-half idea (at figure 12) of the scherzo's principal theme; and the second simply adopts the main subsidiary theme ⓒ of the first movement, transforming its original crotchets into dotted minims. Also, as a further subtlety, the repetition of the second 'trio' theme (from figure 26) is underpinned by a short ostinato figure, drawn from the opening two bars of the first 'trio', which is repeated, with only slight pitch alterations, no less than thirty-six times.

The finale, which is linked to the scherzo, is a fully-fledged sonata movement in F sharp major in which there are first and second subject groups, with orthodox key relationships, an extended development, and a grandly climactic coda. Living up to the 'concertans' description of the work's title, the keyboard writing is vigorous and virtuosic, ranging widely over the keyboard and involving several thunderous chordal and double-octave passages. The recurrence of music from earlier movements occurs at two main places: in the development section, where the 'motto' elements ⓓ and ⓑ from the first movement reappear, initially in a very loud, grandiose manner at figure 39 , and subsequently in a soft and delicate fashion a semitone higher at figure 40 ; and in the coda at figure 53 , where the combination of the scherzo's second 'trio' theme with the ostinato bass from the first 'trio', mentioned above, returns in the tonic major as a splendid final paean, with the strings doubling the piano at the octave and unison. The strings, it may be added, have generally independent and 'chamber-idiomatic' parts, though there are a few places, notably at strong climaxes, where they are lured by some particularly uninhibited piano writing into a mock-orchestral style.

After the Op. 1 trios, Franck abandoned chamber composition for some thirty-eight years, returning to it only in 1879, when the first of his masterpieces in this branch of composition, the F minor piano quintet, appeared—to be followed during the ensuing decade by the A major violin sonata (1886) and the string quartet in D (1889). In these later works Franck, whose racial origins were somewhat more German than Belgian or French, continued to provide for his numerous pupils the example of a style richly compounded of German and French romantic elements, and structured repeatedly according to the cyclic principles which both he and Liszt had cultivated so successfully. Not surprisingly, his influence on the next generation of French composers was immense.

A more specifically Gallic strand was provided a little earlier in the century by Lalo and Saint-Saens, both of whom made significant contributions to French chamber music, not least with piano trios. Although their styles differ considerably, the two composers had in common a wide knowledge of, and love for, the classical Viennese repertoire (Lalo as viola player, from 1855, in the Armingaud Quartet) which is strongly reflected in their creative work. Saint-Saens, the younger of the two by twelve years, produced two piano trios dated 1869 and 1892, of which the earlier, Op. 18 in F major, is the more effective. Notable for its classical elegance of style, the work deploys many charming, though never profound, musical ideas. Structurally, it has the merits of simplicity and clarity, and shuns stereotyped 'cyclic' procedures as much as it does romantic rhetoric. The later trio, Op. 92 in E minor, is more ambitious but less successful. More self-consciously 'learned' in style it loses impetus, particularly in the outer movements, through its repetition of empty-sounding melodic gestures. The most effective parts are the middle two movements, a cleverly contrived scherzo in 5/8 time and an elegant Andante of Schumannesque character, with expressive string solos and duets. Of Lalo's three piano trios the most outstanding is certainly the last, Op. 26 in A minor, which was composed in 1880. In addition to the quality of its thematic ideas, it impresses by its firmly controlled structure in which a classical sense of unity is achieved without recourse to thematic recall or other special devices. The slow movement is particularly beautiful and subtle; in it there is combined a romantic warmth of expression with a texture of great refinement. The brief extract given in Example 46 conveys something of the composer's breadth of conception, and the delicacy and precision of his scoring for the ensemble. The lively scherzo, which the composer scored four years later for orchestra, contains a 'trio' section which is not a little indebted to the equivalent movement from Fauré's first piano quartet, completed only a year previously in 1879. The 'borrowing', whether conscious or not, suggests the

Ex. 46

likelihood of a close artistic link between the two composers, both of whom were prominent members of the Société Nationale.

At least equally cordial was the relationship between Fauré and Saint-Saens, his greatly respected teacher, the man who had set before him ideals of classical grace and polished craftsmanship and had given him, incidentally, his first introduction into Parisian musical life. Traces of Saint-Saens's early manner are apparent in Fauré's initial ventures into chamber composition, particularly his first violin sonata, Op. 13, and his C minor piano quartet, Op. 15. But the pupil quite rapidly outgrew the master's rather shallow, though certainly very attractive, forms of neo-classicism, and by greatly refining his style and technique soon assumed the leadership in French chamber music of the younger generation. Apart from his string quartet, which he completed in the year of his death, all his chamber works are for piano with one or more stringed instruments; and, with one notable exception, they include pairs of each of the forms which he cultivated—the violin sonata, cello sonata, piano quartet, and piano quintet. The one exception is his solitary piano trio, completed just before his string quartet in 1923. This remarkable work, which will be considered in more detail in the next chapter, constitutes one of the most impressive examples of the genre, of any period.

Prominent among the composers who sought to emulate Franck and d'Indy in the field of chamber composition were Chausson, Lekeu, Roussel, Magnard, Ropartz, and Migot. Rarely, however, were they able to equal, let alone surpass, the achievements of their models. All too often in their works richly spiced chromatic harmony and the 'crutch' of cyclic organization were expected to do duty for genuine individuality of ideas and precision of expression. Typical of this tendency is Ernest Chausson, who studied with Franck from 1880 to 1883, and produced before his early death in 1899 a small crop of chamber works written in the somewhat overripe romantic style of the period. These include a piano trio (1881), a work entitled *Concert* for violin, piano, and string quartet (1891), a piano quartet (1897), and a string quartet (1897/9) left unfinished at his death but completed eventually by d'Indy. His G minor piano trio, Op. 3, is too early a work to be fully representative, but it gives a good general idea of the stage of development the genre had reached in France at this time. Comprising four large-scale movements, which are not interconnected, the work is unified by an elaborate system of cyclic repetitions; only the scherzo, placed second, contains no thematic allusions from other parts of the work. Dominating the whole conception is a twenty-bar slow introduction, in which portentous motto themes are somewhat stagily presented, on cello and violin in succession, in the manner of texts solemnly presaging a sermon of profound significance (see Ex. 47(i)ⓐ). To counterbalance this, at the end of the work, a grand peroration is devised, during which the motto themes return, virtually unaltered apart from fortissimo dynamics and greatly expanded scoring. The effect of this blatant type of motivic reprise tends to be crudely theatrical, especially since the transference of the themes involves so little transformation. At various other points in the work an almost equally literal type of repetition occurs. In the slow movement, for instance, the opening theme, in 6/4 time (Ex. 47(ii)), is simply an echo of the first violin motif of the introduction (Ex. 47(i)ⓐ) set a fourth lower, with doubled note-values; and in the finale, the second main subject (Ex. 47(iii)) is borrowed, similarly, from the equivalent theme in the Allegro of the first movement (Ex. 47(i)ⓑ), with only slight adaptation. Chausson in 1881 was still powerfully in thrall to Wagner, an influence he was not to shake off or even greatly dilute until the late 1880s, when he began a conscious

Ex. 47

attempt to de-Wagnerize his style. As a result, his trio, despite its undoubted technical merits, is inclined to be overreliant on second-hand rhetoric and a near-exhausted vein of melodic and harmonic expression. Furthermore, the very thoroughness of his post-Franckian cyclic procedures leads often to an excess of unity, and to an attenuation of the natural conflict of ideas which should rightly lie at the heart of the sonata process.

An interestingly different line of approach is apparent in the E flat piano trio by Albert Roussel, composed some twenty years later in 1902. Roussel was a late starter, having embarked on a naval career before turning to music as a profession. His serious commitment to composition began only in 1898 when, at the age of 29 he entered the Schola Cantorum in Paris and worked under d'Indy's supervision for ten years, eventually as a member of the teaching staff. Thus his Op. 2 trio, despite his age at the time of its composition, is an early work, and not surprisingly shows his inexperience in the wide range of styles it draws on—from Lalo to Ravel, including hints of modal and whole-tone writing—and in its use of lushly romantic harmonies alongside more astringent forms of expression. Although overlong and discursive, the trio is aptly conceived for the medium and more delicately scored than many others of the period. Like Chausson, Roussel adopts a cyclic structure which involves much thematic recall; but he differs from his predecessor, partly by providing strongly shaped, independent themes at the start of each of his three main movements, and partly by combining his thematic recall with a wide variety of subtle transformations, exchanging plain statements for discreet allusions. In this latter respect he is aided greatly by the simplicity of his basic motto theme (Ex. 48(i)). This, like Chausson's, is stated in an opening slow introduction, and recurs during the work in numerous guises, such as that in Ex. 48(ii), an adroitly concealed instance from the slow movement, eight bars before figure ⑨ .

Theme transformation also occurs during the course of individual movements, where melodies are moulded progressively to a variety of shapes with an ingenuity comparable to that of Fauré— of the G minor piano quartet, for example. Particularly striking is Roussel's handling of the second main theme of his opening Allegro (Ex. 49(i)), a gentle, bucolic melody of somewhat Ravellian cast, ostensibly in G major, but with a markedly modal (E

Ex. 48

Ex. 49

Aeolian) flavour. Two of its more significant later appearances are shown in Ex. 49(ii) and (iii), the first forthright in character, exploiting the richness of the violin's bottom string and the tritone interval which the composer specially favoured, and the second soft and expansive, and cleverly designed to combine at its halfway point with a motto-theme entry on the piano. One effect of such transformations is to create a 'patchwork-quilt' type of structure in which a large number of contrasted sections are closely juxtaposed. And it is testimony to the degree of skill which Roussel had attained, early in his career, that he succeeds in avoiding the diffuseness of form which such a procedure rather readily invites.

Writing some twenty years later than Chausson, Roussel was able in his trio to eliminate much of the overcharged type of romanticism which affected his predecessor's work, and indeed that of many end-of-century French chamber composers, in the wake of César Franck. Open at the start of his career to a wide range of influences, old and new, Roussel contrived to combine Fauré's virile linearity with the elusive impressionism of Debussy, and to provide in the process prophetic glimpses of the way French music, and particularly chamber music, was to develop. The chamber works of his maturity include a trio for flute, viola, and cello (1929), a string quartet (1932), and a string trio (1937), but unhappily no second piano trio. It remained, therefore, to another of Fauré's disciples, Maurice Ravel, to produce, as we shall see in the next chapter, the first indisputably great piano trio of the new century.

The practice of thematic transference, cultivated so assiduously by the French chamber composers of the period, was adopted with almost equal alacrity by those of Slavonic origin. Among the leading Czechs and Russians of the time there were few who were able to resist entirely the attractions of the method, not even Dvořák, the most classically-minded member of the group. Early evidence of the trend can be seen in the chamber works of Smetana, the founder of Czech nationalism. Already in his first chamber composition, his piano trio of 1855, he begins each movement with a variant of a single motto theme; and in his string quartets, written over twenty years later, he again uses motivic recall and related devices as a means of achieving unity. Smetana, however, moved some way beyond the standard cyclic practices of his day by also incorporating overtly 'programmatic' elements into his chamber works, in line with the methods applied in orchestral music by Liszt and his 'new German' followers at Weimar. His pursuit of these techniques enabled him not only to give expression to nationalist ideals but also to disclose in his music intimate thoughts and feelings in an autobiographical manner, and thus realize simultaneously both political and personal aims. However, by adopting such advanced concepts in chamber music he committed himself to a decidedly unorthodox path and inevitably caused a strong critical reaction among the purists of his time. And even nowadays, despite the obvious sincerity of his approach, it is hard not to regard as excessively laboured the minutely detailed 'programme' (almost rivalling that of Berlioz for the *Symphonie fantastique*) which he provided for the first of his string quartets, the E minor work entitled *Z mého života* (From my life). It is, of course, possible to ignore the 'programme' entirely and simply accept the music on its own terms; but this may present too easy a solution to the problem, since it involves disregarding what is undeniably a significant aspect of the composer's creative thought.

The particular event which prompted the composition of Smetana's G minor trio was the sudden death from scarlet fever of his elder daughter during the summer of 1855, before she had reached her fifth birthday. In a touching entry in the catalogue of his works the composer describes the trio as 'written in memory of my first child, Bedřiška, who enchanted us with her extraordinary musical talent, and yet was snatched away from us by death, aged four-and-a-half years'. And in his diary he fondly tells how the little girl, at the age of 3, was able not only to 'learn songs with their texts and sing them well in tune' but also to 'play the C major scale on the piano with both hands in direct and contrary motion'.[5] The trio is thus an elegiac work, the first in a quite lengthy succession of such compositions for the medium by both Czech and Russian composers, including Dvořák, Förster, Tchaikovsky, Arensky, and Rachmaninov. Curiously enough, the Czech trios appear in every case to have been conceived as personal expressions of grief over the loss of a close relative, whereas the Russian ones were designed, somewhat more for-

[5] See notes provided in the Eulenberg miniature score (No. 335) of the work.

mally, as tributes on the decease of distinguished professional colleagues or predecessors.

Written between September and November of 1855, the Smetana trio was first performed on 3 December of that year at the Konvict Hall in Prague, with the composer as pianist, and Antonin Bennewitz and Johann Goltermann as violinist and cellist respectively. The relatively short time taken over its composition, together with its somewhat unusual structure, suggests that the trio may have been finished in a hurry, and perhaps not altogether in accordance with Smetana's original intention. Two particular aspects of the work indicate the possibility of an enforced change of plan. One is the unorthodox formal arrangement whereby all three movements are in quick tempo and in the tonic key, from which it may be inferred that a slow movement in some related key was originally intended; and the other is that the finale is known to be an 'imported' movement, drawn from an early piano sonata in G minor which the composer had discarded. Taken together these features suggest that some external reason, probably pressure of time, may have caused the composer to modify his original scheme. One result of the importation of a 'foreign' finale was to provide some uncharacteristically primitive scoring in the presto sections, where the strings fulfil only a very elementary function against a highly active piano part; and another was to give a somewhat indecisive role to the basic motto theme of the work at the final stage of its structure. It seems likely that Smetana's original intention was to unify the whole trio through systematic recurrences and transformations of the opening motto idea (see Ex. 50(i) and (ii)ⓐ), but that this plan was to some extent frustrated by his need to introduce a previously composed finale. As an ingenious solution to the problem, he devised a simple six-bar introduction to the finale, played in tempo and mainly by the strings, in which he provides the recognizable essence of the motto theme in the form of a chromatic scale pattern, falling from d'' to g' (see Ex. 50(iii)). And as a means of enhancing the overall effect of unity, he cleverly foreshadows this introductory phrase by inserting towards the end of the central movement another, even more basic, though clearly related, version of the motto's chromatic descent (see Ex. 50(ii)ⓑ). Despite its apparently rhapsodic, 'heart-on-sleeve' character, the motto theme must certainly have been

Ex. 50

(i) 1st movement: motto theme
Moderato assai

(ii) 2nd movement: transformed motto
(a) [Allegro, ma non agitato]

(b)
Bar 232

(iii) 3rd movement: motto introduction
Presto

devised with its considerable contrapuntal potential in mind—as becomes clear during the first movement's long and stormy development section, in which stretto-like imitative passages, based on the main theme, are tossed between piano and strings. The influence of Liszt hangs a little heavily over the piano writing in this opening movement, partly in the tumultuous double-octave passages in the development, which come near to imperilling the chamber character of the work, and partly also in the delicate *fioratura* passages of the tiny cadenza which precedes the start of the recapitulation.

Nationalist elements are evident mainly in the dance-like character of the second and third movements, based respectively on the polka and the *skocna*, the latter a type of reel in 6/8 time with regular eight-bar phrases. The second movement is cast in a form favoured by Schumann—the scherzo, with two contrasted 'trios'—but otherwise has little that is Germanic about it. Smetana, in fact, avoids the term 'scherzo' and marks his two 'trios', both of which are considerably slower in tempo, as *Alternativo I* and *II*. The resultant movement is strongly sectionalized, but avoids excessive formality by means of some delightful cross-rhythms and unexpected turns of harmony. One notable example of the latter is found at the point of return of the 'scherzo' after

Alternativo I, where a sustained D flat on all the instruments, reached as the submediant in F minor, is quitted as C sharp, the third of the chromatic supertonic seventh in G minor, forming a modulation of great wit and charm. The second *Alternativo* section is sombre in expression, with persistent dotted rhythms and vivid dynamic contrasts, and provides the chief elegiac element in the movement. Elsewhere, the dance-like style of the music suggests that the composer may have been seeking as much to portray the delightful personality of his child as to mourn her loss.

In the finale contrast is provided to the lively, piano-dominated opening, with its persistent combination of duplet and triplet figuration, by a radiantly beautiful second theme. Set in the unusual key of the flat supertonic (A flat major) this appears first on the cello and violin in turn against a very light chordal background on the piano. The melody has something of the character of a national hymn, but there is no reason to suppose that it was taken from any pre-existent source. Later in the movement, by a heart-rending twist of obvious programmatic significance, the rhythm and general melodic shape of this fine theme are transformed to a funeral march (of Chopinesque cast) over a prolonged dominant pedal. However, in the coda which immediately follows, the original 'hymn' melody is restored in brilliant style to translate the mood of despair into one of hope and exaltation.

Whatever the problems may have been which surrounded its original creation, the Smetana trio must certainly be regarded as one of the most important examples of the genre of the second half of the nineteenth century, as striking for the individuality of its ideas as for the powerful sincerity with which they are expressed. Beyond the general portrayal of sorrow and mourning, it is hardly possible to detect in the work any consistent underlying 'programme'. Unity is achieved by largely traditional methods, partly through balanced key-schemes and thematic development, and partly through the connective role played by the basic motto. However, the prevalent folk elements in the work and its early date of composition place it among the most significant attempts in mid-nineteenth-century chamber music to break free from German domination towards a more individual form of nationalist expression.

Despite the success of his piano trio, and the first at least of his two string quartets, Smetana seems never to have found chamber music as natural a form of expression as opera or the symphonic poem. Abstract forms appear to have held relatively little appeal for him; and, as he must surely have recognized, the scope for further descriptive or autobiographical ventures in the area of chamber composition was severely limited. Dvořák, on the other hand, seems to have accepted the chamber style, for all its formidable emphasis on structural logic and textural integrity, as an entirely congenial medium, one which, by providing for the expression of new ideas within well-tried frameworks, could fruitfully encourage both freedom and discipline. It fell to him, therefore, to enlarge upon the nationalist concepts established by Smetana, and through technical means drawn from the central German tradition, particularly of Beethoven, Schubert, and Brahms, to evolve a distinctive new role within the classical sonata concept for folk-style melodies and dance-rhythms of Slavonic character. In the process he added significantly to the repertoire of all the principal chamber forms, creating a body of work commensurate in nearly all respects with that of Brahms.

Brahms, it is generally accepted, was a principal influence on the music of Dvořák; and this is certainly true of the later periods in the Czech composer's career. But at earlier stages it is not inappropriate to regard the two composers as both subject to the same or similar influences—Beethoven and Schubert, consistently, Liszt and Schumann in their younger days, and in Dvořák's case, Wagner during a heady phase in the 1870s. A brief look at the chronology of various chamber works by the two composers, while clearly proving nothing, shows their joint growth in quite an interesting perspective. The earliest of the Dvořák string quartets, for example, were composed at the same period, 1873–6, as the Brahms quartets; while his first two piano trios, those in B flat (1875) and G minor (1876), predate all those of Brahms except the B major trio, Op. 8, in its first version of 1854. Furthermore Dvořák's third trio, the large-scale work in F minor, Op. 65, was completed in the same year, 1883, as Brahms's C major trio, Op. 87, and his great A major piano quintet appeared in 1887, at the same time as the Brahms C minor trio, Op. 101. It seems therefore that, in some of their chamber music at least, there was a considerable element of parallel development between the two composers. Nevertheless, Brahms's role as the 'senior partner' is unquestionable: partly because he was by eight years the older of the two, and, from 1877, a powerful supporter of the Czech composer who brought his work valuably to the notice of the publisher Simrock; partly because he belonged by birth to the German mainstream and Dvořák to a tributary; and perhaps most significantly, because he was nearer to the fountain-head, Beethoven, in his grasp of formal structure. What Dvořák had to offer is a Schubert-like spontaneity, colourful scoring, and an altogether different—nationalist—vein of expression, in melody, harmony, and rhythm. One can hardly doubt that he had to wrestle with problems of style and structure, just as Mendelssohn and Schumann did; but, standing as he did outside the central German tradition, he seems to have been less burdened by these difficulties, and to have been able to produce uncomplicated solutions to them almost by intuition.

Central in importance to Dvořák's small group of piano trios is the F minor work published in 1883 as his Op. 65. Though in no sense 'autobiographical' in the manner of Smetana's trio, it clearly related to certain pressing events in Dvořák's life at the time, notably the death in December 1882 of his mother, to whom he had remained deeply attached. Although the trio was not formally designated as a memorial tribute to her, it is clearly elegiac in character, as its dark colouring and intensely emotional tone, particularly in the beautiful slow movement, signify. Also at this time some intense pressure was being put on the composer to widen the international appeal of his work. To various of his German friends and colleagues it seemed that the 'barbarous' folk colouring in his work—and in particular his use of Czech rather than German librettos for his operas—was jeopardizing his chance of gaining the wider recognition that he merited, particularly in Germany.[6] Dvořák clearly took their advice very seriously and thought deeply about it, since it involved a crucial conflict of loyalties—to his nationalist inheritance on the one hand, and to the full scope for development that his genius demanded on the other. The outcome was a deepening of his style, and the acceptance of a greater Germanic, and specifically Brahmsian, element in his writing, but no significant decrease in its nationalist

[6] V. Fischl, 'The Life of Antonin Dvořák', in V. Fischl (ed.), *Antonin Dvořák: His Achievement* (London, 1942), 26–8.

characteristics—all of which contributed to a highly successful compromise solution to the problem. Apart from the piano trio, three other major compositions resulted immediately from the resolution of this crisis: the Symphony No. 7 in D minor, the orchestral *Scherzo Capriccioso*, Op. 66, and the dramatic cantata, *The Spectre's Bride*.

In the F minor trio Dvořák appears at his most Brahmsian. This is evident not so much in the overall melodic style, which remains as resolutely Slavonic as ever, but in the handling of transitions, developments, and codas, where the composer cultivates an unusually detailed motivic approach, using variation techniques and closely woven imitative patterns in the Brahms manner in order to tighten the joints of his structure. The problems of stylistic conflict, referred to earlier, and the means of their resolution, are epitomized in the exposition section of the first movement, where the first subject group, with its grave, finely sculpted first theme and dramatic and powerfully Brahmsian linking passages, is starkly contrasted with a second theme of extreme lyricism and markedly Slavonic character, presented initially by the cello. The potential source of conflict lies not solely in the excessively song-like nature of the second theme, but also in the momentous way in which it is introduced, as an exquisite but isolated 'event' in the flow of ideas, beautiful without doubt, but absorbable only with difficulty into the sonata argument. As Dvořák must certainly have been aware, it is at points such as this that the fusion of romantic and classical elements, and the creation of convincing structural logic, come near to the edge of breakdown. However, the skill with which the composer, from bar 82, tightens control over his material, recovers momentum, and leads on through rising sequences, imitations, and remote harmonies into a closely reasoned development section, shows how carefully he had calculated the risk and how confident he was of his ability to handle the structure on his own terms.

In place of a scherzo Dvořák (perhaps again following Brahms's example) provides a more sedate movement, a graceful dance in C sharp minor (the minor submediant) with folk-style repetitions and a curiously irregular disposition of rhythmic accents. The opening dominant–tonic leap of the main theme implies an anacrusis, despite occurring on the first beat of the bar, and the subsequent pattern of accents suggests, at least to the unwary ear, a charming scatter of unequal bar-lengths (see Ex. 51 for an outline of the opening bars). Nothing could be less Brahmsian, or indeed less classical, than the pattering accompaniment of quaver triplets which the strings supply against the piano's melody during the first forty-six bars of this movement. But, as so often, Dvořák's judgement is fully vindicated by the result, the very monotony of the ceaseless cross-rhythms serving as an admirable foil to the perky precision of the main theme. Dvořák's scoring generally is so adept that it is strange to find an apparent miscalculation in the 'trio' section of this movement. This occurs at letter ⬚G⬚ where, against a softly arpeggiated chordal passage in the piano right hand, the cello supplies pizzicato semiquavers and the violin an unbroken sequence of off-beat, two-note chords. On paper it looks delicate and imaginative, but in practice it is virtually impossible to make the violin's contribution sound other than clumsy and obtrusive. Comparison with the preceding version of the same passage (from two bars after letter ⬚F⬚), where the piano has the syncopated chords, shows how easily writing which is fully idiomatic for one instrument can go adrift when transferred to a different one.

Ex. 51

The slow movement, in A flat major, starts like those in both of Dvořák's earlier trios with a solo passage for cello with piano accompaniment. The warmly eloquent opening idea, clearly inspired by the tone quality of the instrument, falls naturally into a five-bar phrase, which is then echoed a tenth higher by the violin. A subsidiary idea ensues, consisting of only one bar for the violin alone, and with these slender resources the composer builds up a structure of notable richness, which, despite its reliance on short-scale repetitions, creates a remarkable effect of expansiveness. Broadly ternary in form, with a middle section in the tonic minor (notated as G sharp minor), the movement is cleverly designed to embrace within its static overall scheme of tonality many temporary shifts to 'foreign' key-areas. One such is the move to F major (the major submediant) in the first section for a return of the opening cello theme, now allotted to the violin and more elaborately accompanied; and another the memorable moment in the middle section, where B (= C flat) major is briefly touched upon for the enchanting piece of Dvořákian romantic ecstasy shown in Example 52, which is derived with perfect logic from earlier motifs. When this idea recurs in the coda, the subdominant harmony in its opening bar is replaced by a flat supertonic (Neapolitan) chord which imparts a striking note of disquiet to the otherwise nostalgic mood of the ending.

The finale, a large-scale sonata rondo, is based on an exhilarating principal theme in the style of a *Furiant*, an energetic Czech dance characterized by cross-rhythms and off-beat accents and commonly used by Dvořák in major works as a substitute for a scherzo. Despite its prominent folk elements the movement is none the less strongly Brahmsian in character, providing with its grand structure and complex developmental procedures a kind of Czech counterpart to the German composer's Hungarian-style finales, such as the *Rondo alla Zingarese* of his G minor piano quartet, Op. 25. For his second theme Dvořák introduces a more sedate idea of waltz-like character, which actually bears a marked similarity to one of a group of waltzes for piano which he had published in 1880.[7] When restated by the piano alone, with left-hand arpeggios and a simple countermelody above (at bar 127), this theme acquires such a Brahmsian guise that one might almost

---

[7] No. 1 of his set of eight waltzes, Op. 54.

Ex. 52 [Poco adagio]

suspect the composer of introducing an element of satire, were not the idea so foreign to what we know of his uncomplicated nature. Altogether less Brahmsian is the brief moment of thematic recall which Dvořák introduces at the end of the movement, immediately before the coda. Without in any way venturing into the realm of the cyclic designs of Franck and his followers, he simply reintroduces the outline of the opening theme from the first movement, with its original rhythmic features smoothed away, not so much to enhance the unity of the work as to provide a neat rounding-off of its grandiose climax and an elegant lead into the quiet start of the coda.

Dvořák's two earlier piano trios, those in B flat Op. 21, and G minor Op. 26, were written some seven or eight years before the F minor work, at about the same period as his fifth symphony, G minor piano concerto, and first major opera, *Vanda*. Both are substantial four-movement works, richly stocked with individual, often folk-influenced ideas, and effectively scored for the medium. The G minor work, which was completed in only sixteen days, was the first of Dvořák's works to be written after the death in September 1876 of his daughter Josefa, the second child of his marriage to Anna Cermakova; it thus shares with Smetana's trio in the same key a similar elegiac purpose. Though not representative of the composer at his finest the work is purposeful, attractively lyrical, and full of imaginative touches of scoring. What it lacks in powerful transitions and developments in the Brahms style, it makes up for by its freshness of expression and gentle charm. Particularly noteworthy is the confident hand which lies behind the witty scherzo, with its consistent five-bar phrasing and elegantly fashioned canonic entries.

Fifteen years later the composer produced his final work for the medium, the so-called 'Dumky' Trio of 1891, which soon became one of the most admired of his chamber compositions. The *Dumka* (plural, *Dumky*), a musical form which seems to have originated with Dvořák, is an instrumental piece characterized by vivid swings of mood and tempo, between sad (slow) and joyful (fast), expressive of a peculiarly Slavonic volatility of temperament. Its origins, about which Dvořák himself seems not to have been entirely clear, lie in a Little Russian (Ukrainian) type of folk-ballad, often nostalgic or elegiac in character, in which moods varying similarly between dark melancholy and wild elation are closely juxtaposed. The idea of combining slow and scherzo-like elements within a single sonata movement was not, of course, peculiar to Dvořák; an obvious example from another source is the middle movement of Brahms's A major violin sonata, Op. 100. But, by an extreme sharpening of the degree of contrast and the use of vividly colourful folk elements, Dvořák succeeded in fixing a highly personal imprint on the form. Examples of its use for single movements are to be found in several of his chamber works—the E flat string quartet of 1879, for example, and the famous A major piano quintet Op. 81—but only in the trio did he attempt to create an entire composition out of a succession of such pieces. The result is a wayward, spontaneous, but wholly convincing structure, comprising six movements in a progressively changing pattern of keys—from E minor through

C sharp minor, A major, D minor, and E flat major to C minor—
in which any suggestion of a sonata-like tonal unity is avoided.
The most common arrangement of the contrasting tempi is
slow–fast–slow–fast, found in movements 1, 2, and 6. Of the
remaining movements, 3 and 4 keep broadly to a simple slow–fast
pattern, but with several shorter internal passages showing slight
tempo fluctuations, while 5 is continuously fast in the manner of a
scherzo. Some minor instances of theme transformation occur
between the slow and fast sections of the two outer movements,
but it is mainly through its consistency of style and scoring
(particularly in the brilliantly effective piano writing) that the
work achieves its strong feeling of unity. Strictly speaking, the
composition is not properly described as a 'piano trio', since it
lacks the structural, as opposed to the scoring, criteria implied by
the term. Perhaps, without being over pedantic, one might
suggest—on the pattern of Schumann's *Vier Phantasiestück* or,
more recently, Martinů's *Cinq pièces brèves*—that a more appropriate title would have been, *Six Pieces in the form of Dumky* for
piano trio.

After Dvořák, the most important Czech contributions to the
piano trio were those of Martinů, which will be considered later
in their appropriate twentieth-century context. But three other
works merit some attention. One of them is the 'lost' piano trio
by Janáček. This, it appears, was composed in 1908 for a concert
in honour of Tolstoy's eightieth birthday, and based on the
Russian author's short novel *The Kreutzer Sonata*. Its first public
performance took place at Brno, from manuscript parts, in April
1909, and this was followed by a further five or six performances
in Prague and elsewhere up to April 1922; but it seems that the
work was never published. Then, in 1923, at the request of the
Bohemian Quartet, Janáček produced his first string quartet,
which was also subtitled *The Kreutzer Sonata*, apparently completing the work with remarkable speed between 13 October and
7 November of that year; and at that point the piano trio appears
to have vanished entirely from the scene. The whole matter has
been investigated in interesting detail in a recent article by Paul
Wingfield.[8] His view is that the 'extraordinary burst of energy'
which is commonly supposed to have enabled Janáček to com-

[8] P. Wingfield, 'Janáček's "Lost" Kreutzer Sonata', *Journal of the Royal Musical
Association* 112/2 (1986–7), 229–56.

plete his first quartet in about a fortnight is largely a myth. The speed of its creation, he contends on sound evidence, was possible only because the first and third of its movements were transcribed more or less directly from the discarded piano trio. However, it is not likely, or perhaps even desirable, that the trio can now be reassembled in its original form.

Of the remaining Czech works, one is the piano trio in C minor by Dvořák's pupil and eventual son-in-law, Josef Suk, which was composed originally in 1889 and later revised. A work of great charm and assurance, it was written when the composer was only 15, and published finally as his Op. 2. Though lightweight in style and indebted, unsurprisingly, to Dvořák in manner, it has a freshness and vitality of expression which has deservedly kept it continuously in the repertoire. The other work is the D minor trio, marked 'quasi una ballata', by Vítezslav Novák, another of Dvořák's pupils. Novák, who eventually assumed a leading role in modern Czech music, was strongly influenced in the earlier part of his career by Brahms and the late-romantic German school generally. Later, however, after developing close contacts with Janáček and undertaking a detailed study of Slovakian folk melodies, he evolved an altogether more individual, and nationalist, style. His D minor trio, dated 1902, and the second of his works for the medium, is notable particularly for its inventive treatment of form, involving the integration of the four main movements of a sonata structure into a single, continuous piece, bound together by a recurrent motto theme, according to the following plan: Andante tragico; Più mosso quasi doppio movimento; Allegro burlesco quasi scherzo; Tempo dell'Andante tragico; Allegro; Andante. As can be inferred from the section headings, the style is somewhat fantastic and theatrical, and may even involve—ballad-wise—some hidden 'programme'. The general scheme, however, is clearly analogous to that used by Berwald in his piano trios, and owes an even more basic debt to the formal innovations of Liszt. But it is also of special interest for the way it anticipates, like the *Trio-Phantasie* of Joseph Marx discussed in the last chapter, the single-movement 'Phantasy' chamber compositions produced in considerable numbers by British composers early in the twentieth century (see Chapter 7).

By comparison with the Czechs, the Russians of the late nineteenth and early twentieth centuries made only rather sporadic contributions in the field of chamber music. In the absence of a chamber composer of the commanding skills and fecundity of Dvořák, their output lacked a central and unified corpus of work, and comprised the largely isolated products of men whose principal creative activity lay in other areas, notably opera, orchestral music, and solo piano music. The result of this is observable readily enough in the sphere of the piano trio. Among the relatively small number produced, many are single additions to the genre by their composers, and many again are characterized by the overweight keyboard parts and quasi-orchestral scoring which betray, in varying degrees, the main predilections of their creators. The body of works produced is, however, by no means lacking in interest and value. Included are the products of such relatively minor composers as the Rubinstein brothers (Anton and Nikolay), Arensky, Taneyev, and Grechaninov, all of whom composed in a manner which is distinguished more for its effectiveness and craftsmanship than for its individuality. But chief in importance, inevitably, are the contributions of Tchaikovsky and Rachmaninov, whose immense and highly idiosyncratic examples of the trio genre still retain a firm place in the repertoire, despite some manifest shortcomings as 'pure' chamber music.

Pressure on Tchaikovsky to write a piano trio, a task for which he seems to have regarded himself as poorly equipped, appears to have come originally from his indefatigable 'pen-friend' and patroness, Nadezhda von Meck. During the summer of 1880, while staying with her family at the Villa Oppenheim at Fiesole, near Florence, she engaged a young student from the Paris Conservatoire to give piano lessons to her children, and also to act as pianist—with Pachulski (violin) and Danilchenko (cello)—in a trio which performed regularly at her musical evenings. The young Frenchman, whom she habitually referred to as Bussy, but who is better known in musical history as Debussy, delighted his employer by composing a trio himself during that summer, which was duly performed by the resident ensemble. In a letter to Tchaikovsky, dated 29 September,[9] she wrote that 'Bussy is still here, and Danil'tschenko, and they play trios for us every evening. My Frenchman has also written a very beautiful trio. I

[9] The dates given are those applicable under the old calendar. New calendar dates are twelve days further forward: e.g. 29 Sept. = 11 Oct.

regret, dear friend, that it is not possible to send the work to you for your expert opinion, but he [Debussy] is returning to Paris in a few days time.' And some three weeks later, she wrote again, still with reference to the work of 'her Frenchman': 'Every day trios are played to me, and every day I regret that you have not written one.'

The trio by the eighteen-year-old Debussy was long believed to have been lost; but some four or five years ago the missing manuscripts turned up at auction, and in a private collection, and made possible an almost complete reconstitution of the work. The editorial work, including the reconstruction of various missing parts, was undertaken by an American musicologist, Ellwood Derr, who eventually published the work in Germany in 1986.[10] The trio is a substantial four-movement work, somewhat in the style of Massenet, but with features derived also from Schumann and from César Franck, whose class at the Paris Conservatoire Debussy was then attending. Skilfully scored, it is an effective piece and has considerable melodic charm. But Debussy was very immature at the time, and apart from the interesting light it sheds on his early development it is difficult to regard the work as other than *un péché de sa jeunesse* which is probably best left in decent obscurity.

Tchaikovsky, it seems, was never able to see Debussy's work; and, for all Madame von Meck's urgings, he did not turn seriously to the idea of composing a trio himself for over a year. During the intervening period two particularly sombre events overshadowed his life and rendered him incapable, temporarily, of pursuing further creative work. One was the death in March 1881 of his friend Nikolay Rubinstein (1835–81), the famous pianist and composer, and first director of the Moscow Conservatoire, who had been at once his severest critic and most ardent supporter. And the other was the serious illness of his much loved sister Sasha, from which, happily, she recovered in due course. However, by the end of the year the idea had formed in his mind of writing a piano trio as a memorial to Nikolay Rubinstein, and by December he had begun work on what was destined to be a large-scale work in A minor, with the dedicatory subtitle, '*A la*

---

[10] C. Debussy, *Piano Trio in G major*, ed. E. Derr (Munich, 1986): see also E. Derr, 'Sein erstes überliefertes Instrumentalwerk zur Erstöffentlichung von C. Debussys frühen Klaviertrio', *Neue Zeitschrift für Musik* (Dec. 1985), 10.

mémoire d'un grand Artiste'.[11] Although it was not without considerable misgivings that he entered upon his task, he soon appears to have become whole-heartedly involved in it, and to have worked at an almost feverish pace. Writing from Rome to his brother Anatol in January 1882, he declared himself to be 'completely engrossed in my trio, and attracted by this form of music, which I have not tried previously, and which is quite new to me'. And by the middle of that month he had completed it.[12]

One can hardly fail to connect the speed with which he completed the work with the curiously unfinished—in the sense of 'unpolished' or 'unrevised'—nature of its final version; and to wonder whether, under pressure to complete in good time for the projected first performance in March 1882, on the anniversary of Rubinstein's death, he may not have been impelled to hurry the final stages of his work even more than was his usual custom. But, whatever the circumstances, the promised début took place at the Moscow Conservatoire on the appointed day, with J. Grymalji and W. Fitzenhagen as violinist and cellist respectively, and Sergey Taneyev as pianist. After the performance, Taneyev sent the composer a copy of S. V. Flerov's criticism of the work in the *Moscow News* (1882, No. 290), an offering which is said to have given him 'no pleasure at all'. It is clear, however, that Tchaikovsky was himself equally stern in his criticism of the work. 'I fear', he wrote to Madame von Meck in January 1882, 'that I may have arranged music of a symphonic character as a trio, instead of writing directly for my instruments.'

Tchaikovsky can scarcely have been much surprised by the predominance of 'symphonic' writing in his trio, since this represented so surely his normal mode of musical expression. Had he written more 'directly for his instruments' he might conceivably have produced a work of more classical orientation, but almost certainly at the sacrifice of much of the vigour and

[11] An earlier example of an elegiac chamber work by Tchaikovsky is his string quartet No. 3 in E flat minor, of 1877, composed in memory of his violinst friend Ferdinand Laub. Its third movement is a funeral march marked *'Andante funebre e doloroso ma con moto'*.

[12] In further correspondence with Anatol (from Rome, 9–21 Jan., 1882) the composer wrote: 'I am finishing my trio and hope to get completely free of it tomorrow (Sunday), and to take a long walk for relaxation. To this end I have been at work from 9 am. to 4 pm., and so intensely that I cannot think properly any more. This excessive haste at the end of a composition always has a bad effect on it, but I can't change my nature.' Quoted in *Pyotr Ilyich Tchaikovsky: Letters to his Family: An Autobiography*, tr. G. von Meck, (London, 1973; rev., with addit. annotations by P. M. Young, 1981), 271.

individuality it was in his nature to impart. Not surprisingly it is
the grand, sweeping climaxes, inseparable from the Tchaikovsky
style, which afford the most obvious scope for quasi-orchestral
treatment; at such moments powerful dynamics, high pitch,
virtuosic piano-writing, and string chords or repeated notes
combine to produce an effect of almost overpowering intensity.
But often the 'symphonic' effect is evident as much in the stuff of
the music as in its scoring. Repeatedly, in ascents to, or descents
from, the grand climaxes there are extensive phrase repetitions
and prolonged sequences which are natural enough as a 'theatrical' effect in symphonic writing, but which sound forced, and
even somewhat coarse-grained, in chamber music. A striking
example—which, interestingly, is not heavily scored—occurs
between bars 182 and 194 of the trio's first movement, where the
piano, accompanied by cello alone, provides two matching and
consecutive sequences—ornamenting the rising note-series: C, D
flat, E, F, and F, G flat, A, B flat—which proceed through a vivid
crescendo to a fortissimo climax. At this point the violin enters
and after several exalted phrases, vehemently repeated, leads the
music gradually downwards in pitch and dynamics to settle in E
flat minor, two octaves lower. There is nothing about the passage
or its scoring which is fundamentally alien to the trio medium,
but the style of the writing seems to cry out for orchestral weight
and variety of instrumental colour. Climaxes, however, are not
the only points at which the chamber style is jeopardized. At the
other extreme are those passages, often quiet and lyrical in
character, where a basically orchestral approach is betrayed by a
lack of textural variety. One example is variation 9 in the second
movement, where muted string solos, marked *lamentoso*, are
accompanied continuously by pianissimo arpeggios on the piano.
Here again, the writing is perfectly well adapted to the medium;
but its static, unvaried disposition suggests an orchestral rather
than a chamber motivation, as if the composer had at the back of
his mind an oboe and a bassoon as soloists, with a harp supplying
the arpeggios and shimmering tremolando strings, perhaps, the
sustaining pedal effect. The example just given emphasizes a
problem which is endemic in Tchaikovsky's work generally, and
in his chamber music in particular: how to preserve a satisfactory
balance between melody and accompaniment. A style such as his,
which so powerfully emphasizes melodic beauty, necessarily

creates a matching demand for characterful accompanying material; and this, as we have seen in relation to many earlier trios, is something much less easily achieved in chamber music than in orchestral writing. Generally, in the Tchaikovsky trio, when the strings have the principal melodic interest there is little difficulty, and the composer is able to exploit the keyboard's natural aptitude for accompanying with much imagination. But in the inevitably more problematic reverse situation his custom is either to leave the piano entirely unaccompanied or else fall back on string figuration of an orchestral character. a typical example of the latter (mentioned in Chapter 4) is the cello's arpeggio pattern of rapid sextuplet semiquavers, provided as an accompaniment to the piano's restatement of the opening theme, from bars 20 to 34 in the first movement. At the same time one should not overlook the many places where free imitation and theme combination in the string parts are linked with finely etched piano figuration to produce textures of a wholly convincing chamber character: for example in bars 95 to 104 in the first movement.

The structural plan of the work—a sonata movement followed by a set of variations—is somewhat unusual, and suggests Beethoven's Op. 111 piano sonata as a possible model, though the stylistic gap between the works could hardly be wider. For the first movement Tchaikovsky adopts a broadly classical pattern, with more or less conventional key adjustments for his second subject group; but he departs considerably from normal by elaborating his themes piecemeal, within individual parts of the exposition, rather than in a clearly separate development. The overall framework is typically sectional, but the joins are achieved with considerable skill and make for a generally convincing sense of continuity. At the point where a clear-cut break becomes necessary—between the end of the exposition and the start of the recapitulation—a short solo violin link is inserted (perhaps in emulation of Smetana's trio) as an elegant means of relaxing the momentum temporarily, and at the same time filling the gap. In his search for unity the composer provides for a great deal of repetition; sometimes by means of an immediate repeat, and sometimes with a long-range one, as for example in the final coda, where the elegiac melody from the opening returns as an expressively recalled motto theme. But an even greater sense of cohesion results from a strong family likeness which exists between many of the work's principal themes. The connecting factor is a 'hidden' scalic figure—a descending motif to suggest grief—which (whether by design or not it is impossible to say) contrives to exert a strong influence on significant melodic elements in both movements, as shown in Example 53.

The second movement is both less and more problematic in structure than the first; less because of the straightforward nature of its variation treatment, and more because of the gross imbalance it creates with the rest of the work by its huge dimensions. The extreme length of the movement, and particularly of its repetitious finale, is one cogent reason for supposing that the composer may have been hurried over the work's completion: that he may have had, as the familiar paradox goes, too little time to make it shorter. In the event he sought to remedy things with the scalpel rather than the pen, by sanctioning the omission, ad lib, of two of the variations (usually Nos. 7 and 8), and of no less than 136 bars from the finale. The result is far from satisfactory, not least because the 'cut' in the sonata-form finale involves the omission of large parts of both its exposition and development sections, and thus the elimination of virtually all balance and variety from its key scheme. A slight programmatic intention appears to lie behind the series of variations, each of which was said by the composer to refer to some particular event in Nikolay Rubinstein's life. The only clue to the nature of these 'events' is contained in a letter which Tchaikovsky wrote to his brother

Ex. 53

Modest in October 1882: 'the variations', he declared, 'are only memories. One is a memory of a trip to an Amusement Park out of town [perhaps No. 5], and another of a ball we both attended [perhaps No. 6], and so on.' There is no good musical reason for attempting to identify the scene or happening associated with each variation; but it is not unlikely that the fugue (No. 8) was intended as a joking reference (of somewhat damaging prolixity) to an agreeable academic pursuit at the Conservatoire, and the finale theme, apparently modelled on the parallel finale opening in Schumann's *Études symphoniques*, as a reminder of a work of special significance to the deceased pianist and composer.

With one exception the variations cling closely to the original theme, moulding its note-pattern to a wide range of new rhythmic shapes, in major and minor keys. The exception is variation 6, a charming waltz in A major, in the composer's most typically balletic vein, which has its own independent theme. But even here the original theme maintains contact, its opening two bars reappearing in an amusing combination with the waltz theme, initially in the distant key of C major (see Ex. 53 for a brief outline, transposed to A major). The counterpoint is somewhat brash, and the combination, at each appearance, short-lived; but it provides a bold and imaginative stroke, typical of the composer at his most theatrical. To end the work Tchaikovsky provides what are in essence two separate codas, both concerned with recalling the motto theme from the first movement. In the first of these the entire motto is allotted to the strings, *fff* and two octaves apart, while the piano contributes a tumultuous accompaniment of chords and flashing arpeggios, providing the *ne plus ultra* of heavyweight scoring for trio. At the other extreme, dynamically and stylistically, the second 'coda' contains only soft, plaintive fragments of the motto theme scored separately for solo strings, and a simple pattern of chords in funeral march rhythm for the piano. The effect of the latter setting, it has to be said, is as impressive as that of the former is excessive.

Eleven years later, on 6 November 1893, Tchaikovsky died at the age of 53, and on the same day the 20-year-old Rachmaninov began to compose a piano trio in his memory. This was the second of two trios, both entitled *Trio élégiaque*, which the young composer produced at about this time. The earlier one, completed in January 1892, is a single-movement work in sonata form of rather modest pretensions; no reason is known for its '*élégiaque*' sobriquet, but its style is appropriately gloomy. The later trio, commemorating Tchaikovsky's death, is an altogether grander work, in three movements, and gives a powerful impression of sincere grief. In recognition of the example set by his great predecessor the youthful Rachmaninov also marked his score: '*A la mémoire d'un grand Artiste*'.

The remarkably prompt start which Rachmaninov made on his memorial work suggests not only an understandable frenzy of sorrow and admiration but also a wholly level-headed desire to complete his composition while its elegiac purpose was still fresh in people's minds. As it turned out the trio took him just over seven weeks to finish, and cost him, on his own admission, infinite pains in its creation. 'I trembled for every phrase', he wrote on 19 December to Natalia Skalon, shortly after finishing the work, 'and sometimes crossed out everything and started over again to think, think.'[13] However, after all such searching self-criticism, the work failed to satisfy him after its initial performance, and was subjected to considerable later revisions. Significantly enough, these included substantial cuts, introduced for later performances in 1907 and 1917, which strongly suggests that, as in Tchaikovsky's own case, overhaste in its original completion had led to excessive length.

In structure and general conception the work is markedly similar to the Tchaikovsky trio, yet sufficiently independent to show the young composer's growing confidence in his own powers. The opening movement is the grandest of the three, with powerful, dramatic writing and colourful solos for all three instruments. While displaying broad sonata characteristics, it is even more sectional than Tchaikovsky's equivalent movement, its exposition alone comprising no less than seven separate sections in different tempi. Furthermore, the transitions between the sections are by no means all equally convincing; indeed, some of them sound almost like cruel parodies of Tchaikovsky's feebler structural joins, though we can safely assume that this was not the intention. Following this, in obvious homage to Tchaikovsky's second movement, there is an extended set of variations based on a theme from Rachmaninov's own orchestral fantasia, *Utyos* (The

[13] S. Bertensson and J. Leda, *Sergei Rachmaninov: A Lifetime in Music* (London, 1965), 63.

rock) Op. 7, which follows the older composer's example in the use of contrasted tempi and keys to suggest a combination of slow movement and scherzo. Rachmaninov however avoids the contentious type of variation-finale which caused his predecessor so much trouble, replacing it by an entirely independent third movement. In the original version of the work the simple theme of the variation movement was marked, very strangely, to be played on a harmonium; but happily, this idea was discarded in the first of the later revisions. The individual variations are of mixed quality, No. 3, for instance, with its rippling passage-work for the piano and chordal pizzicato accompaniment, being especially fine and No. 4 decidedly dull. The scoring, generally, is biased heavily in favour of the piano, particularly in the showy, but very empty-sounding, finale, where the strings remain entirely silent for the first twenty-four bars and are later allotted much simple orchestral-style writing, mainly in octaves. At the end, in an isolated but very effective use of thematic recall, the plaintive opening theme from the first movement returns, with its drooping chromatic patterns harmonically enriched, to provide a moving epilogue.

Despite its early place in his output, Rachmaninov's trio well represents his rather limited stylistic range. It has characteristics which, not unfairly, have been criticized as inappropriate to a mature chamber style—its heavyweight piano writing, naturally, and its notably theatrical brand of emotional expression; and undeniably it stands at the opposite end of the spectrum to the classical chamber style of the late eighteenth century. But, in attempting to 'place' it within the whole continuum of trio development, several circumstantial differences need to be taken into consideration; in particular that the composer was writing for performance in large public halls rather than private chambers, for the huge tonal resources of the modern concert grand piano and richer-toned stringed instruments, and for highly accomplished professional performers rather than amateurs. When allowance has been made for such 'physical' factors, there remains a considerable residue of the essential criteria of the classical style. The instrumental parts are each in their own way interesting and independent, though full equality of interest can hardly be claimed; and each contributes in a thoroughly integrated fashion to the sonata argument. What, in fact, is most crucially lacking is the sonata argument itself, as opposed to a loose assemble of contrasted episodes. And in this regard Rachmaninov was by no means untypical of the 'sunset' period in which he worked. As in Germany and France so also in Russia, an overripe romantic style of expression, evident equally in the near contemporary piano trios of Arensky, Grechaninov, Taneyev, and Zolatariev, was beginning to turn to decay, making the accession of fundamentally new modes of musical thought inevitable. The nature of the changes involved, and how they affected the piano trio, will be the concern of the final chapter.

7 The Twentieth Century

To the eye of the historian, eager to trace clear patterns of development, the piano trio's progress during the twentieth century presents a complex and varied picture. A large number of composers of many nationalities have been involved, and their combined output has been very substantial. Some have shown progressive and others conservative inclinations, and their works, naturally, have revealed wide divergences of style and technique. Some have turned to the piano trio very early, and others very late, in their careers, and many have produced only single examples of the genre. Nationality has remained a significant element, as much if not more than in the previous century; but the wars and revolutions of the period, by their resultant migrations, have introduced, also, a significant strain of cosmopolitanism. Not only have composers from mainland Europe moved as refugees to Britain and the United States and exercised a powerful influence in their new environments, but others, again, have travelled in the reverse direction in search of intellectual stimulus, particularly to Paris where the teaching of Nadia Boulanger (up to her death in 1979) proved a constant magnet.

The radical changes which took place in the musical language during the first half of the century had surprisingly little immediate effect on the piano trio. Among the principal revolutionary composers of the time only Bartók added significantly to the trio repertoire, and his contribution, *Contrasts* (1938), splendidly original though it is, stands outside the normal pattern of works by virtue of its unusual scoring—for violin, clarinet, and piano.[1] It is difficult to see any fundamental reason why the trio genre should have been regarded as less adaptable to the innovations of the period than, for example, the string quartet, which was

---

[1] Specially commissioned by Benny Goodman (clarinet) and Joseph Szigeti (violin) for performance with Bartók as pianist, the work has three movements—Verbunkos (recruiting music), Pihenos (relaxing), and Sebes (quick)—the last of which requires in performance both A and B flat clarinets and a 'spare' violin tuned to G sharp, D, A, and E flat.

widely cultivated by composers of an experimental tendency. Possibly the medium was thought to be too restricted in colour and articulation to offer much scope for technical development, or too closely tied to a long and somewhat adipose romantic tradition to be capable of sustaining impressive new modes of expression. But there seems, with hindsight, to be nothing in the nature of the ensemble, not even its linking of instruments of non-equivalent tonal character, to have created misgivings about its adaptability to the disciplines of twelve-note composition, or to the lean textures and austerely dissonant contrapuntal styles typical of the neo-classicism of the period. In the event, with its openness to change largely untested by the experimentalists, the genre's flexibility remained in doubt and its traditionalist profile, however unjustly, was substantially compounded.

A further factor, affecting the modernist image of the trio, was the absence, from the pen of a major composer, of an extended sequence of works for the medium, comparable to the string quartets of Bartók, Hindemith, and Shostakovich. As a result of this no definitively 'progressive' forms of trio writing emerged and the genre continued to be represented by a quantity of somewhat isolated works which, though often of the highest quality, simply reflected the varied styles and fine technical skills of their largely conservative composers.

In more recent times, however, signs of a somewhat different picture have begun to emerge. Although the piano trio has remained the preserve mainly of traditionalists, it has also, since the end of the Second World War, attracted the interest of a small number of more experimental composers (particularly in Britain and America), who have discovered in the medium considerable scope for the promotion of new textures and sonorities. In the process, as we shall see, fresh emphasis has been placed on novelties of instrumental colour, new rhythmic concepts have affected the traditional bases for cohesion in the ensemble, and a drastic realignment has taken place of the piano's role in relation to the strings. Whether in the long run these and other similar developments will prolong the life of the genre remains to be seen; the only alternative seems, unhappily, to be a slow decline towards museum status.

Despite the antipathy of the progressives the piano trio was fruitfully cultivated during the first half of the century by a number of prominent composers, including Ravel, Fauré, Martinů, and Shostakovich. And virtually for the first time, important contributions were made by Britons and Americans of international repute, such as Frank Bridge, John Ireland, Aaron Copland, Roy Harris, and Walter Piston. It is interesting to observe the wide range of nationalities involved, and also to note that the distinguished French, Czech, and Russian successors to Franck, Dvořák, and Tchaikovsky, respectively, were not matched by a German composer of comparable stature to follow in the tradition of Brahms and Reger, a situation which has since remained largely unaltered. Also noteworthy are the contributions which have been made by composers of 'new' nations (ones, that is, which were not involved during the previous century), such as Pizzetti, Malipiero, and Casella in Italy; Granados and Turina in Spain; and Pijper and Andriessen in the Netherlands. An example of interesting formal innovation is found in Malipiero's *Sonata a Tre* of 1927, in which different scoring is used for each of the movements (cello and piano, and violin and piano, respectively, for the first two, and the full ensemble for the third), the effect of symmetry being enhanced by the recall of themes from the first two movements in the finale. And a particularly attractive nationalist flavour is evident in the third of Turina's trios, a Fantasia, dating from 1942, entitled *Circulo*, Op. 91, the three movements of which—*Amancer* (daybreak), *Melodio*, *Crepúsculo* (twilight)—provide vivid scene-painting, full of Spanish life and colour.

Among the earliest works which have a special claim on our attention are the trios of Ravel and Fauré, the former completed in 1914 shortly after the start of the First World War, and the latter in 1923 some eighteenth months before its composer's death. In their refinement of thought and expression these two works represent a splendid culmination to the older French chamber tradition, traceable from César Franck through Saint-Saens, Lalo, and Chausson to Roussel and Ropartz; but, though without rivals in their time, they were essentially 'terminal' works, the respective styles of which offered little if any scope for further development.

Ravel's A minor trio is his third chamber composition, standing between the Introduction and Allegro for flute, clarinet, harp, and string quartet of 1906, and the violin and cello sonata of 1922.

Classical in its poise and precision of expression, the work preserves the outline framework of the traditional sonata concept with its provision of four self-contained movements, each sharply contrasted with its neighbours. But in place of the motivic development and dramatic key schemes typical of the German sonata style, it substitutes eloquent phrase repetitions, extended ostinatos, contrasted tempo blocs, and a striking combination of modality and progressive tonality. As a way of contributing to the work's overall unity, Ravel provides an unusual type of 'head-motif'—involving a simple step downwards and back of a whole tone—which features prominently in the opening themes of each movement except the last, where the pattern is inverted. The method clearly owes something to the system of thematic recall, so assiduously cultivated by Ravel's predecessors, but it is simpler and altogether more subtle in effect. Also strikingly original is the composer's exploration of new sonorities in relation to the trio medium. Calling upon his experience in other fields he combines the brilliant string techniques of his early string quartet—double-octave spacing, harmonics, tremolandi, and extended pizzicato passages and trills—with the powerful and evocative piano writing developed in *Miroirs* (1905) and *Gaspard de la nuit* (1908), in order to achieve some entirely new effects of colour and expression in trio-writing.

The first movement is based on themes of a special melodic and rhythmic character, derived from the folk music of the composer's Basque homeland; originally, they were intended for a concerto entitled *Zaspiak-Bat* which Ravel had planned in 1912 but subsequently abandoned. Folk elements are apparent not only in the modal style of both the principal melodies but also in their general fluidity of rhythm, expressed notationally in each bar by eight quavers grouped in patterns of twos and threes—usually 3 + 2 + 3—to produce a gentle swaying motion. The resultant music is stately and dance-like, rather than dynamic in the normal sonata fashion, though sharp contrast is achieved by lively transitions in fast demisemiquavers, and some near-traditional development tactics are employed, such as the contrapuntal combination of the two main themes (the second in diminution) at the point of climax after figure ⑨. In a key scheme of unusual design both the principal themes are set originally in a modal A minor (the first with Dorian and the second Aeolian characteristics) over dominant and tonic pedals, respectively; then, at the recapitulation, the pedal notes shift their relative positions, so that the first theme, now in E minor, is placed over a C sharp (the sharp submediant) while the second theme, again in A minor, is set above a D (the subdominant). Finally, prolonged emphasis on a pedal C draws the whole movement to a gentle close in C major.

The somewhat languid ending to the first movement contrasts admirably with the extreme vivacity of the scherzo which follows. The title given to this, *Pantoum*, refers to an ingenious poetic form, allegedly of Malayan origin, in which two distinct ideas are presented in each quatrain, one for each pair of lines, and developed by a system of line repetition in the succeeding stanzas. In the process each poetic idea is advanced by only one line in each verse, accompanied by, and integrated with, its 'fellow' idea; and to end the whole poem there is a simple recurrence of the opening line. The form had been adopted for their own purposes by several of the French Romantic poets during the second half of the nineteenth century, including Théodore de Banville, Verlaine, and Baudelaire, and may well have attracted some special attention during the vogue for oriental culture which followed the Exposition Universelle in Paris in 1889. Ravel's interest in it for musical exploitation is not surprising in view of his leaning towards exotic cultural ideas in general, and his known predilection for problem-solving as a source of inspiration. In fact, as Brian Newbould has shown, he followed the poetic scheme through in remarkable detail, providing a well-contrasted pair of themes, the first spiky and fantastic and the second smooth and surging, and a system of 'overlaps' to correspond closely to the basic poetic pattern.[2] Particularly skilful is his introduction (for desirable musical contrast) of a central 'trio' section, with a broad cantabile theme, which provides, as Newbould writes, 'the perfect backcloth against which the interwoven fortunes of the twin scherzo themes can be worked out'. In order to accommodate all three themes, at least in outline, and at the same time maintain the visual as well as the audible integrity of his musico-poetic form, Ravel uses an ingenious system of unequal bar-lengths in the manner shown in Example 54. In the effect of brilliant energy and excitement which it generates this movement

[2] B. Newbould, 'Ravel's Pantoum', *Musical Times* 116 (Mar. 1975), 228.

Ex. 54

is even more electric than the scherzo of the composer's earlier string quartet, which clearly served as a model for it.

For his third movement the composer goes to the opposite extreme in expression, and provides a slow 'baroque' passacaglia, comprising ten free variations on an eight-bar theme. Starting deep in the piano bass with a grave modal melody centred around F sharp, it builds in an arch shape towards a powerful central climax containing some of the richest harmony and scoring in the work, before retracing its steps, both in pitch and dynamics. From bar 32, the fourth of the variations introduces, on cello and piano alone, a new thematic idea akin to a second subject, which is later developed in various different keys and provides a valuable contrast element in the structures. An 'enchainez' link connects this movement to the finale, a spirited affair, which starts most attractively in a 'chinois' style, with an opening theme in 5/4 time and harmonized in fourths and fifths. Scored high on the piano against rapid violin figuration in harmonics and chordal tremolo patterns for the cello, this initial idea creates an aura of bustling energy and excitement; but for reasons we shall consider in more detail, the freshness and drive engendered are not maintained consistently as the movement proceeds.

It is clear that Ravel completed the work under abnormal pressure. On the outbreak of war, on 4 August, he seems to have been torn between a desire to finish the trio and a powerful urge to enlist and contribute as best he could to the war effort. After working 'avec une rage folle' he succeeded in completing the trio by the end of August,[3] but to his great disappointment was turned down by the recruitment board because he was too short and underweight. Writing early in October from Saint-Jean-de-Luz to the composer Florent Schmitt, he referred bitterly to his predicament: 'As for me, I remain here, alas, and seethe with anger. I hurried to finish my trio so that I could join up. But they have found me too light by two kilograms.'[4] Whether or not shortage of time and psychological pressure were the reasons, the final movement of the trio seems to lose a good deal of its momentum and drive as it unfolds. The weaknesses lie partly in an excess of short-scale repetition, always a Ravellian characteristic, but one rarely exploited so mechanically as here; and partly in the rigid metrical patterns—5/4 and 7/4 time—to which he commits himself throughout the greater part of the movement. There are some exquisitely beautiful examples of trio writing (for instance bars 12 to 16) and some which are surprisingly ugly and ineffective, such as the passage between figures 3 and 4, where the rising octaves on the strings are all but smothered by tremolando chords in the piano right hand, and the section starting at figure 6 with its overworked accompanimental trills

---

[3] R. Chalupt, *Ravel au miroir de ses lettres* (Paris, 1956), 113.

[4] Chalupt, *Ravel*, 120.

and arpeggios on the strings. Also beyond the scope normally accepted in chamber music are the final pages of the work, where the '*toujours ff*' marking, the massively scored piano part, and the continual high trills on the strings suggest a striving for an orchestral effect which is as unwieldy as it is inappropriate. This type of extravagance is unusual in Ravel, normally the most precise and fastidious of composers. It is symptomatic of what may be seen as a distinctive finale problem, prevalent in, though not of course peculiar to, the piano trio. In essence, the problem is how to achieve an effect of climax and culmination without overstepping the bounds of the chamber style. The solutions most usually proffered involve a choice between, or combination of, increased speed and more extravagant scoring and dynamics, the former being the 'safer' of the two. The intemperate effect of overscoring, coupled with powerful dynamics, is plainly evident at the end of the Tchaikovsky trio; and the brilliant result achievable by a progressive accelerando, in the '*nach und nach schneller*' of the finale to Schumann's D minor trio. Ravel's solution is by no means a total failure; but the scale and expressive range of the preceding movements seem to demand a more expansive, perhaps more thoughtful, ending. The noisy one provided (possibly prompted by war fervour) conveys in the context an unduly conventional impression.

Subsequently, the composer found an outlet for his patriotic aims as an army truck-driver; and his trio secured its first performance at a concert in aid of the Red Cross early in 1915, with Alfredo Casella taking the formidable piano part and Willaume and Feuillard the string roles. Immediately it was recognized for the remarkable masterpiece it is, and soon became absorbed into the repertoires of those ensembles capable of doing it justice.

Very different in conception is the D minor trio, Op. 120, by Ravel's former teacher, Gabriel Fauré, his only essay in the medium, which appeared in 1923 when he was in his seventy-eighth year. The differences are apparent in virtually every aspect of style and technique. Where Ravel employs vividly colourful scoring, brilliant piano writing, and a highly sectional construction, Fauré prefers a studied simplicity of texture, a gentle, unostentatious piano style, and a seamless continuity in the presentation of his ideas. Where Ravel relies upon phrase repetitions, contrasted tempo blocs, and progressive tonality to provide momentum, Fauré allows his music to unfold gradually, in the manner of a skilled organ improvisation. And where Ravel clearly takes dance, both stately and lively, as a prime source of inspiration, Fauré turns with equal naturalness to song, particularly in the first two movements of his work. Restraint in Fauré's scoring is evident not only in the large amount of two-part writing he allots to the piano but also in the many octave and unison doublings provided in the string parts. Typical is the opening of the first movement, where the cello presents a long-drawn theme, moving by simple steps from tonic to dominant, against an oscillating, two-note figure for the piano, right hand alone. Not until bar 23 does the violin enter, and three bars later the piano left hand, to establish a plain four-part texture of quartet-like clarity. Particularly unusual in advanced trio writing is the use of string unisons. As employed by Fauré the supplementary string parts in each case add emphasis and warmth to low-lying passages, much in the way that the drawing of an additional stop imparts extra colour to a melodic line in organ music. With such simplicity of means the composer is able to achieve a raising and lowering of the intensity of expression by only slight variations of texture, coupled commonly with a significant enrichment of the harmony. A striking example of this occurs in the approach to the recapitulation in the first movement, where a build-up of excitement results as much from the sudden introduction of augmented triads (with their whole-tone harmonic implications) as from the use of slightly enlarged leaps in the string parts and modestly heightened dynamic levels.

The slow movement, which was completed at Annecy-le-Vieux in September 1922, was the first section of the work to be written—and it is interesting to notice that the composer referred to it in his correspondence at that time as part of a clarinet trio, with the violin mentioned only as an alternative treble instrument. Set in F major, the movement is an extended, song-like meditation on three themes, the first of which appears to be related, at a considerable distance of time, to the orchestral countermelody in the Agnus Dei of the composer's *Requiem* of 1883 (see Ex. 55④). Containing very little variety of texture, the movement makes its effect by subtle thematic metamorphosis and a remarkably wide-ranging, almost improvisatory, modulatory

Ex. 55

scheme. At times the wind of key-change seems to blow where it lists, for example in bar 65, where the composer finds himself on the dominant of C sharp (= D flat) minor as he approaches the reprise of his first theme in the tonic. As the eventual point of return is reached, it requires a truly remarkable piece of modulatory sleight-of-hand to restore the home tonic (see Ex. 55ⓑ).

After so much solemn contemplation the strenuous third movement, a combination of scherzo and finale, comes as a major surprise. Though remaining light in texture, it provides scope for much lively pianism in the form of very rapid semiquaver figuration and some sharply etched string passages with powerful cross-rhythms. Much comment has been generated by the superficial, and certainly quite unintentional, resemblance between its opening theme and the well-known aria 'Ridi Pagliaccio' from Leoncavallo's *Pagliacci*, if only because the latter's somewhat tawdry staginess is so comically at odds with the French composer's known refinement of taste.[5] In the trio the 'offending' theme, which is confined entirely to the strings, and set invariably in loud octaves or unisons, functions as an essential rhythmic pillar. This not only marks out the three-bar pattern ($3 \times \frac{3}{8}$ time) underlying much of the movement but also provides, with its

[5] See R. Orledge, *Gabriel Fauré* (London, 1979), 187.

many repetitions, a stable background against which the piano's flying semiquavers can best make their effect. Like the first movement, the finale builds gradually to a resounding fortissimo climax, and then just stops; with his customary fastidiousness the composer, avoiding any trace of bombast, makes do, as much horizontally as vertically, with no more notes than are absolutely necessary. The moderation and refinement which mark this penultimate work of Fauré cannot be taken as evidence of failing powers in the ageing composer. Such characteristics are common enough in his works generally (though they are by no means the only ones) and appear emphasized in the trio mainly because of the slenderness of the medium's resources. No doubt the gentle, ruminative style of much of the work reflects to some extent the cooled ardour of old age; but any suggestion of diminished creative energy is readily refuted by the vigorous, challenging nature of the work's finale. Also, it is worth observing that a 'burnt-out' composer would hardly have proceeded, immediately on completion of the trio, to embark on the composition of his first string quartet.

It was during 1923, the year of the composition of Fauré's piano trio, that the Czech composer Bohuslav Martinů, at the age of 33, settled in Paris to study privately under Roussel. By that time Roussel had left well behind him the late romantic influences which we observed earlier in his E flat piano trio, and had turned, somewhat under the influence of Stravinsky, to leaner, neo-classic forms of expression, evidenced progressively in such works as his second violin sonata (1924), his orchestral suite in F (1926), and his third symphony (1930). Under his guidance Martinů rapidly gained in technical assurance, developing a highly personal style of expression which, for all its newly acquired Parisian traits, retained strong links with the folk idioms of his Czech homeland. Always remarkably prolific, he produced, following his time with Roussel, a series of works of increasing maturity, including his first piano concerto (1925), his second string quartet (1926), his earliest opera, *The Three Wishes* (1929), and in 1930 his first piano trio. This initial essay in the trio genre, subtitled *Cinq pièces brèves*, comprises a series of well-contrasted character pieces, in a power-fully athletic style, with vivid motor rhythms, closely-wrought counterpoint, and a bitter-sweet harmonic palette. Wholly characteristic of the composer are the colourful effects which result from the combination of octaves, thirds, and sixths, striding purposefully together in apparent disregard of passing harmonic clashes, as illustrated by Example 56 which is taken from the first of the pieces. Although any sense of key is almost totally obscured by the intensive use of chromaticism and dissonance, the composer attempts to create an illusion of tonal organization by ending each piece with a plain tonic chord, usually approached very obliquely in the manner of Hindemith. In the process a broad key sequence is suggested, consisting of C major, E flat major, C major, F major, and G major. Brilliantly scored, the pieces create a general impression of somewhat steely efficiency. A softer approach is found only in the second piece, the only slow section in the work, where a warmly expressive duet for the string duo, unaccompanied, is commented upon by the piano in quiet chordal passages with subtly dislocated rhythms.

Eleven years later in 1941, Martinů moved to the United States where he stayed until 1953; and it was there that he produced, in 1950 and 1951, his two later piano trios. These are considerably

Ex. 56

different in character from the *Pièces brèves*; in place of the studied brilliance and excitement of the earlier composition, the two mature works show, equally, a striving towards a classical openness of structure, clarity of texture, and sobriety of expression. Conceived apparently as a matching pair, they have many formal features in common: three-movement structures, sonata-form first movements, central slow movements (one in rondo and the other in ternary form), and *perpetuum mobile* finales. Also shared in common is a striking use of 'progressive' tonality, of the type already seen in the first movement of Ravel's trio. In the titles he provides— *Trio en ré mineur* and *Grand Trio No. 3 en ut*— Martinů appears quite unequivocal about his conception of the works' overall tonalities; yet in practice it is rare for a movement in either trio to end in its original key. In the D minor work, for example, a flatwise tendency in both outer movements results in the original tonic being gradually overpowered by B flat; while in the central movement, by even more tortuous means, the original G minor is supplanted finally by E major. In the C major work a similar system operates, which carries the tonality progressively through B flat and E flat, as two of its main centres, to a final cadence in F. Also very characteristic of the composer is the deceptive harmonic style which he employs. Frequently passages of straightforward diatonic writing are interrupted by strangely 'irrational' dissonances and harmonic *non sequiturs* which add a powerful tang to the music, of decidedly French orientation.[6] The works belong clearly enough to the lean, economical school of trio writing, but are far from being arid or austere. Czech elements are evident in the song-like melodies found in the two slow movements, and particularly in the brilliant passage-work of the toccata-style finales, with their headlong ostinato rhythmic patterns and dance-like verve. In the last movement of the D minor trio, for example, the passage beginning at figure $\boxed{3}$ seems to reach back momentarily, for all its harmonic pungency, to the world of Smetana and Dvořák at their most exuberant.

Strong nationalist expression, heightened at times by the

---

[6] The 'irrational' element, it may be mentioned, extends in some cases to the printed scores of the works, where the presence of discrepant notes in various parallel passages, and the not infrequent omission of precautionary accidentals, leave the composer's precise intentions in doubt. For example, in the D minor trio, first movement, violin, bar 4, it is likely that note 4 should be d' to correspond to bar 107; and in the second movement, piano right hand, bar 64, that note 6 should similarly be g' natural to match bar 16.

experience of war, is apparent even more markedly in the work of Shostakovich. Wide though the stylistic gulf is between his music and that of his nineteenth-century predecessors, he nevertheless shares with them an awareness of a common national heritage, both of culture and temperament, which constantly shapes his creative thinking. And among his works, few are more profoundly Russian, or more redolent of contemporary experience, than his E minor piano trio, Op. 67.[7] Composed in 1944, at one of the darkest periods of the Second World War, it is dedicated to the memory of Ivan Sollertinsky, a talented musicologist and close friend of the composer, who died in a Nazi concentration camp during that year. Thus, like many of the earlier Russian piano trios, it is an elegiac composition, intended to give expression to deep personal sorrow. However, it is hard not to feel that, from a wider point of view, the work is also a lament for the sufferings of the whole nation. Although the composer provided no official 'programme' for the trio, its aura of mingled bitterness and forced gaiety, of wild hysteria and despair, together with its prominent use of a 'Jewish' theme, suggest strongly that, like the seventh and eighth symphonies, it was chiefly inspired by the agony of wartime Russia.[8]

Traditional in its overall conception, the trio comprises a standard four-movement structure, with the scherzo placed second; and in keeping with the composer's normal practice, it preserves a strong sense of tonality, despite the use of an astringent harmonic palette, with much vivid dissonance and chromaticism. Altogether unusual, however, is the composer's handling of the trio medium. Expanding its normal scope to embrace quasi-orchestral sonorities, often of a bizarrely extravagant kind, he attains a degree of expressionism which strains at the limits of the chamber style, but none the less stops short of breaching entirely its necessary restraints. The result is a work which achieves, despite the intensity of the emotions expressed in it, a near-classical equilibrium between form, content, and the means of

[7] This is actually the second of Shostakovich's piano trios. His first essay in the form, entitled *Poem* for violin, cello, and piano, was written in 1923 when he was 17 and still a student at the Leningrad Conservatoire. A one-movement work, it comprises eight interlinked sections, alternately in slow and fast tempi. In style it owes something to Glazunov, but already shows the beginnings of a striking originality of approach.

[8] For an account of Shostakovich's wartime music, see B. Schwarz, 'Dimitri Shostakovich', in S. Sadie (ed.), *The New Grove, Russian Masters 2* (London, 1986), 179 and 187.

communication. Immediately impressive is the impact created at the opening of the work, where a six-bar theme in a modal E minor, the so-called 'Jewish' theme, is presented unaccompanied in harmonics high up on the cello. Capital is made out of the extreme difficulty of the passage which, even in the most skilled player's hands, produces the chilling effect of a shrill and tortured voice. Subsequently, the violin and piano in turn contribute mock-fugal answers to the theme, each pitched a thirteenth below the previous entry, and emphasize in the process the vital role which counterpoint is destined to play throughout. The first movement is analysable in sonata terms, though its themes and their deployment lack the clear elements of contrast one would normally expect to find. Instead the process involved, as very often with Shostakovich, is one of organic growth, in which every new feature can be related in some degree to the opening theme. At the beginning a relentless pulse is established, which adds to the generally doom-laden character of the music; but subsequently the speed gradually increases until bar 107 where with the emergence of the main subsidiary theme, the original tempo is doubled.

The strong forward drive apparent in the first movement is continued even more intensely in the scherzo. Set in the remote key of F sharp major, it exudes an air of forced jollity, its loud, emphatic themes and calculatedly crude scoring conveying a deliberate impression of brashness and insensitivity. A vivid contrast is created between the opening theme, with its wide-ranging arpeggio patterns, and two ideas which are introduced later, the first a tight-fisted, knotted theme at figure 31 and the second a surging motif at 37. Subsequently, each of these is combined contrapuntally with the main idea to provide a complex of ingenious cross-references. And still further contrast is provided by a radiant 'trio' section in G major at figure 45, which has some of the giant simplicity of late Beethoven, recalling, for instance, the equivalent section in the scherzo of his A minor string quartet, Op. 132. Shostakovich's alternation of tonic and dominant harmonies on the piano, against a largely unyielding tonic motif in the string parts, conveys in its way almost as much charming rusticity of character as Beethoven's drone bass effect on the violin's A string.

The slow movement, designed as a chaconne or passacaglia, is based on a fixed series of eight chords, constantly repeated at different dynamic levels on the piano, which provides the basis for a set of five variations; and these, linked together, are built into an extended elegiac duet for the strings, involving a formal procedure similar to that used by Ravel in the slow movement of his trio. The key, ostensibly, is B flat minor, but over its eight-bar span the chordal pattern moves unpredictably to end on a chord of B (natural) minor, though without its fifth degree. The absence of the F sharp is significant since, each time round, it allows for the insertion of an F natural on the second beat of the bar as a dominant leading back to B flat minor. Particularly curious is the effect produced by the third of the chords, a major 6/4 over a bass G, which is reluctant to shed the powerfully cadential effect it naturally suggests in diatonic harmony. Each time it occurs it provides a momentary oasis of warm repose which is immediately dispelled by the darker, more dissonant harmonies that follow. After the final variation, which contains recalled thematic motifs from the start of the movement, a short extension with sombre repeats of the final B minor chord leads directly back to E major for the rondo finale. This returns, with its pattern of lively dance rhythms, to the general style of the scherzo, but conveys an altogether harsher mood of bitterness and despair, in contrast to the ironic gaiety of the earlier section. Tightly organized, the movement has three principal themes which constantly recur in a rich variety of rhythmic and melodic shapes, and frequently in contrapuntal combination with each other. A bizarre scoring element is introduced from the start by the persistent use of pizzicato, for both strings, in the presentation of the main themes and their accompaniment, producing an effect which is both etioliated and somewhat macabre. The violin, in fact, is bowed only from bar 58, and the cello not until bar 100 when it introduces the third main theme. Repeated motifs and persistent ostinato patterns lead to a wild climax at figure 86 , after which, at 91 , a striking effect of disintegration is achieved by a swirling piano cadenza, the arpeggios of which outline exactly the solemn chordal progression from the slow movement. This leads directly to a recall of the entire fugal section from the opening of the first movement, rescored and with halved note-values, against which the piano maintains its continuous pattern of rapid demisemiquavers. After a short reprise of the finale's opening ideas, the work ends with a further reference to the slow movement's chordal sequence, the final B minor chord of which moves home with perfect logic to the central E major tonality. And high above this the strings provide plaintive, half-whispered reminders of the main rondo theme, and conclude impressively with quiet pizzicato chords. The emphasis on thematic recall at the end of this movement is perhaps the weakest, and in a sense most old-fashioned, structural feature of the work. But from a subjective viewpoint, its function in heightening the trio's powerful expressive message provides a wholly convincing justification for it.

The principal piano trios of the first half of the century, which we have been considering, reflect clearly the diversity of styles current at the time, and underline the significant role which nationality continued to play in shaping them. It would be a mistake, however, to regard the works in question as isolated contributions, entirely unrelated to each other; behind each of them, despite obvious surface differences, it is not difficult to detect a shared conceptual basis deriving from a common European tradition. But outside mainland Europe, particularly in Britain and the United States, the situation was very different; and in the almost total absence of any similar tradition, especially in the field of chamber composition, a high premium was necessarily placed on the work of such pioneers as emerged. It cannot, therefore, be regarded as other than a strange quirk of fate that the most important initial impetus, in their respective countries, was entrusted to a British businessman, Walter Willson Cobbett, and an American insurance agent, Charles Ives.

Ives, whose particular significance to our survey resides in the remarkable piano trio he composed early in the century,[9] is generally regarded as the great 'primitive' of modern American music. Coming from the New England background which had earlier nurtured such original thinkers as Hawthorne, Emerson, and Thoreau, he is a 'primitive' in the sense that he almost totally disregarded the accepted musical conventions of his time and instead turned for inspiration to the sights and sounds of everyday life, such as town bands, drawing-room ballads, hymn tunes, and the music of country fiddlers. With these he endeavoured to build entirely new sound patterns, in which such features as free

⁹ C. Ives, *Trio for Violin, Violoncello and Piano*, ed. J. Kirkpatrick (New York, 1955). This edition includes an extended and detailed critical commentary.

dissonance, the random combination of rhythms, the clash of unrelated keys, and the products of chance were taken as normal. But primitive though his bases for musical organization undoubtedly appeared to his contemporaries, when indeed they bothered to consider them at all, their results in the longer run proved sophisticated in the extreme, foreshadowing by several years many of the fundamental ideas which were to shape the later development of twentieth-century music, such as atonality, polyrhythm, the use of quartertones and chord clusters, and the aleatory approach. Thus, in historical perspective, he came to be regarded as a prime mover in modern American music, and, if not widely influential, at least much respected in European circles.

His trio was begun in 1904 but, because of his business preoccupations, and the demands of other compositions on which he was engaged at the time, was not completed until 1911. The work is in three movements and is intended, according to a letter written by his wife in 1948, to portray aspects of the composer's college life at Yale during the 1890s. In a characteristically self-deprecatory way Ives attempted to hide the basic seriousness of his musical intentions by attaching amusing and eccentric headings to the work, rather in the manner of Erik Satie: 'Yankee Jaws at Mr (or Eli) Yale's School for nice bad boys', for example, as an alternative title for the whole trio, and 'TSIAJ' (this scherzo is a joke) as a superscription for the middle movement. But none of these could disguise the substantial nature of the composition and the deeply considered character of the innovations it contained. Immediately striking is the experimental structure of the opening movement, involving a first section for cello and piano (treble range only), a second for violin and piano (bass range only), and a third in which the two previous sections are combined, the cello and violin retaining their original parts and the piano joining together its previous treble and bass elements. Curiously enough, in view of the essential rigidity of the scheme, the two opening sections are unequal in length, respectively 24 and 27 bars, so that some small but not insignificant adjustments have to be made in the final combination. Whether this happened by accident or design it is difficult to tell, but possibly the composer may have sought by this means to avoid over-symmetry and an excess of simple repetition in the second section. The final combined phase produces some harshly dissonant and decidedly arbitrary music—

perhaps inevitably if, as seems likely, no preliminary care was taken to ensure any sort of logical 'fit'. Clearly enough the whole plan was purely experimental and must be accepted as such; but the overall effect is indisputably somewhat contrived—or academic, even.

By contrast, the second movement is an uninhibited rampage of sound, providing a remarkable pot-pourri of student songs and popular songs and hymns preceded by a short introduction. The tunes, some of which still remain unidentified, are normally presented in a straightforwardly diatonic form, but heavily disguised by an accompaniment which involves bizarre chord progressions, note-clusters, bitonal clashes, and the imitation of drum patterns. A free piano cadenza over tremolando strings produces some effective contrast towards the end, but the final presto coda, comprising a six-bar chordal passge in which the piano 'doubles' the strings at the distance of a semitone (E major against F major) provides what seems to be an excessively laboured brand of humour. The movement is scored with remarkable fullness; out of a total of 217 bars, the cello is silent for eight, the piano for two, and the violin for only one.

Shorter and more concentrated in style, the last movement consists of eight sections at varying tempi, and contains gapped sectional repeats and thematic cross-references, some of the latter reintroducing motifs from earlier movements. One of its more significant ideas is shown in Example 57(i), together with various of the forms (Ex. 57(ii) and (iii)) in which it appears in other parts of the work. In order to expand the scope of the finale, a comprehensive repeat at a slower tempo is indicated immediately before the final coda, after a massive climax, marked *fff*, with strings and piano playing together in unison. The final section itself is concerned largely with the 'derived' theme from bar 68 (see Ex. 57(i)) in combination with a straightforward version of the well-known tune to Toplady's hymn, 'Rock of Ages', allotted first to the violin and finally to the cello.[10] As it reaches its penultimate note the hymn tune breaks off, apparently with some hidden symbolic significance, and the work concludes with a *ppp* dissonant chord on the piano which gradually dissolves into silence. (See Ex. 57(iv)).

[10] See C. Ward, 'Hymn Tunes as "Substance and Manner" in Charles Ives', Univ. of Texas diss. 1969.

Ex. 57

Ives's piano trio, together with his two string quartets and four violin sonatas, provided an important foundation for later American chamber composition in the twentieth century. Although during the 1920s and 1930s his music was often ignored or ridiculed, it was not long before various of the more discerning musicians of the time began to recognize the value of his pioneer work in freeing American music from the grip of various debilitating forms of foreign influence. Nevertheless, the path of musical isolationism—the basing of a distinctive American style purely on indigenous, folk-derived, or picturesque elements—which Ives appeared to support, was not one which appealed uniformly to the succeeding generation of composers. For them there could be little significant future for an American style which ignored the exciting developments which were taking place in Europe at the time, the importance of which was continually manifested by the distinguished *émigré* composers who had settled in their country: Varèse, Bloch, and Rachmaninov among others. As a result, during a significant period of interchange, the number of enterprising young American musicians travelling to Europe for study began to correspond roughly with that of composers from the old world removing to the United States as refugees. And inevitably styles were enriched, and national differences attenuated, on both sides of the Atlantic.

Among the Americans who made contributions to the piano trio at this time were Walter Piston, Roy Harris, and Aaron Copland, each of whom studied with Nadia Boulanger in Paris during the 1920s. The Harris and Piston trios, which date respectively from 1934 and 1935, are somewhat dryly neo-classical in manner, and lack the sharp edge of characterization which distinguishes the near-contemporary first trio of Martinů. Essentially 'period pieces' they reflect a little palely the predominant influences of the time—Stravinsky, Hindemith, Prokofiev, and Milhaud—and reveal American traits mainly in their occasional touches of rhythm and harmony of jazz derivation. More characterful is Aaron Copland's trio, a single-movement work entitled *Vitebsk*, which dates from 1929. The title refers to the birthplace of the Jewish writer Ansky (1863–1920), who incorporated into his play *The Dybbuk* (1916) a Jewish folksong which he had encountered there in his youth. Copland heard the melody first while attending a performance of the play, and at once conceived the idea of basing a trio on it. At the time the composer was fresh from his studies with Madame Boulanger, and rapidly gaining a reputation, at least in his home country, as a notable young *avant-gardiste*. Basing his approach in the trio on the experimental techniques employed by Alois Hába in his string quartets of the early 1920s, Copland makes an extensive use of quartertones, both above and below the written note, as indicated by special symbols. In fact it may well be that he was the first to exploit the system in a piano trio. The technique is used particularly in an extended introductory paragraph and a matching final section, where descending, quartertone-inflected thirds on the strings, delivered fortissimo in 'snap' rhythms and in octaves, are interspersed between ringing chords on the piano like a clashing peal of bells. The scoring sonorities which result are quite strongly reminiscent of the tolling-bell effects which Stravinsky creates with four pianos and percussion at the end of *Les Noces*, a work which received its first performance in Paris in 1923, while Copland was still studying there. Arranged as a sequence of closely knit sections, the trio, which is more specifically Jewish than American in style, comprises a number of contrasted meditations on the central folk tune. The melody itself, which appears in various minor key versions, has an unambiguously modal character; but by the use of extreme dissonance and quartertone patterns in the surrounding material a fully atonal effect is produced throughout the work. Copland has never again attempted a piano trio; but later in his career he contributed significantly to the chamber repertoire with a violin sonata (1943) and a piano quartet (1950). In these he discarded many of the more exploratory features of style and technique found in *Vitebsk* in favour of complex, finely devised textures, not infrequently constructed on serial lines.

In parallel with these American developments there began in Britain also a remarkable upsurge of creative activity in chamber composition early in the century, in which a prominent part was played by Walter Willson Cobbett. In addition to founding a medal for services to chamber music, and compiling and publishing in 1929 his renowned *Cyclopedic Survey of Chamber Music*, a reference work of much continuing value, Cobbett instituted a series of competitions designed to encourage the production of new chamber works by native composers. Competitors were invited to submit one-movement compositions for various media, in which, in any way of their own free devising, the successive sections should correspond broadly to the movements of a full-length sonata work. Described by the term 'Phantasy' the works were intended to recall the spirit, though not of course the actual form, of the English 'Fancy' of Elizabethan and Jacobean times. There is something peculiarly, not to say eccentrically, English about the idea of using a competition as a spur to artistic creation; but, under Cobbett's guidance, the venture was hugely successful, eliciting new works over a fifteen-year period from a host of rising composers, including William Hurlstone, Frank Bridge, John Ireland, Eugene Goossens, Herbert Howells, Ralph Vaughan Williams, and Benjamin Britten. At the second of the contests in 1907 entries were invited specifically of Phantasy piano trios, and for their contributions on this occasion prizes were awarded to Bridge, Ireland, and the Scottish pianist-composer

James Friskin. All three men were at the time in their twenties, though Friskin was seven years junior to the others, and all were pupils of Stanford at the Royal College of Music.

The Phantasy trios produced by Bridge and Ireland for this event are attractive, skilfully written works which have readily retained a place in the repertoire. Bridge's movement, which is the more individual of the two, comprises an arch structure in which outer allegro sections, representing formally the exposition and recapitulation, enclose a central slow–scherzo–slow pattern which does duty for a development. Particularly striking is the almost continuous use of thematic metamorphosis, by which nearly every idea in the work is drawn, with notable (and almost unnoticeable) ease and naturalness, from the dramatic motif announced at the start. The style, which involves broad melodies and colourful harmony, owes at least as much to French influence—of Chausson, d'Indy, and early Fauré—as to that of Stanford. A similar degree of melodic elegance and harmonic luxuriance is apparent in Ireland's trio, which shows clearer evidence also of indebtedness to Stanford. His structural treatment, however, is rather less enterprising than Bridge's, involving a single slow section at the centre, and relying more for the progress of the sonata argument on simple repetition than on the imaginative refashioning of the thematic material. Subsequently, in 1917, Ireland gained a further Cobbett prize for a Phantasy trio, and proceeded many years later to crown his output for the medium with a full-scale, four-movement work, his trio in E minor, of 1938, which he dedicated to William Walton. Written in the grand manner, and supremely confident in tone, this last of his trios shows great technical accomplishment with its sweeping melodies, colourful harmonies, and masterly control of structure. But what it fails to reveal, surprisingly, is any significant degree of stylistic growth, even over the very earliest of his trios. All the exciting new developments in European music, which had so attracted the Americans of the period, seem to have passed the composer by, making little or no impact on his creative thinking.

With Frank Bridge, however, the case was very different. His second trio, a four-movement work published in 1930, shows a remarkable advance on his earlier chamber music, revealing the outcome of his search for a thoroughly individual style, enriched by a close absorption of the most recent new ideas and techniques from abroad. Turning right away from the Stanford tradition from which he had started, he embarked, disconcertingly to his British contemporaries, on a darkly emotional, expressionist mode of writing akin to that found in the earlier works of Schoenberg and Bartók, in which he deploys a degree of chromaticism which borders on atonality. In order to compensate for any loss of cohesion resulting from his loosened grip on tonality, he introduces many thematic cross-references and trans-formations, and makes a particularly extensive use of ostinato patterns, as in the passage in Example 58 from near the start of the haunting slow movement, with its air of stillness and timelessness. Retaining some contact with the Phantasy concept, Bridge joins his four movements together in pairs, linking the opening allegro to the scherzo, and the slow movement to the finale, so that an impression is created of two long and strongly contrasted move-ments. In the course of some brilliant trio writing he places effective emphasis on both extremes of the keyboard, particularly in the vivid scherzo, a counterpart, with its exciting use of pizzicato and '*pointillisme*', to the equivalent movement in the Ravel trio. The ghostly, somewhat tenebrous character of the work in general is effectively dispelled in the finale which, though still largely atonal, provides a broader melodic sweep and conveys a stronger, more confident mood. However, by means of a brief but impressive return of the mysterious opening idea from the first movement, a powerful overall sense of unity is imparted to the work. Wholly convincing in style and substance, the second Bridge trio is one of the most notable examples of the genre of the first half of the twentieth century, worthy of a place beside the trios of Ravel, Fauré, and Shostakovich. The fact that its com-poser was an Englishman, and its style alien to British sensibilities in the 1930s, led to its almost complete neglect for many years. Only quite recently has it begun at last to gain some of the recognition it deserves.

Ex. 58

The 'Cobbett' composers, and others not directly influenced by the competitions, gradually built up during the first half of the century a corpus of new British chamber music of a distinctively national character which, within the somewhat narrow historical perspective of the time, was recognizably modern and original. Initially, in the absence of a firm native tradition they turned to the current French style, and particularly that of Ravel with its finely pointed dissonances and brilliant instrumental writing, to give a sheen of modernity to their music; and by combining these techniques with melodies and rhythms of an English folk-song cast, began to progress towards a genuine individuality of expression. As early as 1920, in his D major piano trio, E. J. Moeran provided an elegant conflation of the folk style with the shimmering, impressionist harmonies of the French school. And in the following year Rebecca Clarke, in an entry for a competition organized by Elizabeth Sprague Coolidge,[11] produced her rugged, cogently argued E flat piano trio in which an English forthrightness combines most effectively with advanced French traits of the period, including a stylish use of whole-tone patterns. Gradually, as composers increased in confidence, the French influence became diluted; but even as late as 1938 a residual element of the Ravel style is still evident in the third Ireland trio, though overlaid by the broad gestures of a typically English brand of romanticism. Altogether more unusual for the period, however, are the German-style 'expressionist' features which we have seen in the second of Bridge's trios, indictive of the radical change in his style which had occurred after the end of the 1914–18 war. Apart from the piano trio, the new orientation in Bridge's thinking is apparent in his piano sonata (1924), string trio (1928), violin sonata (1934), and fourth string quartet (1937), all of which can be seen now, with hindsight, to have contributed significantly towards the internationalism which increasingly characterized British music during the 1940s and 1950s.

Of the generation of British composers who were coming to prominence at the start of the Second World War, three in particular were later to make notable contributions to the piano

---

[11] Elizabeth Sprague Coolidge (1864–1963), one of the most outstanding musical patrons of the twentieth century, was a fervent supporter of chamber music. The organizer of festivals, and originator of numerous commissions to leading composers, she also had many works dedicated to her, including several piano trios.

trio form: Edmund Rubbra, Lennox Berkeley, and Alan Rawsthorne. Rubbra's first trio, dated 1950 and thus of the same period
as his fifth symphony, is described as being 'in one movement',
but actually comprises three short movements linked together
without break, rather in the manner of a Cobbett Phantasy. His
more substantial second trio, written some twenty years later, has
two large interconnected movements in contrasted styles, and
well demonstrates his main style characteristics: a largely linear
approach, with seamless contrapuntal textures propelled by some
powerfully dissonant harmony and an ingenious system of continuous thematic variation. The work contains music of substance
and dignity, but its lack of the clear instrumental differentiation
characteristic of trio scoring suggests that the medium may not
have been entirely congenial to the composer. Lennox Berkeley's
contribution is an effective horn trio, composed in 1954. After
studying with Nadia Boulanger in Paris from 1927 to 1933,
Berkeley gained an initial reputation for the 'Gallic' wit and
precision of his music, in which offshoots from the somewhat
ironic neo-classicism of early Poulenc and Stravinsky are plainly
evident. Later, however, a deeper, and indeed more English, note
became apparent in his work, most decisively in his full-length
opera *Nelson*, which was completed in 1953. In the horn trio
(written, perhaps as a relaxation, a year later) variety and textural
clarity are achieved by employing the instruments more often in
pairs than as a full ensemble, some particularly charming effects
resulting from the use of duets for unaccompanied violin and
horn. Specially noteworthy are the variations with which the
work ends. Based on a sixteen-bar theme, with a falling minor
seventh as its main melodic feature, the ten variations are sharply
characterized by contrasts in mood and tempo, and emphasize
instrumental timbres in various horn and violin solos, supported
by a richly eventful piano part.

Rawsthorne's trio was commissioned by the Worshipful Company of Musicians for the Festival of the City of London in 1962,
and first performed there on 12 July of that year by Yehudi
Menuhin, Gaspar Cassadó, and Louis Kentner. Its three movements—Introduction, Capriccio, and Theme and Variations—are
interlinked (the second and third by an *attacca*) to form continuous
and highly unified music over an extended time-span. The sense
of unity is further enhanced by the use of thematic transference

and metamorphosis, often in widely spaced contexts. For example, the scalic ideas which characterize the Introduction, while in no sense forming a 'motto' theme, return in fragmentary form during the link, from letter Ⓜ, to the start of the variation movement, and again at the end of the whole work; and features of the striding opening theme of the Capriccio (Ex. 59(i)) return, transformed in rhythm, first as a fugue subject initiated by the cello at letter Ⓙ (Ex. 59(ii)), and secondly as the principal idea at letter Ⓥ (Ex. 59(iii)) of the last of the variations which make up the final movement, in the latter case suggesting, also, some hidden interconnection with the basic variation theme. Colourfully scored, the work contains some unusual passages for unaccompanied strings. A particularly notable example is the seventeen-bar section between letters Ⓖ and Ⓗ, where double-stoppings on both instruments, together and separately, establish a consistent string texture in three and four parts and in the process impart a markedly concertante air to the solo piano section which ensues. Rawshorne's tough, somewhat gritty harmonic style—non-diatonic, but not fully atonal—and his strong contrapuntal lines combine to provide a decidedly 'internationalist' manner, which leans unmistakably on Bartók and Hindemith. In his work, as increasingly in British music of the time, there remains little which can be identified as specifically national in character.

More recently, the British composers who have written piano trios are separable into three main categories. There are those, in the first place, who have maintained a traditionalist line by adopting, in a host of personal ways, the musical lingua franca of

Ex. 59

the times, traceable back through Rawsthorne and Walton to its roots in the work of Hindemith, Milhaud, and Bartók. In the dissemination of this style in Britain a not unimportant role was played by the Hungarian-born Mátyás Seiber and the German-born Franz Reizenstein, both of whom settled in England in the mid 1930s. Reizenstein, whose large output of chamber music includes a piano trio, actually studied with Hindemith in Berlin before he left for England in 1934: and later, from 1958, he became particularly influential through his teaching at the Royal Academy of Music. Secondly, there are those who have been drawn initially to the methods of Schoenberg and his pupils, and subsequently to the developments in the post-Webern era engendered by Messiaen, Boulez, Stockhausen, and others, including ametrical rhythms, the serialization of durations and dynamics, and the use of aleatory and improvisatory techniques. In some cases the British composers involved have expanded their horizons by study abroad, both in Europe and the United States, with such leading composers as Messiaen, Petrassi, Lutoslawski, and Milton Babbitt. But once again the foundations for this departure in British music were clearly laid half a century earlier by refugee musicians from Europe who settled here in the 1930s, notably Egon Wellesz, Roberto Gerhard, and Walter Goehr, all of them one-time pupils of Schoenberg. And the third of our categories comprises a small group of what may be called 'radical revisionists', who, in very recent times, have turned away from the extreme complexities of avant-garde composition towards simpler melodic and rhythmic styles, and sparser textures, while remaining essentially innovative in their approach.

Two works of contrasted character which illustrate the 'traditionalist' style of the later twentieth century are the piano trios of William Mathias and Kenneth Leighton, both of which were composed in 1965, three years after the Rawsthorne trio. Each of them was written for a special purpose, the Mathias for performance by the Tunnell Trio at the Cheltenham Festival in 1965, and the Leighton for a competition in Hanover in the same year, where it was awarded the Bernhard Sprengel Prize for Chamber Music. Despite considerable differences of style the two trios share a number of features which are typical of the neo-classical approach. Both are basically tonal in orientation (and both, in fact, in D) despite a free use of chromaticism and dissonance; and both adopt a lean, athletic style of writing, with Stravinskyan ostinato patterns and sharply etched rhythms to create a vivid sense of forward propulsion. Octave writing between the strings is frequent in both works, together with much two-strand writing (sometimes amplified by octaves) for the piano; and chordal patterns are correspondingly rather less common. Furthermore, both works are predominantly contrapuntal in conception and make extensive use of imitative, canonic, and fugal procedures. Mathias's trio is notable for its compactness; its four movements (of the traditional type, with the scherzo second) are clear and economical in structure, and exploit simple thematic ideas in a variety of ingenious ways. Particularly striking, in the sonata-form first movement, is the telescoped recapitulation, at bar 153, where both first and second subjects enter together (the former inverted) in a delightful, pre-planned contrapuntal combination, producing an irresistible impression of a good-natured argument between the participants. A deeper mood is established in the slow movement, in which meditative string solos and duets are set against a resonant background of sustained, arpeggiated piano chords, creating an oasis of calm between the Waltonesque scherzo and fugal-style finale, both of unbridled energy. The lilting folk-song style of the central melody and its harp-like accompaniment provide a clear reflection of the composer's allegiance to his Welsh origins and background.

The Leighton trio, despite having only three movements—an interlinked allegro, scherzo, and finale—is longer and more complex in structure. Throughout the work a great deal is made of certain 'contradictory' motifs—particularly ones involving tone and semitone intervals and conflicting major and minor thirds—which are linked together to provide firmly characterized thematic material. Strong contrasts are developed between various extended sections, some in a thoughtful contrapuntal style and others in which dynamic energy is built up by means of sharply pointed rhythms, in the manner of Walton. In the process an overriding sense of excitement is generated, particularly in the central scherzo, which is then gradually relaxed in the slow finale (entitled *Hymnus*) and resolved most memorably in the eloquent closing paragraphs. The trio exhibits much resourceful scoring. Though by no means prodigal with his notes the composer succeeds in cultivating an impressive variety of textures, showing his clear awareness as a performer of the medium's rich potential, and is particularly successful in creating strong climaxes without overloading the ensemble.

In their inventiveness and technical assurance these two works provide worthy samples of the 'traditionalist' types of trio composed during the last twenty-five years. Their qualities, however, are shared equally by numerous similar works of the period, in which a musical language and structure of traditional orientation are deployed with a refreshing lack of conventionality. Two further examples may be briefly considered. One is the trio in three movements—Sonata, Rondeau, and Finale—by Trevor Hold, which was composed for the resident ensemble (the Archduke Trio) at Leicester University. The title of the slow middle movement possibly holds some special significance, since this meditative section seems to owe as much, structurally, to the verse form of the medieval rondeau as to the instrumental rondo pattern of later times. An opening 'refrain', comprising a simple chordal progression on the piano, occurs four times, in conjunction with expressive counterthemes for the strings, at first separately on violin and cello in turn and later in an ingenious contrapuntal combination. And between the recurrences of the 'refrain' there are inserted contrasted episodes for the full ensemble, in a manner comparable to the addition of new 'lines' to a poetic text. The resultant music is unusual in form and elegant in expression, and provides, within its modest limits, a miniature compendium of quietly effective ways of writing for the medium. In splendid contrast, the finale adds a new dimension to the concept of the exuberant ending, with its employment of Charleston tempo, with a pattern of $3 + 3 + 2$ quavers to the bar, and consistently paired notes in 'swung' rhythm.

The other example is the second trio, Op. 111, by Alun Hoddinott, which was written for the Stuttgart Trio in 1984 and first performed by them in Cardiff in March of that year. Yet another three-movement work, but this time with a central scherzo and an adagio finale, the trio is in every way as spare in texture and finely pointed in rhythm as the other neo-classical works we have been considering. However, it departs interestingly from usual practice in both its second and third movements by its use of free-rhythm note patterns for the piano, which provide, with the aid of the sustaining pedal, a shimmering, impressionist type of accompaniment. First heard in the middle section of the trio's macabre sounding scherzo, the note patterns are derived from the principal melodic ideas on the strings that they support; and when recalled in the finale, either in direct or inverted form, they add considerably to the cohesion of the structure as a whole (see Ex. 60 for a section from bar 18 of the third movement).

The rarity of piano trios which employ Schoenbergian twelve-note techniques is very marked; indeed, before the middle of the century such works are practically non-existent. It is not easy to see why composers working with this system should have avoided the trio genre so completely. Possibly the mixed nature of the medium, with its two essentially melodic instruments pitted against one more naturally biased towards harmony, proved a deterrent, since it may have seemed to provide less scope for a strict application of serial principles than, for example, a string quartet with its more purely linear procedures. Certainly,

Ex. 60

those few composers who actually attempted trios in serial form tended to employ the system with much freedom. Two examples of contrasted character from the middle of the century show the methods involved and their application in piano trio terms. One is the *Kammersonate* for piano, violin, and cello by Hans Werner Henze, which was written originally in 1948 when the composer was studying twelve-note techniques with René Leibowitz in Darmstadt, and subsequently revised in 1963. The work has four short movements—fast, slow, slow, and moderately fast—followed by a separate slow epilogue, all of which are based on two distinct note-series, one for movements 1, 3, 4, and the epilogue and the other for movement 2. The presentation of the melodic material, and consequently of the principal note-rows, is allocated largely to the strings, with the piano supplying a varied chordal accompaniment. However, a notable exception occurs at the start of the fourth movement where the piano maintains a whimsical variant of the basic note-series for four bars before the entry of the strings, and then leads on into a ghostly waltz, involving much delicate scoring and shared melodic interest, the intense, febrile character of which echoes early Schoenberg, of the Op. 25 Suite for piano, for example, or parts of *Pierrot Lunaire*. Also of particular interest is a passage for keyboard alone at the beginning of the second movement, in which pianissimo chord clusters support a purely diatonic melodic fragment which sounds, in context, like the bearer of a secret message; the mysterious, whispered response is a two-strand section for muted strings, in which all the notes of the second series used are given in a tightly-knit contrapuntal pattern. In its overtly expressionist manner, the trio is as much a 'period piece' as Frank Bridge's second trio, but it makes a convincing use of serialism and is distinguished by its colour and delicacy of scoring

The other work of the period is the one-movement trio by the American composer Earle Brown, entitled *Music for violin, cello, and piano*, which dates from 1952. Brown is one of a group of composers, including Morton Feldman and Christian Wolff, who became, under the aegis of John Cage, leaders of the American avant-garde, with a special interest in graphic scores and the products of chance in the compositional process. In his trio the element of chance is restricted to certain aspects of ensemble and rhythmic notation. Against a crotchet pulse, varying in speed between ♩=40 and ♩=120 the players are required to observe the mathematical durations of the notes in their parts as precisely as possible, and in the absence of regular rhythmic patterns, to achieve a sufficient degree of ensemble by 'hearing' their relationship to each other. The obvious difficulty of this is intended to produce, in the composer's words, 'a rather flexible, floating quality in performance'. In other respects the trio is precisely organized, using fairly strict serial procedures, vivid pointillist textures, and a large amount of extreme octave displacement. Some impression of its general character may be gained from the opening bars of the work (given in Ex. 61). This shows the first complete statement (and the first ten notes of the second) of the basic note series, expressed in asymmetrical rhythms and in bars comprising twelve, sixteen, and eighteen semiquavers, respectively. Also shown is the extremely dislocated melodic style, with its continually changing dynamics.

It seems likely that, in the judgement of history, this American trio will appear more significant for its experimental features than for its artistic merits. Yet, with its early date of composition, it pointed the way forward, interestingly enough, to several later developments. In Britain, where a 'time-lag' so frequently affects the rate of artistic progress, it was a number of years before piano trios of a similarly advanced nature began to appear, in parallel with more traditionalist works. Two of the earliest and most important examples are the trios of Alexander Goehr and Jonathan Harvey, the former commissioned by the Bath Festival

Ex. 61

and first performed there in June 1966 by Yehudi and Hepzibah Menuhin with Maurice Gendron (cello), and the latter composed for the Orion Trio and premièred by them in Southampton in December 1971. Though hardly less experimental than Earle Brown's trio, these two works far outstrip the American one in musical substance.

A radical rethinking of the potentialities of the trio medium is evident in Goehr's work, with its intensive exploration of new techniques and sonorities—including scordatura tuning, the use of quarter- and three-quarter tones, skeletal piano writing, and various subtle forms of rhythmic organization. Yet, equally, it shows a continuing allegiance to the classical traditions of trio composition in its clear structure, finely articulated scoring, and essentially direct manner of expression. Stylistically the music is refreshingly difficult to categorize. Certain influences, notably early Schoenberg and Messiaen, are traceable readily enough; but they are distilled, through Goehr's wide-ranging musical sympathies, into a personal and very distinctive musical language which, though complex and intellectually challenging, is always intensely communicative. The work is in two movements of strongly contrasted character, the first sectional, with numerous immediate and long-range repeats, and the second 'through-composed' in a more freely improvisatory manner. In the opening movement the systematic use of repeats (often involving only a double-bar and repeat sign) imparts a remarkable openness to the form, which is closer in outline to that of a baroque ritornello movement than a classical sonata. In order to create a sense virtually of tonal stability, the same pitch is nearly always adopted for the spaced repeats as they occur; and to replace the dynamic contrasts of the sonata style, a simple decorative system is employed which involves the colourful ornamentation of various relatively static harmonic patterns. The method of adding decorations to a repeated section may be seen in Example 62, a passage from figure 9 of the first movement which, at its original appearance fifty-one bars earlier, consisted of the piano part only. The string parts added here provide a good example also of the unusual system of rhythmic notation which Goehr employs at several places in the first movement. The aim, quite simply, is to allow each of the string players to adopt a different metrical pattern from either one or both of his partners; thus, in appropri-

Ex. 62

ate contexts, the separate instrumental parts are given a time-signature and barring which conflict with those in the piano part. But in order to simplify the *appearance* in the score and thus facilitate ensemble, a lay-out is used for the piano part in which all the time-signatures and bar-lines are made to coincide, while the 'real', conflicting metre is shown only by a cue-line between the staves. In Example 62, an overall 2/4 metre is shown in the score, and to accommodate this the string contributions are notated in triplets; but in the individual parts a 4/8 signature is provided, with independently placed bar-lines which, as the cue-line shows, do not coincide with those in the piano score. The example shown illustrates, in fact, one of the simpler uses of the device; in various other instances, where only one of the players is 'out of step', and the rhythms of the other two are much more complex, it becomes increasingly necessary, as the composer stresses in his preface, for each player to 'realise his own metre . . . unhampered by the demands of precise ensemble'.

The second movement is notable for its lyrical beauty. Quietly contemplative, it exploits a rich vein of solo and duet writing for the strings, against a background of sparse and somewhat reticent contributions from the piano. Particularly remarkable is the passage for the strings alone between figures ⟨3⟩ and ⟨5⟩, where gentle chordal writing, with double-stopping on both instruments, is linked with quarter- and three-quarter-tone slides, marked *sospirando*, to convey a mood of quiet sorrow. Unlike the first movement there is no attempt to achieve unity through spaced repeats, but simply to provide, through the recurrence of tiny melodic cells, an overall sense of thematic integration. And even though twelve-note patterns are introduced at the start, shared between cello and piano, and in some later instances also, they do not appear to fulfil any vital structural purpose.

In Jonathan Harvey's trio, on the other hand, twelve-note techniques play a more significant role. The work was composed very soon after Harvey had completed a period of study with Milton Babbitt at Princeton in 1969–70, and not surprisingly it reflects to some considerable degree the experience he had gained there. The opening movement, entitled 'Song', comprises a long-drawn cantabile melody, played largely in octaves by the strings against a flowing, mainly single-line piano part in demisemi-quavers, involving various twelve-note patterns in whole or partial series. The texture is predominantly two-part but, as the extensive pedalling indications show, the intended effect is frequently more impressionistic than crisply contrapuntal. After this relatively orthodox beginning the ensuing movements show increasing complexity. At the opening of the second movement (enigmatically called 'System') separate four-note chords for strings and piano resound repeatedly against each other like tolling bells, the strings getting gradually softer and the piano simultaneously louder, over eleven and ten stages, respectively. Following this grave introduction the somewhat doom-laden effect is dispelled by an extended, highly ornate section of formidable rhythmic intricacy, much of it unbarred and present-ing, with its fluctuating tempi, extraordinary problems of ensemble for the performers. Certain interconnecting links appear at the start of the finale (entitled 'Rite'). The piano begins with a fragment of its opening phrase in the first movement, and this leads directly to the keyboard's 'tolling bell' chord from the middle movement. Thereafter, as the movement proceeds, both string and piano 'tolling' elements recur in various guises, eventually recombining as the long-held chord of the almost inaudible (*pppp*) ending. Elsewhere, in the main body of the finale, elaborate improvisatory techniques are employed. These involve the allocation of thematic segments, or specified groups of notes, to one or more instruments in the ensemble, to be played in free rhythm and in any chosen order against a stable background of precisely notated rhythms in the other instrumental part(s). The contrast between freedom and restraint is not however confined to these improvisatory passages; in the structure of the movement as a whole a similar dichotomy is apparent between the freely decorative style of the improvised sections and the tightly organized nature of the opening paragraphs, in which closely-knit four-strand textures are worked out precisely on serial lines.

These works by Goehr and Harvey represent the furthest extreme in modernist 'language' and scoring to which the piano trio has so far travelled; and it is arguable, at least, that the radical approaches employed in them impose almost as much of a strain on the medium as did, in their quite different way, the quasi-orchestral methods of many late nineteenth-century composers. The differences, however, are substantial and significant. Whereas in the typical grand romantic trio a certain insensitivity seems to lie behind the overblown approach—an attitude which implies that the medium is only a rough-and-ready means to broader musical ends, rather than a delicate mechanism with its own, wholly individual, expressive capabilities—in the modern works it is an obsessive regard for technical minutiae, together with an intensive search for entirely new sound potentialities in the medium which have tended to alter the traditional balance between the substance of the music and its means of expression. In both cases the trio techniques represent, of course, a reflection of the more general styles characteristic of their respective periods. But in the twentieth-century works the approach has been imaginative and creative in a way which is altogether less apparent in the earlier ones. Also it is worth repeating that the feature which has probably contributed most to the changed concept of the trio is the drastically reduced role of the piano as a subsidiary partner to the strings, often contributing only single notes, chords, or melodic fragments to the texture, or indeed remaining silent for long periods. The contrast which this has produced with the traditional 'concerto-style' trio—without in any way 'straining the medium'—could hardly be more marked.

More recently the piano trio has continued as the vehicle for a remarkably wide variety of styles. Indeed, it is difficult not to conclude that, if a musicologist two hundred years from now were to be confronted by half-a-dozen unidentified trios from the 1980s, he would find the greatest difficulty in determining their authorship and chronology with any accuracy. A work in a latter-day Schoenbergian style, and constructed with excellent crafts-manship, is the trio by Hugh Wood composed during 1982–4 and dedicated to the erstwhile Parikian–Fleming–Roberts Trio. A splendidly characterized 'appassionato' opening, with a powerful descending twelve-note pattern on the strings matched by a similar ascending one (also involving all twelve notes) on the piano, sets the scene for a first movement of much vigour with sensitively varied scoring. The Adagio which follows maintains a free use of twelve-note patterns, but is based on rather less striking melodic ideas and makes a somewhat pale impression. The final movement, on the other hand, shows the composer at his most characteristic—and indeed most English—with its vivid dancing rhythms and gently whispered scoring, leading through a final crescendo to a brilliantly effective close.

Amongst the trios characterized earlier as 'radical revisionist' in style, particular mention may be made of those by David Matthews and Dominic Muldowney, the former published in 1984 as a tribute to Hans Keller, and the latter in 1985 (though completed a few years earlier) to a commission from the Montpelier Trio. In general terms, works in this style take a middle road between the traditionalist neo-classical manner and that of the experimental avant-garde, avoiding on the one hand the seria-lism, disjunct melodic lines, and rhythmic complexities of the progressives, and on the other the clear-cut melodic statements, thematic contrasts, and broadly tonal orientation of the conserva-tives. But they are not, for that reason, any less 'advanced' in language and expression. The Matthews trio is somewhat the more conventional of the two, with four contrasted movements, including a scherzo placed second, and a slow movement which is linked to the finale. In the first movement the themes grow organically from descending arpeggio figures stated in the introduction, and there are clear-cut sections corresponding broadly to those in a regular sonata movement. The textures are characteristically light, and there are some effective examples of interchange of material between keyboard and strings in a markedly 'classical' manner. Pungency is imparted to the fairly plain melodic lines by much sharply dissonant harmony which, in the first three movements at least, effectively dispels any sense of tonality. It is the more surprising, then, that the finale suddenly acquires an F sharp as its key-signature and creates an initial impression of G major. Any sense of tonal stability thus achieved proves illusory, however, and following a last-minute switch to a six-flat signature implying G flat, the movement ends with an oblique shift to a final D flat chord, with colourful accessory notes. By comparison, Dominic Muldowney's trio is more enigmatic in form and 'language'. Cast in a single extended movement, with fourteen sections at differing tempi (ranging from lentissimo to presto agitato) it develops its musical argument from the assembly of numerous tiny intervallic patterns, among which the ascending major sixth is particularly prominent. Special importance attaches also to an opening three-note pattern on the piano—D, A flat, G—spread widely across the keyboard, which recurs seven times at spaced intervals, and in a variety of forms, acting as a type of 'signpost' to map out the progress of the music as it unfolds. This opening figure, together with a sample of the undulating, motivic string texture, and a curious use of the piano to provide quiet echoes of notes just played by the strings, can be seen in Example 63.

As a pair, despite considerable differences of style, these two works point the way towards an interesting new concept in trio writing—one which makes a virtue out of textural simplicity, but does not shrink from a powerful individuality—obscurity, even—of 'language'. However, when stripped of so much of its natural capacity for vivid contrast, and restricted to pastel shades of musical colouring, the character of the medium necessarily undergoes considerable change. And, as a result, if the danger of

Ex. 63

monotony is to be averted, the musical arguments need to be very strongly profiled.

As final testimony to the extreme diversity of styles found in the 1980s, brief mention may be made of three other trios, by composers of Swedish, American, and French origin, each of which could hardly have failed to magnify the detection problems of our hypothetical musicologist in the twenty-second century. All three works were written late in their respective composer's careers, and represent their sole contributions to the genre. The first is the *Trio in One Movement* (1986) by the Swedish composer Sven-Erik Bäck, which provides a vivid example of post–Webernian *Punkt-musik*. Using a wide range of string devices, skeletal piano writing, persistent tempo fluctuations, note-clusters, and passages of improvisation (partly free and partly timed in seconds), it represents one of the more experimental extremes to which notated, as opposed to electronically realized, music may be taken. Stylistically it belongs firmly within the ambit of influence of Boulez and Stockhausen, and shows few if any traits of a nationalist character. In total contrast is the second of our works, a one-movement trio by the American composer Morton Feldman, which was published in 1980. With a duration said to be 'approximately one hour and twenty minutes' the work contrives to create a hypnotic effect of timelessness by means of a succession of isolated notes, chords, and fragmentary motifs, often linked solely by the piano's sustaining pedal. No tempo indications are given, but the impression created is of a slow measured progress, undisturbed by continual changes of time-signature, often one for each bar, which appear designed chiefly to test the alertness of the players. Both strings are muted throughout, and the dynamics are restricted in range from mezzo-piano down to *ppppp*, the softest levels being the ones most frequently cultivated. Reflecting the philosophy of a particular sector of the American avant-garde centred around Cage, the trio possesses the character somewhat of a devotional incantation—meditative, remote, and perhaps consciously related in its manner to the Vedic hymn or mantra.

To turn from this to our third work is to move to an entirely different, more 'corporeal', world—that of France in the 1930s. The trio is one published in 1987 by the septuagenarian composer Jean Françaix, which in four short, thematically-interrelated movements, conjures up delightfully the half-forgotten world of Poulenc, Milhaud, Auric, and others in pre-war Paris. There is no reason to suppose that the work is not newly minted; nor clearly is it simply a piece of pastiche. What it shows, in fact, is a very senior composer applying himself, for the first time in his long career, to a genre which the French, generally, have so greatly enriched; and doing so with wit and urbanity in a musical style which is second nature to him.

Any speculation about the likely future of the piano trio is probably as unwise as it is likely to be unrevealing. Inevitably it will be linked to the whole future development of the musical language, and this from our present viewpoint seems certain to be exceptionally problematic. All that can be said with any confidence is that the large output of trios in recent times (of which the ones considered above represent only a small part), together with the variety of styles contained in them, appear to augur well for the continuing vitality of the genre. Certainly there seems to be no good reason to anticipate its early demise. Complete casualties amongst the major forms of instrumental music are very rare in history, and occasioned in almost every case by the 'obsolescence' of particular instruments—the viol, the harpsichord, and the baryton, for example—a fate which seems unlikely to overtake the piano trio in the foreseeable future. Much more difficult to estimate is the likely style and content of any continuing trio form. In general the trios of the traditionalists, well though they have maintained the constructive aims and technical criteria of the founders of the genre, have begun to suffer some inevitable loss of immediacy and freshness of expression. While those of the avant-garde, exciting though their technical innovations have been, have tended to place excessive emphasis on scoring and instru-mental colour as a largely 'impressionist' means of expression, and to retain in the music itself, for all its deeply buried mathematical logic, only restricted powers of communication. It seems probable, therefore, that some new stylistic *rapprochement* may be expected, somewhat on the lines of the 'revisionist' works we have identified, but more arresting in content and more securely aligned with the natural scoring attributes of the medium.

It is unlikely that, in the process, the piano trio—or, indeed, chamber music generally—will readily regain its historical posi-tion as a performers' medium in the widest sense, able to absorb into its repertoire important new works which are in any way within the competence of even the best amateur players. Although, as we have seen earlier, the trio has caught up only rather belatedly with the more extreme advances in twentieth-century music, the modernist repertoire it has recently begun to acquire is of such a daunting complexity that its accessibility is limited entirely to the virtuoso professional ensembles of the present time—and often only to them with very considerable difficulty. It is noteworthy that the problems involved are not only the 'physical-technical' ones resulting from new perform-ance practices, such as special bowing procedures, pizzicati, harmonics, scordatura tunings, and the rest but also the 'mental-assimilation' ones proceeding from the baffling obscurity of many present-day systems of notation and the difficulties of ensemble they create. Curiously enough, similar, though much less drastic, problems appear to have troubled amateur players in the late eighteenth century; as a reviewer in the *Allgemeine deutsche Bibliothek* put it in 1790, in relation to some recently published Haydn trios, 'it is more the frequent modulations to remote keys—where many accidentals, often double sharps and flats, occur—than any innately difficult passages or ones requiring great technical ability, which demand a trained keyboard player for these sonatas'.[12] No doubt, as in the past, today's musicians, professional and amateur, given a sufficient period of consolidation, will eventually come to terms with the new notational systems and learn to handle them with the same freedom and comparative ease as traditional notation. But the process of adaptation is certain to be very protracted; much more so than in Haydn's day. In the meantime the 'realization' of advanced new scores remains the province of a few specialist groups who are linked with composers in a somewhat inhibiting 'closed circuit' of supply and demand, in which new works are left, often after only a very few performances, to establish what precarious footholds they can within the wider repertoire. And inevitably, that 'wider repertoire' relies heavily—perhaps too heavily for the continuing health of the genre—on the accepted masterpieces of the past. Parallels with history should obviously be drawn with caution; but it is difficult not to observe that, when Mozart in June 1788 suggested 'making a little music again' at Puchberg's place, it was contemporary music he had in mind—specifically his own latest piano trio, K542 in E major—not something written fifty or more years earlier.

[12] *Allgemeine deutsche Bibliothek*, 117/1(1790): cited from H. C. Robbins Landon, *Haydn: Chronicle and Works* ii (London, 1978), 723.

Bibliography

ABRAHAM, G., *A Hundred Years of Music*, 4th edn. (London, 1974).
—— (ed.), *Tchaikovsky: A Symposium* (London, 1946).
ALTMANN, W., 'Beethovens Umarbeitung seines Streichtrios, Op. 3, zu einen Klaviertrio', *Zeitschrift für Musikwissenschaft* 3 (1920–1), 129.
—— *Handbuch für Klaviertriospieler* (Wolfenbüttel, 1934).
ANDERSON, E. (ed.), *The Letters of Beethoven*, 3 vols. (London, 1961; 2nd edn. 1985).
—— (ed.), *The Letters of Mozart and his Family*, 2 vols. (London, 1938; 2nd edn., rev. M. Carolan and A. H. King, 1966).
BADURA-SKODA, E., 'The Chronology of Schubert's Piano Trios', in E. Badura-Skoda and P. Branscombe (eds.), *Schubert Studies: Problems of Style and Chronology* (Cambridge, 1982), 277.
BELL, A. Craig, 'An Introduction to Haydn's Piano Trios', *Music Review* 16 (1955) 191.
BENTON, R., 'A Résumé of the Haydn-Pleyel Trio Controversy, with some Added Contributions', *Haydn-Studien* 4 (1978).
BERTENSSON, S. and LEYDA, J., *Sergei Rachmaninov: A Lifetime in Music* (New York, 1956; 2nd edn. London, 1965).
BICKLEY, N. (ed. and tr.), *Brahms's Letters to and from Joachim* (London, 1914).
BLUME, R., *Studien zur Entwicklungsgeschichte des Klaviertrios im 18. Jahrhundert*, University of Kiel dissertation, 1976.
BRAND, F., 'Das neue Brahms-Trio', *Die Musik* 32 (1938–9), 321.
BROCK, D. G., 'The Instrumental Music of Hummel', University of Sheffield dissertation, 1976.
BRODER, N., 'Mozart and the Clavier', *Musical Quarterly*, 27 (1947), 422.
BROWN, A. P., 'The Solo and Ensemble Keyboard Sonatas of Joseph Haydn: A Study of Style and Structure', Northwestern University dissertation, 1970.
BUKOFZER, M., *Music of the Classic Period, 1750–1827* (Berkeley, 1958).
CARPENTER, T. L., 'Brahms: Progressive or Regressive? An Analysis of the Piano Trio Op. 101 in C minor from other Schoenbergian perspectives', University of London dissertation, 1983.
CESARI, G., 'Origini del trio con pianoforte', *Scritti inediti a cura di Franco Abbiata* (Milan, 1937), 183.
CHALUPT, René, *Ravel au miroir de ses lettres* (Paris, 1956).

CHUSID, M., 'The Chamber Music of Franz Schubert', University of California, Berkeley, dissertation, 1961.

CLAPHAM, J., 'Blick in den Werkstatt eines Komponisten: die beide Fassungen von Dvořáks Klaviertrio in f moll', *Musica* 13 (1959), 629.

—— *Dvořák* (London, 1979).

CLOSSON, E., *A History of the Piano*, English edn. (London, 1947).

COBBETT, W. W., (ed.), *Cyclopedic Survey of Chamber Music*, 3 vols. (London, 1929; 2nd edn., 1963).

COOPER, M., *French Music from the Death of Berlioz to the Death of Fauré* (London, 1951).

DEANE, B., *Albert Roussel* (London, 1961).

DERR, E., 'Sein ersters überliefertes Instrumentalwerk zur Erstveröffentlichung von C. Debussys frühen Klaviertrio', *Neue Zeitschrift für Musik* (December 1985), 10.

DEUTSCH, O. E., *Mozart: A Documentary Biography*, 2nd edn. (London, 1966).

—— *Schubert: A Documentary Biography*, tr. E. Blom (London, 1946).

—— *Schubert: Thematic Catalogue of All his Works in Chronological Order* (London 1951). Revised and enlarged German version in the *Neue Schubert Ausgabe* (Kassel, 1978).

DUNHILL, T. F., *Chamber Music: A Treatise for Students* (London, 1925).

EHRLICH, C., *The Piano: A History* (London, 1976).

EINSTEIN, A., *Mozart: His Character, His Work* (London, 1946).

—— *Schubert* (London, 1951).

EPPSTEIN, Hans, 'J. S. Bachs Triosonate G-dur (BWV 1039) und ihre Beziehungen zur Sonate für Gamba und Cembalo G-dur (BWV 1027)', *Die Musikforschung* 18 (1965), 126.

FEDER, G., 'Haydns frühe Klaviertrios: eine Untersuchung zur Echtheit und Chronologie', *Haydn-Studien* 2 (1970), 289.

FELLINGER, R., 'Ist das Klaviertrio in A dur ein Jugendwerk von Johannes Brahms?', *Die Musik* 24 (1941–2), 197.

FILLION, M., 'The Accompanied Keyboard Divertimenti of Haydn and his Viennese Contemporaries, c.1750–1780', Cornell University dissertation, 1982.

—— 'C. P. E. Bach and the Trio Old and New', in Stephen L. Clark (ed.), *C. P. E. Bach Studies* (Oxford, 1988), 83.

FISCHER, W., 'Mozarts Weg von der begleiteten Klaviersonate zur Kammermusik mit Klavier', *Mozart Jahrbuch* (1956), 16.

FORTUNE, N., 'The Chamber Music with Piano', in D. Arnold and N. Fortune (eds.), *The Beethoven Companion* (London, 1971), 197.

FULLER, D., 'Accompanied Keyboard Music', *Musical Quarterly* 60 (1974), 222.

GÁL, H., *Johannes Brahms: His Work, His Personality*, trans. J. Stein (London, 1963).
—— *Franz Schubert and the Essence of Melody* (London, 1974).
GEIRINGER, K., *Brahms: His Life and Work*, tr. J. Weiner and B. Miall (London, 1936).
—— *Haydn* (London, 1932).
GREENWOOD, J. E. P., 'Brahms's trio Op. 8: The Two Versions of the First Movement', University of London dissertation, 1983.
GRIFFITHS, P., *The String Quartet: A History* (London, 1983).
GROSS, E., 'The Chamber Music of František Xaver Dussek', University of Aberdeen dissertation, 1986.
HELM, A., *Beethoven* (Berlin, 1927).
HENROTTE, G. A., 'The Ensemble Divertimento in Pre-classic Vienna', University of N. Carolina dissertation, 1967.
HERING, H., 'Das Klavier in der Kammermusik des 18. Jahrhundert', *Die Musikforschung* 23 (1970), 22.
HESS, W., 'Beethoven's Revisions of his own Works', *Miscellanea Musicologica* (Adelaide), v (1970), 1.
HINSON, J., *The Piano in Chamber Ensemble: An Annotated Guide* (Bloomington, Indiana, and London, 1978).
HOBOKEN, A. van, *Joseph Haydn, Thematisch-bibliographisches Werkverzeichnis* (Mainz, 1957–71).
HOLETSCHEK, F., 'Das Klavier in der klassischen Kammermusik', *Österreichische Musikzeitschrift* 13 (1958), 178.
JANÁČEK, K., 'Smetanova komorni hu' (Smetana's Chamber Music), *Hudebni věda*, 16 (Prague, 1979), 195.
JARDILLIER, R., *La musique de chambre de César Franck* (Paris, 1929).
JOHNSON, D., 'The Artaria Collection of Beethoven Manuscripts: A New Source', in A. Tyson (ed.), *Beethoven Studies* (London, 1974), 174.
JONES, J. B., 'The Piano and Chamber Works of Gabriel Fauré, with particular reference to those works composed after 1890', University of Cambridge dissertation, 1973.
KARSCH, A., *Untersuchungen zur Frühgeschichte des Klaviertrios in Deutschland*, University of Cologne dissertation, 1941.
KELLER, H., 'The Chamber Music', in H. C. Robbins Landon and Donald Mitchell (eds.), *The Mozart Companion* (London, 1956), 90.
KERMAN, J., *Ludwig van Beethoven: Autograph Miscellany from circa 1786 to 1799, Brit. Lib. Add. Ms. 29801, ff. 39–162 (the 'Kafka' Sketchbook)*, 2 vols. (London, 1970).
—— 'Beethoven's Sketchbooks in the British Museum', *Proceedings of the Royal Musical Association* 93 (1966–7), 77.
—— 'Tändelnde lazzi: On Beethoven's Trio in D major, Op. 70 No. 1',

in M. Hamrick Brown and R. J. Wiley (eds.), *Slavonic and Western Music: Essays for Gerald Abraham* (Oxford, 1985), 109.

KEYS, I., *Brahms Chamber Music* (London, 1974).

KIDD, R. R., 'The Emergence of Chamber Music with Obbligato Keyboard in England', *Acta Musicologica* 44 (1972), 122.

KING, A. H., *Mozart's Chamber Music* (London, 1968).

KIRKENDALE, W., *Fuge und Fugato in der Kammermusik des Rokoko und der Klassik* (Tutzing, 1966).

KOMLÓS, K., 'The Viennese Keyboard Trio in the 1780s: Studies in Texture and Instrumentation', Cornell University dissertation, 1986.

—— 'The Viennese Keyboard Trio in the 1780s: Sociological Background and Contemporary Reception', *Music and Letters* 48 (1987), 222.

KULL, H., *Dvořáks Kammermusik* (Berne, 1948).

LANDON, H. C. R., Preface to *Die Klaviertrios von Joseph Haydn*, the first complete critical edition (Vienna, 1970).

LÁNG, P. H., *Music in Western Civilization* (New York, 1941).

LARGE, B., *Martinů* (London, 1975).

LARSEN, J. P., 'Some Observations on the Development and Characteristics of Viennese Classical Instrumental Music', *Studia musicologica* 9 (1967), 131.

LAYTON, R., *Berwald, a Critical Study* (London, 1959).

MACARDLE, D. W., 'Beethoven and Haydn', *Monthly Musical Record* 89 (1959), 203.

MARGUERRE, K., 'Die Violinsonate KV.547 und ihre Bearbeitung für Klavier allein', *Mozart-Jahrbuch* (1959), 228.

—— 'Mozarts Klaviertrios', *Mozart-Jahrbuch* (1960–1), 182.

MERSMANN, H., 'Beiträge zur Aufführungs-Praxis der vorklassische Kammermusik in Deutschland', *Archiv für Musikwissenschaft* 2 (1919–20), 99.

MOLNAR, A., 'Die beide Klaviertrios in D moll von Schumann (op. 63) und Mendelssohn (op. 49), *Sammelbände der Robert Schumann Gesellschaft* i (Leipzig, 1961), 79.

MOSER, A., *Johannes Brahms im Briefwechsel mit Joseph Joachim*, 2 vols. (Berlin, 1908).

NEWBOULD, B., 'Ravel's Pantoum', *Musical Times* 116 (March 1975), 228.

NEWMAN, W. S., 'Concerning the Accompanied Clavier Sonata', *Musical Quarterly* 33 (1947), 327.

—— *The Sonata in the Classic Era*, 2nd edn. (New York, 1972).

NICHOLS, R., *Ravel* (London, 1977).

NORRIS, C., *Shostakovich: The Man and his Music* (London, 1982).

NORRIS, G., *Rakhmaninov* (London, 1976).

NOTTEBOHM, G. *Beethoveniana* (Leipzig-Winterthur, 1872)

—— *Zweite Beethoveniana; nachgelassene Aufsätze* (Leipzig, 1887).

OREL, Alfred, 'Franz Schuberts "Sonate" für Klavier, Violine und Violoncell aus dem Jahre 1812', [D.28] *Zeitschrift für Musikwissenschaft* 5 (1922–3), 209.

ORLEDGE, R., *Gabriel Fauré* (London, 1979)

PAYNE, A., *Frank Bridge: Radical and Conservative* (London, 1984).

PIRRO, A., *Les Clavecinistes* (Paris, 1925).

PLANTINGA, L., *Schumann as Critic* (New Haven, Conn., and London, 1967).

REED, J., *Schubert* (London, 1987).

—— *Schubert, The Final Years* (London, 1972).

REESER, E., *De Klaviersonate met Vioolbegleiding in het parijische Musieleven ten Tidje van Mozart* (Rotterdam, 1939).

RIEMANN, H., 'Mannheimer Kammermusik des 18. Jahrhundert', preface to *Denkmäler der Tonkunst in Bayern* 15/6 (Leipzig, 1915).

—— 'Johann Schobert, ausgewählte Werke', preface to *Denkmäler deutscher Tonkunst* 39 (Leipzig, 1909; repr. 1958).

ROBERTSON, A. (ed.), *Chamber Music* (London, 1957).

ROE, S. W., 'The Keyboard Music of J. C. Bach: Source Problems and Stylistic Development in the Solo and Ensemble Works', University of Oxford dissertation, 1982.

ROSEN, C., *The Classical Style* (London, 1971).

SAINT-FOIX, Georges de, 'Histoire de deux trios ignorés de Michel Haydn: Leur influence sur Mozart', *Revue de musicologie* 12 (1931), 81.

SCHINDLER, A., *Biographie von Ludwig van Beethoven*, 3rd edn. (Münster 1860); Engl. version *Beethoven As I Knew Him*, ed. D. W. MacArdle (London, 1966).

SCHMID, E. F., *C. Ph. E. Bach und seiner Kammermusik* (Kassel, 1931).

SCHÖKEL, H. P., *Johann Christian Bach und die Instrumentalmusik seiner Zeit* (Wolfenbüttel, 1926).

SCHUMANN, R., *Erinnerungen an Felix Mendelssohn-Bartholdy*, ed. G. Eismann, (Zwickau, 1947; enl. 1948; Engl. edn. London, 1951).

—— *Gesammelte Schriften über Musik und Musiken*, 2 vols., 5th edn. (Leipzig, 1914).

SCHWARTUNG, H., 'Über die Echtheit dreier Haydn-Trios', *Archiv für Musikwissenschaft* 22 (1965), 191.

SCHWARZ, B., 'Dimitry Shostakovich', in S. Sadie (ed.), *The New Grove, Russian Masters II* (London, 1986), 179, 187.

SHEDLOCK, J. S., 'Beethoven's Sketch Books', *Musical Times* 33 (July 1892), 394.

SHELDON, D., 'The Transition from Trio to Cembalo-Obbligato Sonata in the works of J. G. and C. H. Graun', *Journal of the American Musicological Society* 24 (1971), 395

SMALLEY, D., 'John Ireland's Chamber Music', University of Wales, Aberystwyth, dissertation, 1982.

SOUREK, O., *The Chamber Music of Antonin Dvořák* (1956), an abridged version in English of *Dvořákovy skladby komorni* (Prague, 1934).

TEMP. ˜ˎEY, N., 'Instrumental Music in England, 1800–1850', University of Cambridge dissertation, 1960.

THAYER, A. W., *Life of Beethoven*, rev. and ed. Elliott Forbes, 2 vols. (Princeton, 1964).

TOVEY, D. F., *Beethoven* (London, 1944).

—— *Essays in Musical Analysis: Chamber Music* (London, 1944).

TURRENTINE, H. C., *Johann Schobert and French Clavier Music from 1700 to the Revolution*, University of Iowa dissertation, 1962.

· TYLER, H. M., 'The Harmonic Language of Mozart's Chamber Music, 1785–91', University of Sheffield dissertation, 1969.

TYSON, A., 'Beethoven's "Kakadu" Variations and their English History', *Musical Times* 104 (1963), 108.

—— (ed.), *Beethoven Studies* (New York and London, 1973–4)

—— (ed.), *Beethoven Studies 2* (London, 1977).

—— 'Haydn and Two Stolen Trios', *Music Review* 22 (1961), 21.

—— 'New Light on a Haydn Trio (XV: 32)', *Haydn Yearbook* 1 (1962), 203.

—— 'Stages in the Composition of Beethoven's Piano Trio, Op. 70 No. 1', *Proceedings of the Royal Musical Association* 97 (1970–1), 1.

—— 'The Authors of the Op. 104 String Quintet', *Beethoven Studies* (London, 1974), 158.

ULRICH, H., *Chamber Music: The Growth and Practice of an Intimate Art* (New York, 1948).

WALTER, H., 'Haydns Klaviere', *Haydn-Studien* 2/4 (Munich and Duisberg, 1970), 256.

WARD, C., 'Hymn Tunes as "Substance and Manner" in Charles Ives', University of Texas dissertation, 1969.

WEBSTER, J., 'Towards a History of Viennese Chamber Music in the Early Classical Period', *Journal of the American Musicological Society* 27 (1974), 212.

WEISE, D., *Beethoven: Ein Skizzenbuch zur Pastoralsymphonie, Op. 68, und zu den Trios, Op. 70*, 2 vols. (Bonn, 1961).

WEISMANN, W., 'Zur Urfassung von Mozarts Klaviertrio, KV 564', in W. Vetter (ed.), *Deutsches Jahrbuch der Musikwissenschaft für 1958* (Leipzig, 1959), 35.

WESTRUP, J. A., *Schubert's Chamber Music* (London, 1969).

WHITTALL, A., 'The Sonata Crisis: Schubert in 1828', *Music Review* 30 (1969),124.

WILLFORT, M., 'Das Urbild des Andantes aus Schuberts Klaviertrio, D. 929', *Österreichische Musikzeitschrift* 33 (1978), 277.

WINGFIELD, P., 'Janáček's "Lost" Kreutzer Sonata', *Journal of the Royal Musical Association* 112/2 (1987), 229.

ZHDANOV, V. A., and ZHEGIN, N. T. (eds.), *P. Chaykovsky: perepiska s N. F. von Meck*, correspondence with Nadezhda von Meck (Moscow and Leningrad, 1934–6).

Index of Piano Trios

(Principal references)

General Index

Abel, Karl Friedrich (1723–87) 1
Abraham, Gerald 65, 105, 106 n.
Albrechtsberger, Johann Georg
  (1736–1809) 46, 47
Anderson, Emily 3 n., 10 n., 14 n., 16 n.,
  53 n., 59 n.
André, Johann 9, 22
Andriessen, Hendrik (1892–1981) 173
Ansky, Shloime 191
Apponyi, Count Anton 44
Arensky, Antony Stepanovich
  (1861–1906) 148, 161, 170
Armingaud Quartet, The 141
Artaria, Domenico 9, 18 n., 25 n., 44,
  45 n., 52 n., 53
Auric, Georges (1899–1983) 132, 211
Avison, Charles (1709–70) 8
  sonatas for harpsichord, two violins,
  and cello, Op. 7 8

Babbitt, Milton (b. 1916) 198, 206
Bach, Carl Philipp Emanuel (1714–88) 1,
  5 n.
Bach, Johann Christian (1735–82) 1, 9,
  11, 12
  sonatas Op. 2 11; sonatas Op. 15 11, 12
Bach, Johann Sebastian (1685–1750) 5,
  98, 99, 110
  gamba sonata in G (BWV 1027) 5
  and trio sonata in G (BWV 1039) 5
Bache, Francis Edward (1833–58) 134–5
Bäck, Sven-Erik (b. 1919) 210–11
Badura-Skoda, Eva 71 n., 80 n.
Banville, Theodore de 175
Bargiel, Woldemar (1828–97) 98, 116,
  117
Bartók, Bela (1881–1945) 171, 172, 194,
  197
Bartolozzi (née Jansen), Theresa 38–9
Baudelaire, Charles Pierre 175
Beethoven, Ludwig van (1770–1827) 13,
  14, 17, 18, 37, 38, 41, 42, 43, 44–70,
  72, 83, 84, 85, 86, 87, 88, 92, 93, 99,
  105, 110, 111, 122, 152, 153, 185

string trio arrangements 53; septet
  arrangement 52; symphony
  arrangements, No. 1 47, Nos 2 and
  3 53; string quartets 53, 55, 58, 60,
  66, 67, 86, 185; violin sonata, Op. 96
  66; cello sonatas 47, 54, 61, 88 n.;
  piano sonatas 47, 58, 67, 83 n., 165;
  symphonies, No. 3 42, No. 5 51,
  54, No. 6 54, No. 9 58; piano
  concertos, No. 4 67, No. 5 55;
  Choral fantasia 54
Bennett, William Sterndale
  (1816–75) 134–5
Bennewitz, Antonin 149
Berg, Isak 75
Berkeley, Lennox (b. 1903) 196
Berlioz, Hector (1803–69) 148
  Symphonie fantastique 148
Bertensson, Sergei 168 n.
Berwald, Franz (1796–1868) 98, 130,
  135–7, 160
Billroth, Theodor 122
Bloch, Ernest (1880–1959) 191
Boccherini, Luigi (1743–1805) 8
Bocklet, Carl Maria von 70, 71
Boehm, Joseph 70
Bohemian Quartet, The 14, 159
Boulanger, Nadia (1887–1979) 171, 191, 196
Boulez, Pierre (b. 1925) 198, 211
Brahms, Johannes (1833–97) 14, 52, 54,
  88, 92–3, 97, 112, 115, 117–28, 129,
  132, 134, 152–3, 154, 155, 156–7,
  158, 173
  string quartets 54, 152; string quintet
  in F 119; piano quartet in G
  minor 165; violin sonata in A 119;
  clarinet sonatas 54; piano variations,
  Op. 21 125; 3rd symphony 109
Branscombe, Peter 71 n.
Breitkopf and Härtel 34, 54, 118
Bridge, Frank (1879–1941) 130, 173, 192,
  193–4, 195, 202
  piano sonata 195; violin sonata 195;
  string trio 195; string quartet 195